# VIRTUE AT WORK

# Virtue at Work

*Ethics for Individuals, Managers,*
*and Organizations*

GEOFF MOORE

OXFORD
UNIVERSITY PRESS

# OXFORD
UNIVERSITY PRESS

Great Clarendon Street, Oxford, OX2 6DP,
United Kingdom

Oxford University Press is a department of the University of Oxford.
It furthers the University's objective of excellence in research, scholarship,
and education by publishing worldwide. Oxford is a registered trade mark of
Oxford University Press in the UK and in certain other countries

Published in the United States of America by Oxford University Press
198 Madison Avenue, New York, NY 10016, United States of America

British Library Cataloguing in Publication Data
Data available

Library of Congress Control Number: 2016957139

ISBN 978-0-19-879344-1

# *Acknowledgements*

My first and most significant debt is to Alasdair MacIntyre whose work forms the organizing framework for this book. Over a period of some twenty years, his writings have challenged and inspired me, so that my intellectual journey has been largely informed by grappling with, and seeking to apply, the key concepts of virtue ethics which he introduced principally in his ground-breaking book *After Virtue*. I am sure that he will not agree with everything I have written here, but I hope he would acknowledge that my presentation of his work is, at least, reasonably accurate as well as compelling, and that working out its practical implications for virtue at work is a worthwhile project.

My second debt is to those scholars who have accompanied me on this journey. Most notable among them is my former colleague and continuing friend Ron Beadle, with whom I have collaborated and deliberated over many years. Others, particularly those involved with the International Society for MacIntyrean Enquiry, have contributed to my understanding of MacIntyre's work, and within this society and beyond there are now a large number of scholars who have explored MacIntyre's concepts in a wide range of occupations and organizations. Many of these studies appear in this book, and again I hope that my presentation of this work is reasonably accurate. In addition, there are those academics, in the roles of editors and reviewers, who have assisted in honing my work, and to whom I am, almost without exception, extremely grateful.

My third debt is to co-authors who have worked with me on the various empirical studies I have been involved with, and to the organizational members who have been willing to give of their time to these studies. This book is intended for a practitioner audience, and I hope that it repays some of those debts. One manager, who read an academic paper of mine based on a study of his organization, said that his head hurt as a result. It was partly that comment which made me realize that there was a need to explain this approach in a more accessible way; I hope that reading this book does not hurt heads any more than it needs to.

My fourth debt is to David Musson, formerly of Oxford University Press, who heard me make a presentation at a conference and approached me with the question I was, at that moment, asking myself: 'Have you thought of writing a book on the subject?' It was a happy coincidence, and I hope the end product repays the trust David placed in me.

I wrote the early part of this book while on a period of research leave from Durham University, when I was based in the School of Management at the University of South Australia in Adelaide. I am deeply grateful for the space (literal and metaphorical) which both universities gave me to work on this project.

At a more personal level, various people have helped in the writing of this book. Notable among them have been my two brothers. Andy, a former senior civil servant, read the manuscript and provided very helpful comments from the perspective of just the kind of person I have in mind as the audience. He even said that he enjoyed it (which is pretty high praise from a brother). Nigel, a practising civil engineer, helped me to understand better how architectural practices work. And, more generally, my wife Alison has been a source of continuing support, and has held firmly to the belief that I might just be on to something quite important here. She also possesses and exercises the virtues in abundance, and so has been a practical inspiration in what might otherwise have become a rather intellectual endeavour. It is to her that I dedicate this book.

Geoff Moore

*Durham, October 2016*

# Contents

# List of Figures

# 1

## Introduction

Consider Elaine's story.

Elaine works as a middle manager in a medium-sized company of architects—DesignCo. The main projects which DesignCo works on are office buildings, often in city centres. Sometimes, these are rather utilitarian buildings, fit for purpose but not very inspiring to design, to build, or (so Elaine has discovered) to work in. Occasionally the company wins a bid for a new corporate headquarters, a building which is designed to be a 'statement' which 'says something' to the world around about the scale and ambitions of the client. Here, opulence and functionality go side by side. But many of the projects Elaine works on are somewhere between these two extremes—spaces where 'value for money' is the key.

Elaine trained as an architect, passed all her exams first time, and gained experience in a number of architectural practices before moving to DesignCo. One of the things which marked her out from the very beginning was her creativity; she won the creative design prize in her final year at university for her work, tempered only by the fact that the judges (who included practising architects) thought the design might be rather difficult to build and thus rather expensive. Since then, she has been involved in several of the more glamorous projects the companies for which she has worked have bid for and won, and her ideas about what makes for a 'good' building have, as a consequence, developed and matured. She can design to a brief and stay within the cost parameters she is given. But she still has a creative edge to her work, and often pushes herself and others to come up with better solutions to difficult problems, to design buildings which fit well into their surroundings and enhance them, and to minimize ecological impacts.

Elaine now has a small team of architects working with her which includes a junior architect just out of university as well as some clerical assistants. So she is responsible not only for the management of the parts of the projects which her team is given, but also for managing her team. And that, naturally enough, involves developing those in her team who are architects so that they become better architects, and particularly so in the case of the new recruit who is only just starting out. But, of course, this all takes time, and may not 'pay off' if any of them were to prove to be unteachable or to leave.

DesignCo had been successful in times past and employees, including Elaine, had benefited with salary increases and bonuses. But more recently a downturn in the economy, and a new managing director, have meant that the pressure has increased. Bidding to keep costs within clients' budgets and fees low, in order to win the contract, then designing to try to drive those internal costs even lower and hence maintain not just the business, but also the previous level of profit margins, has become the order of the day.[1] Elaine can almost feel her creative side being squeezed out bit by bit; not only has the atmosphere in the company changed so that it is no longer considered a good thing to come up with innovative designs, but there just doesn't seem to be enough time to do so anyway. Any 'spare' time has to be devoted to reducing DesignCo's costs on the existing designs, not to finding clever solutions to difficult problems. Architecture in general, she reflects, and DesignCo in particular, seem to be becoming more utilitarian—the same old designs fitted into spaces which don't quite 'work' with them.

Occasionally she has a 'run in' with her boss, who seems to have lost the love of architecture he once had (she learned a lot from him when she first arrived at DesignCo); he now seems to be fixated with the 'numbers'. 'What is DesignCo all about?' she asks, only to get a slightly condescending smile in return.

To relate Elaine's story in this way tells us quite a lot about her. We could probably, on the basis of the above account, describe her character quite accurately, although we would obviously need to see her in action at work over an extended period to begin to know who she really is—whether she is generally courteous or clinical, has a sense of humour, whether she forms friendships with others at work or not, and so on. But, of course, this is only part of who Elaine is. She is also a daughter, a wife, mother to three teenage children, a cellist who plays in a local orchestra, an ardent reader of thrillers, quite good-looking, and, somewhat strangely, with a penchant both for white-water rafting and for doing zany deals on eBay.

Consider Elaine's story.

It is worth adding that Elaine, and the other members of her family who we will meet during the course of this book, are fictional characters. But they should be recognizable as typical of people in a modern, industrial, or post-industrial, consumer society. DesignCo is similarly a fictional organization, though also intended to be recognizable as typical of organizations in general.

We still don't know Elaine or DesignCo well, of course, but that will have to do for now. Elaine would have to be a central character in a novel for us to understand her more fully, and this book is not a novel. But even with the

---

[1] Internal costs for architectural practices can be driven down by using more junior architects and reusing parts of designs from previous projects.

limited account of Elaine and her story which we have so far, and the initial insights into her employer DesignCo, the major themes of this book are evident.

## WHAT THIS BOOK IS ALL ABOUT

First, this book is about organizations. Even for those who do not work in an architect's practice, much of what was described above about DesignCo was probably familiar. There were different kinds of work from the mundane to the exotic; there were good times when the economy was booming and it was possible to be creative and innovative, with budgets which were relatively relaxed; through to difficult times when every penny seemed to get counted, creativity got squashed, and questions about the purpose of the company and, indeed, of the industry began to be raised, at least in Elaine's mind. Was it really about architecture, or about the money, with architecture merely as a means to an end all along?

These are questions which seem to be about rather more than 'Corporate Social Responsibility' as it is often called, or about creating value for different stakeholders, even though we could have described much of the above in stakeholder terms (the shareholders of DesignCo Ltd, senior management, employees, clients, the environment broadly defined, for example), and discussed how they create value for one another and how that value, once created, is shared.[2] The way Elaine's story was described seemed to have something quite fundamental to do with what we will come to call the 'practice' of architecture, but also about the structural form of the company—DesignCo Ltd—which provides an organizational framework within which the practice of architecture takes place. Clearly, these two—the practice and what we will come to call the 'institution'—are interrelated. You couldn't really have one without the other, or at least not for any length of time. But already in Elaine's mind was a question of priority—which comes first, particularly when the chips are down? And what sort of organization was DesignCo turning into? Is it still (was it ever) a 'good' organization?

Second, this book is about management and managers (we will clarify the distinction later). Elaine is a manager, responsible both for the work which her team is required to do, and for managing them as individuals. Doubtless, there will be some kind of management control system in DesignCo, and Elaine will be held to account for completing projects on time, within budget, and to the required quality standards. She will likely be subject to an appraisal system and, as well as the basic criteria just described, she will probably have other

---

[2] 'Creating Shared Value' is a common way of describing corporate social responsibility and stakeholder engagement, made (relatively) famous through an article by Michael Porter and Mark Kramer in the *Harvard Business Review* in 2011. We will return to this in Chapter 2, but it is worth noting that it is not without its critics, see Crane, Palazzo, Spence, & Matten (2014).

targets, to do with maintaining her professional qualification, and contributing to the company in ways which do not seem to be directly connected to the job (organizational citizenship behaviour, or OCB, as it is sometimes known). There may also be a target to do with the development of the staff in her team, and particularly of more junior colleagues such as the new architect they have just recruited. She herself has been the beneficiary of that kind of professional development in the past, including from the person who is now her boss and, even if DesignCo does not require it, she would perhaps feel obliged to offer her time and expertise to induct the new recruit not only into the organization, but also into the much broader practice of architecture itself.

Consequently, Elaine seems to have to divide her time between the practice of architecture (making sure the team's designs meet best practice and including her own continued engagement as a professional architect in her own right), the management of that activity (budgets, critical path analyses, and so on), and the management and development of the other members of her team. As with the organization itself, one can foresee tensions between these activities—when time always seems to be tight, does she take time with the new recruit or get those spreadsheets to her boss? What does it mean to be a 'good' manager?

Finally, this book is about individuals and, most particularly, about their working lives in organizations. Elaine was initially educated by an organization—the university she attended. She worked for several more organizations as an employee before joining DesignCo. While the sort of person Elaine is—in particular her creative talent—has had an impact upon her work, the organizations she has worked for have also been influential in creating the person she has, so far, become. Perhaps her natural flair wouldn't have lent itself to designing to a brief, or to keeping projects on time and within budget. But she has learned those things, probably to the point where they are now second nature to her.

But the organizations which have employed her have been important in another way. They have provided the salary which allowed Elaine initially to leave the parental home and provide for herself, and later to contribute to the family income. As well as the functional aspects of life—house, food, car, and so on—the money allows her and the family to do other things, in her case to play the cello and go white-water rafting, for example.

In constructing a narrative (the story of Elaine's life), and in understanding who she has become (her character), organizations have played an important part. An interesting question related to this would be whether she is the same person at work as she is at home (and as she is when the raft is plunging through the rapids). Another interesting question would be whether she has pursued the same kind of projects and ambitions throughout her life, and her commitment to these. Finally, just as we did with DesignCo when asking whether it was a 'good' organization, and when we asked what it means to be a 'good' manager, we might want to ask what it means to be a 'good' person and whether Elaine could be described in that way.

Elaine's story has been told in a way which has deliberately introduced us to what is known as virtue ethics. Later, we will go into this in more detail, but already we can discern some key themes. Ethics in general might be described as being about discerning how we should live and what it means to live a good life. Virtue ethics does this from a character-based perspective, which also necessarily means that it is narrative-based—it involves telling stories about activities and relationships. In the above account, this is most obvious in relation to Elaine herself—what sort of person is she and how has her character developed through the various practices (notably architecture and family) which have shaped her? In more technical language, which virtues does she possess and exercise, and which vices is she subject to? What does it mean to be a good person?

But, so I and others have argued,[3] this virtue-based approach can be extended and applied not just to individuals but also to particular roles. In particular, and of most interest to us, it can be applied to the role of managers. So we can ask what it means to be a good manager and derive some general characteristics which would help us to identify what it might mean to undertake this role well.

More controversially, perhaps, this same way of thinking has also been applied to organizations. Obviously, organizations are different from individuals and individuals-as-managers. In technical language they are ontologically differentiated, which is to say their very nature or essence is different. But, so it has been argued, we might helpfully be able to think about organizations in the same way—in other words, to describe organizations in terms of the virtues and vices which they possess, and to summarize this in terms of the character of the organization, just as we can summarize the virtues and vices which an individual possesses in terms of their character. This way of thinking would lead us to ask what it means to be a good organization.

Why, then, is a book such as this needed, given that there are any number of books which purport to explain how to run successful organizations, how to be a great leader or manager, how to run one's life better, and so on? The answer lies deep, and we will come back to it over the next few chapters. But for now suffice it to say that this approach—to do with virtue at work—is philosophically grounded in a major tradition in ethics, has been worked out in numerous academic papers, has been applied to different kinds of organizations and different types of practice, and has already been the subject of other books (though rather different to this one).[4] And those of us who have been working in this area over many years think it really does have

---

[3] For those who might be interested, references to the academic work which underpins the arguments in this book will be given at the appropriate points.

[4] See, for example, Beabout (2013), Hartman (2013), and Morrell (2012). The first of these is closest to the approach adopted here and will be referred to particularly in Chapter 6. The other two take a more general Aristotelian rather than MacIntyrean approach.

something different and important to say to individuals, to managers, and to organizations.[5]

But the detailed analysis of this way of thinking about individuals, managers, and organizations is to be found only in academic articles published in respectable academic journals, or in books by respectable publishers. This is important because it provides some guarantee of the rigour of this approach, since each of these articles and books will have been peer reviewed to exacting standards by other academics who are experts in the field. (This is to say, in the technical language which we will explore in later chapters, that the practice of research and scholarship has its own standards of excellence to which these articles and books adhere.) But therein lie two problems; these articles are inaccessible in both senses of the word. First, without access to a good university library, and to a mechanism which would allow one to explore these articles and books as a collection over against all the other topics which one might be interested in, it would be impossible to even find this material. But second, even with such access, these articles and books might well remain inaccessible in the sense that, having read them all, the reader may be none the wiser. The technical language in which they are written, while not completely impenetrable, is not necessarily easy to grasp.

So, the purpose of this book is to make this approach to virtue at work, or virtue ethics for individuals, managers, and organizations, accessible. Although we will need to explore quite detailed philosophical concepts, the intention is to make these understandable to those we might call 'everyday persons'.

## WHO IS THIS BOOK FOR?

Who, then, is this book written for? As just indicated, it is for individuals, managers, and organizations. But it is likely to be of interest mainly to those who are engaged in management at whatever level—from the most junior supervisory level to the most senior, from those who are just setting out on a managerial career to those who have been leaders of major organizations for many years.

But let us take this to a rather deeper level. The philosopher with whom we will engage in this book is Alasdair MacIntyre. He has been a key contributor

---

[5] One of the most important academics working in this area is Ron Beadle. I draw on our joint work at various points, his work in relation to meaningful work in Chapter 5, and his work on circuses in Chapter 9. In 2013, he entitled his professorial inaugural lecture: 'Virtue at Work: What everyone should learn from the Circus'. That this book is also entitled 'Virtue at Work' is coincidental.

to the relatively recent rehabilitation and development of virtue ethics, and it will be his approach, and its application in organizations, which we will be exploring. In relation to who both MacIntyre and this book seek to engage with, MacIntyre speaks of 'everyday plain persons', not in a derogatory sense, but to distinguish them from two kinds of philosophers (more of which below). So 'plain' refers to the fact that they are not professional philosophers, rather than to any other attribute which they may or may not have. 'Everyday persons' simply means that these are individuals with a life in what we often term 'the real world', but it also carries with it ideas from virtue ethics which we have already begun to explore—that they engage in various practices (such as architecture and family life), pursue excellence in them by employing and cultivating virtues along the way, and in such a way that their character is developed so that they may find themselves engaged in a quest to understand the deeper questions of life.[6]

This does not mean, however, that they *necessarily* engage in such a quest. They may find themselves in an unreflective mode for lengthy periods of time, in effect living without questioning the prevailing customs and culture of the society, communities, and organizations of which they are a part. But then they may find themselves challenged by particular circumstances— redundancy, a scandal perhaps leading to the failure or near failure of their organization, the near closure of their bank and an associated financial and economic crisis, questions over global ecological sustainability, or, at a more personal level, the death of a close relative or friend, their own morbidity or mortality, the breakdown of a close relationship—which forces a rethink.[7] At this point, everyday plain persons become philosophers, and while MacIntyre is sceptical both about our own society's ability to provide for systematic reasoned debate, and of philosophy's ability to help with this, nonetheless he wishes to encourage everyday plain persons on this quest. As he says, 'philosophy is a matter of concern for plain persons before it is a matter of concern for professional philosophers'.[8]

So, this book is written for the everyday plain person. If, as a reader, you are entirely happy with the way the world is, including your experience of organizations as an employee or manager, then this book is not for you. If, on the other hand, you have even the slightest hesitation when reflecting on life, management, or organizations, and wonder if things could possibly be both clearer and, perhaps, better, and are willing to engage with what might

---

[6] MacIntyre (1992: 3–8).

[7] MacIntyre (1977) refers to these as 'epistemological crises' meaning that they ask fundamental questions about the nature of life, and how we can be sure of what we think we know about it.

[8] MacIntyre (2006: 180).

just turn out to be some of the most comprehensible and practical philosophy you have ever come across . . . read on.


## INTRODUCING ALASDAIR MACINTYRE

Since we will be using Alasdair MacIntyre's ideas as a basis for this book, it is appropriate to give some background to him as a person. Born in 1929 in Glasgow, Scotland, MacIntyre was educated and began his academic career in the UK. In 1970 he moved to the USA and has held academic appointments at a number of universities there, latterly at the University of Notre Dame where he remains, since his retirement in 2010, as a Senior Distinguished Research Fellow in the Center for Ethics and Culture, as well as holding a position as Senior Research Fellow at the Centre for Contemporary Aristotelian Studies in Ethics and Politics at London Metropolitan University.

Politically, the early MacIntyre was a paid-up Marxist, but the experience of what Marxism turned into when put into practice led to him rejecting it as a political project while remaining loyal to many of its tenets as a political philosophy. Thus, he remains a staunch critic of what he regards as the 'modernity' of advanced capitalism, and of modern liberal individualism, influenced as it is by the liberalism of the Enlightenment.[9] In the early 1980s he converted to Roman Catholicism and while the influence of this tends not to be evident in much of his writings (and not in those writings which are most relevant to this book, particularly *After Virtue*), he does his work against that background.

Philosophically, MacIntyre would be principally positioned as a neo-Aristotelian, that is someone who draws from but has developed Aristotle's ideas. As noted above, and following from his neo-Aristotelianism, he is known as a virtue ethicist (even though he would dispute the title), and the book which both fed the developing interest in the rehabilitation of virtue ethics and made his own name was entitled *After Virtue: A Study in Moral Theory*. Originally published in 1981, it is now in its third edition,[10] and has been called 'one of the most influential works of moral philosophy of the late twentieth century'.[11] As its name suggests, it is what might be termed a work of 'meta-ethics', that is an argument about and justification for a particular way of 'doing' ethics, and one which, he argued, became fragmented and lost

[9] See, for example, a recent contribution about investment advising and, as he terms it, the 'irrelevance of ethics'—MacIntyre (2015).
[10] MacIntyre (2007); it is this edition which we will be referring to.
[11] See, for this point specifically and for a more general introduction to Alasdair MacIntyre, the biography provided by Christopher Lutz in the Internet Encyclopaedia of Philosophy available at http://www.iep.utm.edu/mac-over/, accessed 14 September 2016.

as the ethics of the Enlightenment period (principally Kantianism and Utilitarianism) took hold. Probably his most accessible book, and one which develops and makes concrete the ideas expounded in *After Virtue*, is *Dependent Rational Animals*.[12] However, it is *After Virtue* which we will be principally drawing from here.

As noted above, MacIntyre has long held a sceptical view of his own profession of philosophy. He has, for example, distinguished between two different kinds of philosophers—those which we might call 'philosophers as technical specialists' and those who are 'philosophers as seekers of understanding'.[13] Unsurprisingly, he is critical of the first, arguing that they engage in philosophy almost as a diversion from the problems of real life. Philosophers as seekers of understanding, however, are 'engaged by questions about the ends of life', conceive of their work as 'contributing to an ongoing philosophical conversation' recognizing that 'the end of the conversation and the good of those who participate in it is truth and the nature of truth, of good, of rational justification, and of meaning'.[14] MacIntyre is firmly in this latter camp, seeing philosophy as having to grapple with everyday problems for everyday plain persons. A summary of MacIntyre's 'project' is that his 'Aristotelian philosophy investigates the conditions that support free and deliberate human action in order to propose a path to the liberation of the human agent through participation in the life of a political community that seeks its common goods through the shared deliberation and action of its members'.[15] We will come back to a number of the terms in this summary in later chapters.

It is notable that while MacIntyre maintains the respect of his own academic community,[16] he is widely read outside of philosophy—in sociology, politics, theology, organization studies, and business ethics, for example. In 2007 an academic society was formed specifically to pursue and promote MacIntyre's work,[17] and he continues to engage with both proponents and critics of his work. Indeed, he remains committed to the urgency of the task, as he sees it, of

---

[12] *Dependent Rational Animals*—MacIntyre (1999a). If the reader is tempted to explore MacIntyre in the original, this is probably the best book to read. On the other hand, *After Virtue* is his classic and most well-known book, and in educated circles one is much more likely to meet people who have read *After Virtue* than *Dependent Rational Animals*.

[13] This is Beabout's terminology, see Beabout (2013: 140).

[14] MacIntyre (2006: 130–1), see also Beabout (2013: 139–43) for an extended discussion.

[15] Christopher Lutz, Internet Encyclopaedia of Philosophy, available at http://www.iep.utm.edu/mac-over/, accessed 14 September 2016, drawing from *Dependent Rational Animals*, Chapter 8.

[16] For example, MacIntyre is a former President of the American Philosophical Society, has given the prestigious Gifford Lectures in the University of Edinburgh published as *Three Rival Versions of Moral Inquiry* (1990), and was awarded the Aquinas Medal by the American Catholic Philosophical Association in 2010.

[17] See http://www.macintyreanenquiry.org, accessed 14 September 2016.

revolutionizing ethical and political theory in the modern era. He is, as might be evident from this description, quite a character.

## HOW IS THIS BOOK STRUCTURED?

This book is in three parts. Part I (Organizations and Virtue Ethics) has three chapters which lay out the groundwork of the approach. Chapter 2 (Organizations and Ethics) explores the ubiquity of organizations in our present social order, offers a definition of a formal organization, and considers the reasons organizations exist. It then turns to explore how we typically think about organizations (the metaphor approach), before summarizing and critiquing current approaches to organizational ethics.

Chapter 3 (Virtue Ethics and Organizational Ethics) offers an account of ethics which explains and contextualizes the virtues approach at the individual and social levels, as well as exploring two criticisms of this approach. It includes a discussion about 'reasons for action', that is how as individuals we should be able to offer justifications for our actions because they contribute to our own purpose or *telos*. The chapter then explains how we might legitimately extend this way of thinking about ethics to the organizational level, covering the idea of organizational-level *telos* and including a discussion of the question of organizational moral agency.

Chapter 4 (A MacIntyrean Approach to Organizations and Organizational Ethics) is a key chapter which both completes Part I and leads into Parts II and III. It introduces MacIntyre's concepts of practices and institutions, and internal and external goods, showing how these give a novel but powerful way of thinking about organizations as 'practice-institution combinations', and which helps us to see organizations as essentially moral spaces. It also introduces the virtuous organizational mapping as a way of analysing organizations, identifying potential problems ahead of time, and so potentially leading to change in organizations.

Part II (Implications for Individuals, Managers, and Organizations) also has three chapters which focus respectively on the implications of the approach laid out in Part I for individuals, managers, and organizations. Chapter 5 (Implications for Individuals) works through what the virtue ethics approach outlined in Part I might mean both in general at an individual level, and for individuals when working in organizations. It explores the notion of human lives as narratives, and human beings as on a narrative quest towards their own *telos*. It then asks what all of this might mean for our working lives, and hence what we might expect to put into, and get out of, organizations. It thereby links to and explores the notion of meaningful work.

Chapter 6 (Implications for Managers) extends the previous chapter by raising the question of what a MacIntyrean organizational virtue approach might mean for managers. It distinguishes between managers and management, explores MacIntyre's critique of managers and responses to it, locates managers and management within the practice-institution combination framework, and identifies the characteristics of, and the virtues required by, the virtuous manager.

Chapter 7 (Implications for Organizations) takes the previous discussions to the organizational level and explores the characteristics of a virtuous organization. It proposes a taxonomy of organizational-level virtues, and introduces the idea of corporate character. It discusses how to 'crowd-in' virtue through appropriate organizational governance mechanisms, and therefore provides guidance on organizational design and operational issues.

Part III (Organizational Virtue Ethics in Practice) consists of two chapters. Chapter 8 (Virtue Ethics in Business Organizations) draws on the foundations in Parts I and II, to demonstrate the application of this approach to business organizations. The chapter begins with a critical approach in questioning whether all business activities can be practices in MacIntyre's terms, and provides a nuanced answer to this important question. Examples are then drawn from industrial sectors such as pharmaceuticals, health and beauty, garment manufacturing, banking and investment advising, and from particular functions within business organizations such as human resources and accounting.

Chapter 9 (Virtue Ethics in Non-Business Organizations) extends the previous chapter by demonstrating the application of the organizational virtue ethics approach in various non-business settings. These comprise studies of various performing arts (symphony orchestras, circuses, and jazz); examples from the health sector (a revisiting of the 'Bristol Babies' case, the practices of surgery and nursing, and a study of action research involving NHS managers); and finally studies of churches as organizations and of journalism as a practice.

Finally, Chapter 10 (Conclusions) draws together the whole book, summarizing its key themes, and suggesting how those who have read it may apply it to their own lives, their managerial practice, and their organizations.

# Part I

# Organizations and Virtue Ethics

# 2

## Organizations and Ethics

### INTRODUCTION

There are three focal points in this book—individuals, managers, and organizations—each of which will be analysed from a virtues perspective. But the context in which individuals (at least from the work perspective which will be the main consideration here) and managers operate is within organizations. Hence, we first need to understand something more about organizations. This chapter explores the ubiquity of organizations in our present social order, offers a definition of a formal organization and considers the reasons organizations exist. It then turns to explore how we typically think about organizations (the metaphor approach), before summarizing and critiquing current approaches to organizational ethics.

### THE UBIQUITY OF ORGANIZATIONS

Organizations are ubiquitous in our present social order—they exist everywhere. They are 'a pervasive and enduring feature of contemporary society'[1] in every country across the globe. Indeed, we are so used to them that we can easily forget that this was not always the case. Work was, of course, *organized* from the earliest times; one has only to think of the cooperation required in ancient times to hunt large game or to farm, the division of labour associated with the creation of tools and weapons in the Bronze Age, and examples of the large-scale systematic organization of work in, for example, the building of the pyramids and irrigation projects in Egypt.[2] These significant feats of *organizing* (as a verb), together with the political, military, and religious *organizations* (as a noun) of pre-modernity, provide evidence of mankind's ability to collaborate in groups towards some desired end.

---

[1] Scott (2007: 2).    [2] See, for example, Hannan & Kranzberg (no date).

But it was the Industrial Revolution in eighteenth-century Britain, with the technological development of power-driven machinery, which probably had the most significant impact upon the organization of work. With mechanization came the factory and with it came industrial organization, and industrial *organizations*, of a type which had not existed before, enabled, or so it is argued, by the invention of free incorporation and limited liability (in England, the Limited Liability Act of 1865).[3] The history of developments in industrial and post-industrial society from then until the present day need not concern us, except to make the obvious point that organizations have multiplied in both number and form over that period. In the UK for example, the total number of companies on the register with Companies House in June 2016 was 3,741,883, with a net increase in that month alone of 13,067 companies.[4] And the UK Charity Commission had on its register 165,965 charities as of June 2016, an increase of 688 since March 2016.[5] Not only do organizations exist, but we seem to be continually creating more of them.

Today we are familiar with the three-fold division into private-sector business organizations, statutory-sector organizations, and voluntary-sector organizations and, while the picture is considerably more complex than this simplistic division would suggest (state-owned business organizations in China cross the boundaries, as do public-private alliances in the provision of health care in the UK, for example), it at least enables us to appreciate that today we are surrounded by, and move easily between, these different organizational types. It is organizations from which we buy food and other goods, organizations which provide us with health care and 'public' services such as waste collection, organizations which educate us and continue to educate our children. We support charitable organizations such as those engaged in raising money for cancer research or in providing overseas aid and, in some cases such as hospices, we may in time become the beneficiaries of such organizations. One has only to look at a bank or credit card statement to realize that we are employed by, buy from, and give to organizations; nearly all the transactions are likely to be with organizations of one form or another. We are dependent upon organizations from before we were born until after we die. Indeed, it has been argued that we do not live in market economies but in

---

[3] See Ireland (2010: 848) for example, although the argument is made there that this had little initial impact on business activity, which continued to revolve around family firms and partnerships with unlimited liability (2010: 844).

[4] Companies House, available from https://www.gov.uk/government/uploads/system/uploads/attachment_data/file/545611/StatisticalReleaseIncorporatedCompaniesUKJune2016_V1.1.pdf, accessed 14 September 2016. In July 2016 there were 53,949 incorporations and 40,882 dissolutions, giving some indication of the 'turnover' of companies.

[5] Charity Commission, available from https://www.gov.uk/government/publications/charityregister-statistics/recent-charity-register-statistics-charity-commission, accessed 14 September 2016.

'organizational economies'.[6] It used to be said that the only certainties in life were death and taxes. Perhaps, in our day, we should include organizations as one more certainty in life.

But since organizations are ubiquitous in our present social order, impact upon us at almost every moment of our lives, and look as though they are here to stay—in other words, since they are so important to us—then it would presumably be important to have a clear idea as to what an organization is and why organizations exist.

## WHAT ARE ORGANIZATIONS
## AND WHY DO THEY EXIST?

A classic definition of a formal organization, which is broad enough to encompass all of the organizational types which have been mentioned above, is as follows:

> A purposive aggregation of individuals who exert concerted effort toward a common and explicitly recognized goal.[7]

Even a definition as apparently straightforward as this can, however, be questioned. For example, do all members of an organization have a common goal which is shared and towards which they are all explicitly working? What about the potential (and sometimes actual) misalignment between management and trade unions, for example, where management may argue that the goal is profit while the trade union and its members may argue that the goal is (or ought to be) to do with the security, and terms and conditions, of workers' employment? Clearly there can be different understandings of organizational purpose. But, under normal circumstances, these differences will not be so great as to prevent a common effort towards the achievement of some reasonably common understanding of what the organization's goals are. Later on (in Chapter 4), we will come back to the idea of organizational purpose, since it is fundamental to a virtue ethics approach, and suggest a way of conceiving of organizational purpose which might help to resolve the kind of differences outlined in this example. For now, however, the definition of a formal organization given above will suffice. Without specifying what form the aggregation may take (public or private, and with all of the various legal possibilities for incorporation which exist), the key points are that a formal organization involves individuals working together to achieve some common purpose.

---

[6] Ghoshal, Bartlett, & Moran (1999: 10).     [7] Blau & Scott (1962).

But it is worth noting two things which this definition does *not* imply. First, it does not imply that the individuals who aggregate together must remain the same. Organizations are 'indefinite collections of loosely related and constantly changing individuals'.[8] Organizations may well outlast the individuals who currently comprise them so that, in time, an organization may contain *none* of its current members, and yet still be the very *same* organization. Second, this does not imply that the common purpose is fixed for all time. Thus, it does not prevent discussions about what that common purpose is or should be—as we saw in Chapter 1, Elaine was reconsidering why DesignCo existed; was it for the architectural practice which was at the core of the organization or for the profit which might be 'extracted' from its operation? Indeed, it is likely that there will need to be a continuing debate about the purpose of any organization; why does it exist, what good is it serving?

But just because we know that organizations exist in the very broad variety of forms which they may take, and just because we have at least a working definition of a formal organization, still does not explain why they exist in the first place. There have been, as might be expected, various explanations of this.[9] One such explanation, hinted at above in relation to the Industrial Revolution though true even in pre-industrial societies, is that organizations come into being when the technology required becomes sufficiently complex that it is more than one person can handle. It would be difficult to imagine one person designing and making a car, for example, simply because the range of knowledge and skills required would be too much for one person to learn and be able to exercise with the requisite level of skill.

A second explanation is that organizations exist because they may well be able to offer their members inducements (wages/salary and perquisites) which are worth more to them than the contributions it asks of them (principally the time devoted to work). Thus, an organization may be able to create a whole which is greater than the sum of its parts, and therefore be able to reward its members accordingly. At a very simple level, from a personal perspective, individuals might well earn more by working for an organization than they could by working for themselves. Organizations, in the terminology of 'shared value' which was mentioned briefly in Chapter 1, are value-creating mechanisms; we can achieve more together than we can alone.

A third explanation is perhaps the best known and goes under the heading of 'transaction cost economics'. At its simplest this explanation is that an organization 'can mediate economic transactions between its members at lower costs than a market mechanism can'.[10] Take the example of car manufacturing given above, and assume for the moment that there are no

---

[8] Hasnas (2012: 194).
[9] See Ouchi (2007: 13–14) for the three explanations given here.
[10] Ibid.: 13.

organizations in the world. It is, as stated, *difficult* to imagine one person designing and making a car, but it is not *impossible*, even allowing for the fact that a modern car has something approaching 30,000 parts. Because the individual almost certainly could not master all of the technologies which are involved, she would have to contract with many other individuals who each had developed certain other elements of the knowledge and skills which are required—to do with the drive train, body building, braking system, electrical system, and so on. And because each of those individuals probably would not have all the knowledge and skills required in their own sub-systems, it is likely that they would, in turn, have to contract with other individuals. It would become an extraordinarily large network, with each contract having to be negotiated individually. These are the direct 'transaction costs' of the market mechanism, though there would also be other costs in the form of monitoring each contract to ensure everyone does what they agreed to do. And, in addition, there would be capital requirements for most of the technologies (engine design, for example) which would be beyond the capacity of any one individual. So the principal advantage of formal organizations derives from their ability to reduce the costs of creating and monitoring a vast set of detailed contracts under irreducible and inescapable uncertainty. Markets, in this sense, have limits.[11]

It is not difficult to see that the only realistic way of designing and making a car is through an organization which brings many of these transactions and technologies 'in-house', as it were. It is not only more efficient that way, but it also reduces the uncertainty of thousands of market-based contracts. Of course, specialization will mean that it is often best for one organization to focus on certain aspects—perhaps design and assembly in the case of cars— and allow others to undertake other aspects—braking systems, for example. So while it is not impossible for one organization to do everything (it was said of Harland and Wolff shipyard in Belfast, which built the Titanic, that in its heyday it made everything for an ocean-going liner except the gyroscope), it is, of course, unusual. In addition, because organizations normally outlast their members, their longevity is a distinct advantage; buying life insurance from a 65-year-old individual, however experienced he may be, would not be as secure as buying it from a life-insurance organization which happened to employ him.

In summary, organizations come into existence for a combination of reasons—because of the level of complexity which is beyond one person to handle, because of their ability to add value over and above that which any one

---

[11] I am indebted to a speech by Martin Wolf, Associate Editor and Chief Economics Commentator for the *Financial Times*, for these last two points. See https://www.icgn.org/ sites/default/files/Martin%20Wolf%20speech.pdf, accessed 14 September 2016.

individual could achieve, and because of their inherent efficiency and lack of uncertainty over a purely market-based system of individual transactions.

So, we know why organizations exist and we have a working definition of a formal organization. But that is not typically how we *think* about organizations. To understand that, we need to consider a rather different approach.

## METAPHORS AND THEORIES OF ORGANIZATIONS

In an important book titled *Images of Organizations*,[12] from an area of study which is known as the 'sociology of organizations', Gareth Morgan introduced the idea that the way we think about organizations, the images we have of them in our minds, are what we would usually refer to as *metaphors*. In other words, we use metaphors to speak of organizations as being *like* this or that, in just the same way as we use metaphors to speak of individuals. To say that 'Elaine was a brick' would normally be taken as a metaphor, indicating that she had stood firm alongside others in a difficult situation, and therefore as a compliment rather than a criticism.

Metaphors are important because they provide us with ways of thinking and of seeing which have a significant influence on how we understand our world, and therefore also on how we act within it. As Morgan says, 'research in a wide variety of fields has demonstrated that metaphor exerts a formative influence on science, on our language, and on how we think, as well as on how we express ourselves on a day-to-day basis'.[13] Metaphor, therefore, produces insight, enabling us to enhance our understanding of things.

But we also need to recognize that the use of metaphor is *always* one-sided; it tells a part of the story but not the whole story. All we are saying when we use metaphor is that something is *like this* in some respects. Elaine is 'like a brick' in the sense that bricks are solid and dependable objects, things you can rely on to do their job in constructing a building, for example. The compliment paid to Elaine says she is like that as a person, or at least was like that on a particular occasion. Saying that she is like a brick, however, is clearly not meant to imply anything about her size, shape, or colour—she is, presumably, not squat, with square edges and red-skinned! So we have to be careful in using metaphor to recognize that, 'while capable of creating valuable insights, [it] is also incomplete, biased and potentially misleading'.[14]

Allowing for this potentially double-sided and paradoxical nature of metaphor, Morgan goes on to claim that 'all theory is metaphor'.[15] This is quite a big claim, but we can see where he is coming from. The rest of his book is

---

[12] Morgan (2006).      [13] Ibid.: 4.      [14] Ibid.: 5.      [15] Ibid.: 5.

taken up with descriptions of the various ways in which metaphors have been used to enhance our understanding of organizations. He describes them as 'images of organization' (to use the title of his book), but they are also theories of organization. Thus, he covers organizations as machines, implying a mechanistic and bureaucratic approach to understanding and managing them. Organizations as organisms helps us to recognize that the environment is an important determinant on organizations; organizations are, in that sense, open systems which need to be able to adapt to their environment if they are to survive. Organizations as brains takes us into ideas about learning organizations. And so on—organizations as cultures, as political systems, as psychic prisons, as flux and transformation, and as instruments of domination make up the remaining metaphors in the book.

Each of these metaphors has a theoretical base or, in some cases, more than one theoretical base to it. But that begs the question as to what exactly a theory is. Our word 'theory' comes from the Greek word *theoria* meaning viewing, speculation, or contemplation. Theory, like metaphor, is therefore a way of seeing some aspect of the world, which then goes on to contemplate it, and potentially to speculate about it in the sense of seeking some explanation for the phenomenon under consideration. Theories therefore 'may be thought of as capable of formulation, as yielding predictions and explanations, as achieved by a process of theorizing, as answering to empirical evidence that is in principle describable without them, as liable of being overturned by newer and better theories'.[16] While this is a general definition of theory, it clearly applies just as much to organizations and organization theory as to life in general, as well as to particular roles such as that of manager. The key points for our purposes are that theory-as-metaphor needs to be capable of being *formulated*, in other words that key concepts and relationships between them can be defined; that this provides an *explanation* of how things are in such a way as to describe but also interpret the empirical evidence before us; and that it offers *predictions* so that, if the theory is 'correct', it will lead to propositions as to what will follow if particular actions are taken. Within the field of economics, for example, some of these theories are known as 'theories of the firm', and include obvious examples such as the profit maximizing theory of the firm, the sales maximization theory of the firm, as well as what is known as the 'nexus of contracts' view[17] (of which, more below).

The reason for covering these metaphorical and theoretical perspectives is that this book introduces another 'way of seeing', a different metaphor or a different theory of organizations and management and, indeed, of life in general. That, at least, is the claim which is being made concerning

---

[16] Blackburn (1994: 375–6).
[17] The nexus of contracts view is taken from one of the more famous papers in the literature—Jensen & Meckling (1976).

MacIntyre's work and its application in the field of management and organizations. Of course, it would be nice to be able to say that this is *the* theory of organizations and management; that it explains everything; that, if followed, its predictions would lead to some kind of 'truth' such that, because it relates to ethics, would make organizations, management, and us as individuals 'better' in some sense. However, given all that has been said above, this would clearly be an overstatement. So the claim about the way of thinking and seeing, the metaphors and theory which are being introduced in this book, is only that it does have something different and important to say to individuals, to managers, and to organizations. It is *one way of seeing*, not the only one, but, so the argument will go, a very important and insightful one.

## OTHER APPROACHES TO ORGANIZATIONAL ETHICS

The approach which is being introduced in this book is, as already noted above, one which puts ethics at the heart of organizations and of management. In Chapter 3 we will begin to explore this particular approach of virtue ethics in more detail, before applying it to organizations in Chapter 4. By way of contrast, the last section of this chapter explores other approaches to organizational ethics so that, when we come to the virtue ethics approach, similarities and differences between them will become evident.

Ethics has, of course, been a concern for organizations at least from the time of the Industrial Revolution, and a short historical excursion may be helpful in setting the context for the later discussion. Consider, for example, the following comment: 'There can be little doubt that the condition of the workers, especially the women and children, in the early textile factories was miserable: 14 to 16 hours every day spent performing repetitive tasks in noisy, foul-smelling, unsanitary surroundings. The workers' homes were equally unhealthy'.[18] Indeed, there were many such criticisms of early capitalism— Southey's description in 1807 of the exploitation of children in a Manchester cotton mill, for example, makes similarly harsh reading:

> They are deprived in childhood of all instruction and all enjoyment;...their health physical and moral is alike destroyed; they die of diseases induced by unremitting task work...or they live to grow up without decency, without comfort, and without hope, without morals, without religion, and without shame, and bring forth slaves like themselves to tread in the same path of misery.[19]

---

[18] Hannan & Kranzberg (no date).     [19] Cited in Simmons (1951: 209–10).

The effect of the Industrial Revolution on workers' lives led to a general critique of the world of business.[20] In D.H. Lawrence's essay *Nottingham and the Mining Countryside*, for example, he condemned the impact of industrialization on housing and community:

> The great crime which the moneyed classes and promoters of industry committed in the palmy Victorian days was the condemning of the workers to ugliness, ugliness, ugliness: meanness and formless and ugly surroundings, ugly ideals, ugly religion, ugly hope, ugly love, ugly clothes, ugly furniture, ugly houses, ugly relationships between workers and employers. The human soul needs actual beauty even more than bread.[21]

And Lawrence added that, 'the industrial problem arises from the base forcing of all human energy into a competition of mere acquisition'.[22] Lawrence's concern for the effects on workers finds rather more subtle but perhaps even more melancholic echoes in T. S. Eliot's *The Waste Land*:

> Unreal City,
> Under the brown fog of a winter dawn,
> A crowd flowed over London Bridge, so many,
> I had not thought death had undone so many.
> Sighs, short and infrequent, were exhaled,
> And each man fixed his eyes before his feet.[23]

The conflicts which are painted in these extracts are analysed in terms of virtue and vice (the terminology we will be using in this book) in John Maynard Keynes' words in his essay *Economic possibilities for our grandchildren*, written in 1930. In suggesting that, within a century, we would have found a solution for the 'economic problem' of the human race, as he termed it, he saw a time when we would be able:

> to return to some of the most sure and certain principles of religion and traditional virtue—that avarice is a vice, that the exaction of usury is a misdemeanour, and the love of money is detestable ... [that] we shall once more value ends above means and prefer the good to the useful.

But then he warned:

> But beware! The time for all this is not yet. For at least another hundred years we must pretend to ourselves and to everyone that fair is foul and foul is fair; for foul is useful and fair is not. Avarice and usury and precaution must be our gods for a little longer still. For only they can lead us out of the tunnel of economic necessity into daylight.[24]

---

[20] See Pollard (2000) which offers a detailed but largely negative critique of business as represented in English literature.
[21] Lawrence (1974: 119–20).        [22] Ibid.: 120.        [23] Eliot (1969).
[24] Keynes (1932).

*Virtue at Work*

While this brings to an end our historical excursion (though interestingly Keynes' prediction still has a few years to run), there has continued to be a genuine concern for the impact of organizations (and not just business organizations) on workers and society. There is at least a perspective, implied in the quotation from Keynes, that organizations may not be locations where moral behaviour takes place, but that they are, almost ontologically, the opposite—that is to say that *in their very nature* they are locations for *immorality*. Take, for example, the child sexual abuse scandals which have hit many organizations in recent years. Writing in relation to such scandals in the Catholic Church, but exploring initially two organizational tragedies in Canada[25] for which commissions of inquiry concluded that the tragedies were due to organizational shortcomings, the authors comment:

> There is another explanation for these tragedies that, despite being much more difficult to accept, is equally plausible. Simply stated, the alternative explanation is that the events in question were in fact *made possible* by well-accepted and highly regarded organizational practices. It is because these organizations were as well organized as they were that these events took place, not because they were insufficiently organized. The implication of this explanation is that it applies to the phenomenon of 'organization' itself and, thus, to potentially *all* organizations. What they suggest is not that we have failed to organize, but, rather, that *organization has failed....* If this is the case, what it suggests is that it is organization rather than the lack thereof that leaves us vulnerable to these sorts of moral failures.[26]

In writing this, these authors draw on the work of the eminent social theorist Zygmunt Bauman, and begin their piece with a quote of his: 'the organization as a whole is an instrument to obliterate responsibility'.[27] They then refer to Bauman's inquiry into the Holocaust, in which Bauman 'makes clear [that] complex organizations thwart our moral impulses in numerous ways':

> At the most general level, they accomplish this by facilitating action at a distance. They serve to separate the thought from the deed and, in doing so, they result in decisions being made in relation to abstract entities as opposed to the real Others that those who carry out these decisions must confront. And, conversely, they enable the latter to absolve themselves of responsibility for their actions by virtue of the fact that the decisions that prompted their actions were not their own. Thus, we can see that, by separating decision-making from implementation, the moral impulse is for all intents and purposes by-passed.[28]

---

[25] One involved the contamination of the national blood supply during the late 1970s and 1980s; the other was the so-called Somalia affair, when two Somalis lost their lives at the hands of Canadian military personnel stationed in Somalia as part of a UN peace-keeping force in 1992–3.
[26] Hinings & Mauws (2006: 116), emphasis in original.
[27] Ibid.: 115.    [28] Ibid.: 118.

If this analysis is correct, how do organizations accomplish this separation of decision making from implementation? The answer is that this is commonly achieved through their hierarchical and functional division of labour, in other words it occurs as a natural outcome of the need to impose structure in an organization. And, in relation to the functional division of labour, there arises the substitution of *technical* for *moral* responsibility; the worker is responsible only for making sure the trains run on time, not what they carry (to take an example from the Holocaust where the 'passengers' were, of course, Jews). In effect, this is the means-end argument of morally neutral management which MacIntyre[29] also makes, and which we will revisit in Chapter 6. In summary, 'the triumph of organization is not so much that it thwarts morality, but that it redeploys it toward the pursuit of technical ends', and this is reinforced through the vocabulary of organization with 'its capacity to dehumanize the objects of bureaucratic operations'.[30] In other words, to refer to individuals as groups such as customers or competitors makes them impersonal and no longer 'real Others'.

There is some common ground here with the more recently explored phenomenon of the 'dark side' of organizations. This 'consists of situations in which people hurt other people, injustices are perpetuated and magnified, and the pursuits of wealth, power or revenge lead people to behaviours that others can only see as unethical, illegal, despicable, or reprehensible'.[31] These are not necessarily evil organizations, established for sinister purposes such as those associated with the Third Reich and the Holocaust, but are situations which occur, or can occur, inside otherwise reputable organizations— doubtless much like the organizations in Victorian Britain whose effects were described above. An example, recently reported in a public inquiry,[32] of neglect, physical and sexual abuse, and violence against children in Ireland's industrial schools system over a period of fifty years in the latter half of the twentieth century, demonstrates that this is by no means only historical.[33]

This is not to say that we have to 'buy into' all of this uncritically. The approach in this book, for example, speaks of organizations, when they are in good order and pursuing a good purpose, as '*essentially* moral spaces'.[34] But we should at least acknowledge both the *systemic* possibility (following Bauman), and the rather more *opportunistic* possibility (following the 'dark side'), of corrupting organizations and corruption within organizations. Organizations are ubiquitous *and* have the potential to be deeply dehumanizing, and we would do well to remember this.

---

[29] See MacIntyre (2007: 74) for example.
[30] Hinings & Mauws (2006: 119), emphasis removed.
[31] Griffin & O'Leary-Kelly (2004: xv).    [32] Ryan (2009).
[33] See Kelly (2016) for a summary and analysis of this case.
[34] Beadle & Moore (2011: 103), emphasis in original.

## Corporate Social Responsibility and
## the Stakeholder Approach

Let us, then, turn to an approach to organizational ethics which has attempted
to address some of these rather serious concerns. The most common
approach, at least in the sphere of business, is that of Corporate Social Responsibility and, associated with this, the stakeholder approach, both mentioned
briefly in Chapter 1. Corporate Social Responsibility (henceforth CSR) is
variously termed Corporate Responsibility, Corporate Citizenship, Business
Ethics, and so on. These terms each have similarities and differences in
emphasis so that, for example, the difference between CSR and Business Ethics
can be thought of as a difference in starting points. CSR tends to start at the
'corporate' end of things and tries to work out practical ways in which
companies can respond to issues to do with their role in society and the
kinds of corruption which can take place within them, whereas Business
Ethics tends to start with moral philosophy (in its various formulations)[35]
and seeks to apply various approaches to ethics to corporations and other
business entities. On this understanding, the approach adopted in this book
is closer to Business Ethics than CSR, although the argument will be made
that this approach has very practical implications (along the lines of 'there's
nothing so practical as a good theory').

   CSR has no single agreed definition and, as we shall see below, it has
developed over time as a concept. Academics have defined it variously as:

> Corporate social responsibility encompasses the economic, legal, ethical and
> philanthropic expectations placed on organizations by society at a given point
> in time.[36]

> Situations where the firm goes beyond compliance and engages in actions that
> appear to further some social good, beyond the interests of the firm and that
> which is required by law.[37]

There are similarities in these two definitions. It is noticeable that legal
responsibilities form a basis, but that other responsibilities over and above
the law are expected. These 'ethical and philanthropic expectations' are such as
to 'further some social good'. But there are also differences in these definitions.
The first definition includes economic responsibilities, reminding business
organizations that their fundamental responsibilities lie within their function
as economic actors—in creating products or offering services thereby satisfying customers, in offering employment, in purchasing supplies, and so forth.
The first definition also emphasizes the contingency of CSR—that it depends

---

[35] For a wide variety of approaches in what has been termed 'normative theory' in business
ethics, see Smith (2009).
[36] Carroll & Buchholtz (2000: 35).          [37] McWilliams, Siegel, & Wright (2006: 1).

upon the expectations of society at any given time and so, as these change, CSR will need to adapt.

The second definition implies that CSR is a cost to the organization since the actions in which it might engage go beyond its own interests, while the first definition, although it might be interpreted that way, is silent on this point. On the other hand, there are definitions of CSR, typically from a governmental or intergovernmental perspective (although many businesses also understand CSR this way), which suggest the close alignment of CSR with organizational strategy such that it might be in the interests of both business and society.[38] We will return to this point below.

Even though we have no single definition of CSR, the discussion above gives a sufficiently clear outline of the idea for us to look at it more closely. In particular, a historical analysis of its development is instructive.[39] One possible starting point is the publication in 1953 in the USA of a book entitled *Social Responsibilities of the Businessman*.[40] From this time, and throughout the 1950s and 1960s, the focus of CSR was on what might be termed the 'macro-social' effects of CSR.[41] In other words, the concern was for the kinds of effects on workers and communities which we saw above in the discussion of the Industrial Revolution, and the way in which business was seen both as the source of those kinds of problems and, hence, as responsible for resolving them. CSR, during this period, was characterized as 'a complementary and corrective measure for some social failures inherent in *laissez-faire* economy'.[42] Behind this perspective was a theoretical orientation which was explicitly normative:[43] such impacts on workers and communities were wrong and needed to be put right, and while this might lie within the province of government overall, those organizations which caused the problems, and which potentially had the resources to resolve them, should do so. That there would be costs involved, and that these would have to be met by the businesses themselves, thus lowering profits, did not seem to be a concern.

---

[38] The European Commission and the UK Government have taken these approaches—see, for example, European Commission (2011) and Department for Business & Skills (2014).

[39] The following is taken largely from Lee (2008). Although the article is written from a North American standpoint, the broad thrust of the analysis is in line with developments in CSR elsewhere, particularly in liberal market economies. See also Aguinis & Glavas (2012) for a more recent (and very academic) summary of the CSR literature.

[40] Bowen (1953). Lee (2008: 56, 58) cites this as the pivotal publication in the 1950s and 1960s thinking on CSR. The sexist nature of Bowen's title is worth noting although, of course, most managers were men in those days.

[41] Bowen (1953: 54).      [42] Ibid.: 56, emphasis in original.

[43] Normative is used here in the sense of ethical, i.e., as a norm or a standard. The ethical theory which is most commonly associated with this particular approach is the 'act so that you treat humanity, whether in your own person or in that of another, always as an end and never as a means only' formulation of the Kantian categorical imperative.

Gradually over the ensuing decades, however, this view changed, until by the 1990s CSR had become associated not with the effects of business on society but with CSR's effects on the financial performance of businesses. To understand why this was the case, we need to take a small digression into what is usually termed the stakeholder approach.

One of the criticisms of CSR as a concept is that it is inherently vague. What, precisely, do the 'social' responsibilities of an organization actually mean? It is for this reason that the term social is sometimes dropped, and the more straightforward term 'Corporate Responsibility' used. However, by linking CSR specifically to stakeholders, this became less of a problem. Indeed, Ed Freeman,[44] one of the originators of what became known as stakeholder theory, has suggested that CSR would be better understood as referring to Corporate *Stakeholder* Responsibility.[45]

This move to defining CSR in terms of stakeholders allowed it to become more concrete.[46] It became possible to define which stakeholders the organization felt it owed a responsibility to—typically shareholders, employees, customers, suppliers, and the local community, although recognizing that other stakeholders, such as government, the media, non-governmental organizations, competitors, and perhaps also the ecological environment, could also have an impact and needed to be taken into account in decision making. This was the 'nexus of contracts' approach mentioned above, with managers on behalf of the organization contracting with each of the stakeholders. But this categorization and understanding of stakeholders also enabled the possibility of measuring the impact upon them of various CSR projects or programmes. If an investment was made in some employee initiative, for example, such as providing educational opportunities in work time and at the organization's cost, what return, in terms of increased employee capability, motivation, and retention, did this lead to? Out of this was born the 'business case' for CSR at the project level, and a new area of study at the organizational level to explore whether Corporate Social Performance (CSP) as an amalgamation of all the CSR projects and programmes an organization might have, was related to Corporate Financial Performance (CFP).

This tighter and tighter coupling of CSP with CFP meant, of course, that CSR had moved from its earlier concerns over the macro-social effects of business activity to organizational-level concerns over its effects on financial performance.[47] CSR in its stakeholder formulation had, in other words, been reduced from what might have been regarded as quite a radical idea to become

---

[44] Lee (2008: 58) recognizes Freeman's 1984 book *Strategic Management: A Stakeholder Approach* as one of the pivotal publications in the CSR literature.
[45] See, for example, www.corporate-ethics.org/pdf/csr.pdf, accessed 14 September 2016.
[46] A classic reference in this area is Clarkson (1995).
[47] See Lee (2008: 54).

managerialist and transactional, and ultimately *strategic*. And as such it became a legitimate area of attention for management at all levels, irrespective of their own personal views on the role of business in society. And the theoretical perspective which then became associated with CSR, instead of being explicitly normative (concerned for the impact of business activity on workers and communities, as we noted above), became implicitly normative, based on utilitarian cost-benefit calculations; how does it benefit the *organization*?

There is a criticism which follows from this strategic approach to CSR based on the very nature of the corporation, particularly in its manifestation in the USA and UK, and which connects to the point above about organizations as being instruments to obliterate responsibility. It can be argued that the limited liability attached to corporations enables their shareholders to enjoy, in effect, a position of 'no-obligation, no-responsibility, no-liability' such that shares permit their owners 'to enjoy income rights without needing to worry about how the dividends are generated. They are not liable for corporate malfeasance',[48] or, we may add, need they be interested in the impact of corporate actions on stakeholders except in so far as this contributes to their own financial reward. As another commentator put it, 'the shareholder-centric model appeared to be a recipe for higher economic returns at the lowest possible risk. This was an awe-inspiring combination'.[49] This, it could be argued, enshrines *irresponsibility* into the corporate form. And no wonder then that, 'CSR has been so warmly embraced by so many companies' since it 'leaves untouched the shareholder-oriented model of the corporation and the corporate legal form as presently constituted'.[50]

This is not to say, however, that the strategic approach to CSR does not have its advantages. As noted, by tying CSR into an organization's strategy, and hence potentially leading to a competitive advantage, it encourages the attention of managers, and potentially legitimizes the activity in the eyes of shareholders. This has been encouraged not only by this 'instrumental' stakeholder approach[51] (that stakeholders are means to the end of conventional organizational objectives such as, in the case of business, the maximization of shareholder value), but also by influential papers in the management literature such as those by Michael Porter and Mark Kramer in the *Harvard Business Review*.[52] And while the findings of the large number of academic studies

---

[48] Ireland (2010: 845).     [49] Haldane (2015: 8).     [50] Ireland (2010: 853).

[51] See Donaldson & Preston (1995) for an analysis of stakeholder theory as being capable of analysis along empirical/descriptive, instrumental, and normative lines.

[52] See Porter & Kramer (2002, 2006, 2011). The latter, on 'shared value' was referred to in Chapter 1. There are similar approaches which, in effect, attempt to rehabilitate capitalism. A good example is Beinhocker & Hanauer which argues that 'the crucial contribution business makes to society is *transforming ideas into products and services that solve problems*' (2014: 7, emphasis in original). There are similarities with the idea of *Corporate Social Opportunity*, the title of a practical book by Grayson & Hodges (2004).

which have been conducted into the relationship between CSP and CFP are not totally conclusive, there does appear to be a positive relationship.[53] In other words, an organization which performs well in terms of its social performance *also* performs well in terms of its financial performance.[54] These findings, of course, tend to encourage the strategic approach to CSR; if CSR leads to improved reputation for the organization, increased customer loyalty, attracts a better quality of employees, and improves their motivation and retention, and so increases profitability, why would an organization not engage with it?

However, this is not to say that CSR has become totally dominated by the strategic approach tied to what is generally known as enlightened shareholder value. Just as there were opponents of Bowen's approach in the 1950s, so proponents of the stakeholder approach continue to argue that it is not just an 'instrumental' theory, linking stakeholder management to organizational performance, but that at its core it is a 'normative' theory.[55] In other words:

> Stakeholder theory is a theory of organizational management and ethics … [and] is distinct [from enlightened shareholder value] because it addresses morals and values explicitly as a central feature of managing organizations … attention to the interests and well-being of some non-shareholders is obligatory *for more than the prudential and instrumental purposes of wealth maximisation of equity shareholders.*[56]

As indicated above, this does not mean that this argument has won the day by any means. I suggested a number of years ago[57] that perhaps the best that the stakeholder approach has achieved is not that the organization should be run in the interests of a number of stakeholders besides just shareholders, but that it has added a stakeholder 'tinge' to an otherwise shareholder model of the organization. On this understanding, organizations pursue stakeholder interests only from an enlightened shareholder value perspective.

---

[53] As well as the many individual studies which have been conducted, beginning in the 1970s, there have been occasional review articles and what are known as meta-analyses—studies which conduct a statistical analysis using the data from a number of previous studies. See, for example, Orlitzky, Schmidt, & Rynes (2003) and Endrikat, Guenther, & Hoppe (2014). For an interesting study suggesting that the results of CSP versus CFP studies are socially constructed, such that studies published in business ethics journals find more positive results than those published in economics, finance, and accounting journals, see Orlitzky (2011).

[54] These studies are based on correlations which, of course, do not automatically determine causation. In order to get around this issue, these studies typically include lead-lag analyses taking, for example, CSP in one time period and CFP in a later time period and *vice-versa*. These studies generally find positive results in both directions, i.e., good social performance leads to good financial performance and *vice-versa*.

[55] See again Donaldson & Preston (1995).

[56] Phillips, Freeman, & Wicks (2003: 481), emphasis added.

[57] Moore (1999).

Perhaps a helpful way of looking at this from a practical perspective is that organizations are likely to have a range of CSR projects or programmes.[58] Some may well be generated from a strategic perspective, but others are carried out either because the organization is forced to do them by regulation or, perhaps, because of pressure from particular stakeholder groups, and then there are others besides which are generated because the organization feels it *ought* to do them, akin perhaps to the 'macro-social' altruistic perspective covered above.

Nonetheless, despite these ways in which strategic CSR might be mitigated, there is no doubt that, overall, this is now the dominant approach. And this leads to three immediate concerns. First, the 'business case' approach means that, within the economics of supply and demand, the marginal value of CSR projects will decrease over time. The organization will only 'do' ethics if it pays, and there will come times when it no longer does. Second, there is an assumption behind strategic CSR that what is good for the organization is also good for society. Whereas, in earlier decades, the concern was primarily focused on social ills, now it is focused only on those social ills which also have the potential to benefit the organization. And, as has been said, 'from the perspective of society, the social problems ignored by corporations may well be much more urgent issues that require corporate expertise and operational capacity. Conceiving CSR as discretionary business practices dilutes the meaning of social responsibility in CSR'.[59] Third, this conceives of ethics-as-strategy, rather than ethics-as-ethics. As one commentator has put it, 'This is a morality where maximising shareholder values is the principle that guides the governance of corporations...including how they organize their own ethics'.[60] More technically, ethics, on this understanding, has become purely consequentialist if not Machiavellian. In other words, ethics and its embodiment in CSR and stakeholder theory, has been 'captured' by business and turned to its own advantage. And that should make us profoundly concerned.

There is, however, one other concern in addition to these three which we need to note. While CSR, via the stakeholder approach, gets closer to the 'core business' of the organization, it still leaves unanswered questions about the purpose of the organization, why it exists in the first place, what its *raison d'etre* might be.[61] Creating value and sharing it out among various stakeholders goes

---

[58] See Husted & Salazar (2006) who distinguish between strategic, coerced egoism and altruistic perspectives.
[59] Lee (2008: 65).　　　[60] Rhodes (2016: 1505).
[61] There are other approaches, notably 'Conscious Capitalism', which does claim to address the point about purpose. Mackey & Sisodia make a strong case for purpose-led business arguing that such businesses will fall within (or potentially cross over between) four categories of 'great purpose': the good (service to others); the true (discovery and furthering human knowledge); the beautiful (excellence and the creation of beauty); and the heroic (courage to do what is right to change and improve the world) (2013: 59–64). They then link this to the stakeholder approach as

only so far; what if the 'value' is created from pornography, tobacco, gambling, arms manufacture, and so on? Of course, arguments can be made about the social value of each of these, but the point is that CSR does not distinguish between them and other value-creating activities; so long as organizations are economic actors which create value, they are legitimate players in the CSR field. But surely we might be better with an approach which *does* ask these fundamental kinds of questions, which links directly from the 'core business' of the organization to the common good of society and how the organization contributes to this.[62] It is to just such an approach that we will turn in Chapter 4.

## SUMMARY

In this chapter we noted that organizations are ubiquitous in the present social order, defined what we mean by a formal organization, and have seen why such organizations exist. We then explored the ways in which we think about organizations in terms of the metaphor approach and, linked to this, we came to understand theory as metaphor. In that context, the approach to organizations and management explored in this book can be seen as another theory-as-metaphor, a way of seeing and understanding that is, so the argument will go, different and important because of the way it opens up our understanding of organizations and of ethics, as well as leading to very practical consequences. We then explored alternative approaches to organizations and ethics, noting serious concerns—that organizations might be ontologically (in their very nature or essence) *immoral*—before exploring the most common approach to these issues today, that of CSR and the stakeholder approach. We have seen how this has become a strategic concern for business and, while we noted some benefits of this approach, we also noted several quite serious concerns.

Is there, then, a better approach?

---

'the centrepiece of the conscious business philosophy' (2013: 67), claiming that 'the purpose of business is to improve our lives and to create value for stakeholders' (2013: 20). There is, however, less focus on the development of people than the approach outlined in this book, and there is still a hint that Conscious Capitalism is really tied to success, with the idea that 'firms practicing Conscious Capitalism will *invariably* profit from their actions' (O'Toole & Vogel 2011: 63, emphasis added). Possibly, then, Conscious Capitalism is really closer to the Strategic CSR approach outlined above.

[62] We will revisit the notion of the common good in Chapter 3.

# 3

## Virtue Ethics and Organizational Ethics

### INTRODUCTION

We have already seen that the approach that we will be taking in this book is based on a branch of ethics known as virtue ethics. So it is time to explore what this is all about, and how it can be related to individuals, managers, and organizations. In Chapter 4 we will apply this to organizations and management explicitly, drawing, as noted in Chapter 1, on the work of the moral philosopher Alasdair MacIntyre. Here, the aim is to set out the virtues approach, mostly as characterized by MacIntyre, at the individual level but also at the level of society since the two are interrelated. We will then look at two criticisms of virtue ethics and why, within a virtue ethics approach, we should be able to provide reasons for our actions, before considering whether and how this approach might be applied to organizations.

### VIRTUE ETHICS IN CONTEXT

Virtue ethics has a very long history. One branch traces its origins to Confucianism in the East (based on the teachings of the Chinese philosopher Confucius (551–479 BCE)), and there has, for example, been a comparatively recent attempt to bring this to the attention of the business ethics community.[1] However, the branch of virtue ethics which is more familiar to us in the West is derived from ancient Greece with Socrates, Plato, and most particularly Aristotle (384–322 BCE) as its key proponents. This way of understanding ethics dominated in Western society for many centuries, such that when 'plain everyday persons' thought about ethics they did so in terms of virtues, vices, and character. This all changed, however, as the Age of Enlightenment in Europe in the eighteenth century, based on liberty, progress, reason, and

---

[1] See, for example, Ip (2009, 2011).

tolerance, led to new approaches to ethics—most obviously those associated with Immanuel Kant (1724–1804) on the one hand, and the Utilitarianism of Jeremy Bentham (1748–1832) and John Stuart Mill (1806–73) on the other.

Hence, it is only relatively recently that virtue ethics has re-emerged as a mainstream branch of moral philosophy[2] and, as noted in Chapter 1, Alasdair MacIntyre has become perhaps the best-known moral philosopher associated with this approach to ethics, originating in the publication of his book *After Virtue* in 1981. One way of understanding this development is as a reaction to the deficiencies of what has been called the principle-based ethics of the Enlightenment, typified by Kantian ethics and Utilitarianism.[3]

Both of these principle-based ethical theories take what can be termed an 'action-centred' approach. In other words, confronted with a specific issue over which a decision needs to be taken, they view this as an issue of applying certain principles in order to determine what action should follow. For example, Elaine (who we met in Chapter 1) is married to Fred. What we didn't know then is that Fred is considering separating from Elaine with a view to divorce, and this is, on an action-centred approach, a decision to be taken and then acted upon. Broadly, Kantian ethics would argue in this particular situation that various promises or duties to the other have been entered into and therefore, *irrespective of the consequences*, the conclusion is clear: no, Fred should not separate from or divorce his wife. Because of the way that Kantian ethics approaches decisions, it is characterized as a *non-consequentialist* ethic. Utilitarianism, on the other hand, takes the opposite approach: it depends entirely on the consequences,[4] *irrespective of what prior commitments might exist*. These consequences need to be weighed in terms of the harms and benefits to all those who might be affected by the decision, and the best decision is that which, in the terms for which Utilitarianism is famous, leads to the greatest happiness for the greatest number of people.[5] So should Fred separate from and possibly divorce Elaine? Well, it all depends.

In both cases, however, these ethical theories offer *principles* by which one might come to a decision. But there are problems with this approach. One of the early pioneers of applying virtue ethics to business ethics describes the situation in the following way:

---

[2] See, as a precursor to MacIntyre's *After Virtue*, Anscombe (1958) and Foot (1978) and, for other approaches to virtue ethics, Slote (1996), Hursthouse (2001), and Swanton (2003).

[3] See DesJardins (1993) and Horvath (1995).

[4] There are different approaches even within Utilitarianism, most notably between Act and Rule Utilitarianism. Rule Utilitarianism acknowledges that certain rules (for example, to keep one's promises) generally lead to greater utility, so that, in Fred's case, this might also influence his decision even if he were to adopt a mostly utilitarian mode of thinking. Act Utilitarianism simply focuses on the decision in question.

[5] 'Happiness' is sometimes replaced with the rather more economic concept of 'utility'— hence Utilitarianism.

we should take seriously the fact that in practice, ethical principles seldom give any unambiguous practical advice. Adopting a principle-based approach in business ethics leads to numerous practical difficulties. A seemingly endless series of problems arises when one attempts to derive from such principles as the [Kantian] categorical imperative or the principle of utility [Utilitarianism], solutions to ethical problems faced by business people. Hopeless ambiguity in application, apparent counterexamples, ad hoc rebuttals, counterintuitive conclusions, and apparently contradictory prescriptions create an overwhelming morass in the discussion of particular moral situations.[6]

Another early pioneer of introducing virtue ethics in general, and MacIntyre's work in particular, to business ethics, identified four problems with principle-based ethics: it does not handle well the question of ethical motivation ('why should I be good or do right?'); inherently it offers generalized solutions to specific problems; Kantianism and Utilitarianism, despite their individual claims to an irrefutable logic, often lead to mutually incompatible solutions; and finally, while business ethics tends to be predominantly utilitarian (as we saw in the critique of CSR towards the end of Chapter 2), it tends to a corrupt form of pure Utilitarianism, and so regresses to a kind of Machiavellian calculation in which ends, which have been decided beforehand, justify the means.[7]

In addition to these criticisms, because principle-based ethics can end up with different answers to the same problem, there is the danger of drifting into what might be called 'ethical relativism' where whether a decision is morally correct or not is viewed as being 'relative to the individual (or group) making that judgment, and therefore one person cannot impose moral demands upon another'.[8] MacIntyre says something similar in *After Virtue* where he characterizes the ethics of what he calls 'modernity', based on Enlightenment ethics, as an ethic of 'emotivism' in which 'all moral judgments are *nothing but* expressions of preference, expressions of attitude or feeling insofar as they are moral or evaluative in character'.[9]

However, this is not to dismiss principle-based ethics out of hand. Clearly, we use Kantian and utilitarian principles in our everyday lives as well as in our work in organizations (even if, in the latter, Utilitarianism usually dominates). And somehow we make them work, even using them in combination. But MacIntyre suggests that the reason we are able to reach some kind of agreement on socially important matters (such as in medical ethics), is not because one set of principles (Kantianism, for example) comes to dominate, but because we have some common understanding of what the *substantial good* is which is at stake in any particular decision. To back up his case, MacIntyre gave as an example work by a national commission making recommendations about how to protect people when they are the subjects of biomedical and

---

[6] DesJardins (1993: 137).     [7] Horvath (1995: 500–501).
[8] Horvath (1995: 511).     [9] MacIntyre (2007: 11–12), emphasis in original.

behavioural research. The commission found it relatively easy to reach agreement in concrete cases, while members of the commission continued to hold radically different views on which principles of morality ought to be applied.[10] MacIntyre's point is that there must have been some kind of 'higher' morality at work, beyond the principles, which enabled such agreement.

To return to Fred, we might hope that he would work through *both* his prior commitments to Elaine, the promises he made at the time of their wedding, *and* the consequences of their staying together or separating on him, Elaine, their children, and significant others in their family and community (as well as talking this all out with Elaine, and perhaps getting some counselling, rather than making a decision in isolation). But what might help Fred most is to have some idea of the substantial good, for himself and Elaine and others, which he is trying to achieve. And, associated with this, what Fred might also need is a good dose of practical wisdom to help him (and Elaine) through this agonizing decision. But ideas about 'the good', which is a key idea in virtue ethics, and practical wisdom, which is one of the key virtues, may begin to suggest that a virtues approach might offer a 'higher' morality, and therefore might have something to offer over and above principle-based ethics. So what is virtue ethics all about?

## THE VARIOUS COMPONENTS OF VIRTUE ETHICS

Following on from the above, where we noted that the various forms of principle-based ethics are *action-oriented*, perhaps the clearest distinction with virtue ethics can be drawn by saying that virtue ethics is *actor- or person-oriented*. That is to say that while principle-based ethics starts with the question, 'What should I *do*?', virtue ethics starts with the question, 'What kind of person *am* I or do I want to *be*?', which, of course, links directly to the notion of character. But we immediately need to clarify this by saying that actions are also important to virtue ethics. Actions lead to outcomes which enable us (or perhaps otherwise) to achieve our purpose in life (we will come back to the idea of purpose in a moment). Actions also reinforce character. That is to say, if someone has developed the virtue of honesty, such that we could say she has an honest character, then a series of actions which involve truth-telling under difficult circumstances will tend to reinforce that aspect of that person's character.[11] Elaine, for example, needs to explain to the graduate

---

[10] MacIntyre (1984).

[11] It is worth noting that virtue ethics would allow for occasions where honesty is not the best policy, such as instances where the demands of compassion make it inappropriate to tell the truth. My wife's dress is *always* perfect for the occasion.

recruit in DesignCo that he is not matching up to the demands of the role, and doing so honestly and straightforwardly will strengthen Elaine's character in that respect (although we would, of course, hope that she is also able to do so with sensitivity, to break the news carefully but firmly). But, of course, the opposite may happen. Carrying out a series of subterfuges to avoid telling the new recruit the truth will tend to undermine Elaine's character, and this potentially to her detriment: 'past actions, by moulding character, become the cause of future actions'.[12]

Actions, however, as well as being important in determining character, also play a role in enabling us to achieve our purpose in life. This idea of purpose is an important second component of virtue ethics, so it is worth spending some time on it. Aristotle held that every rational activity should aim at some end or good, in other words that it should have some purpose to it.[13] To illustrate this, let us begin by considering a simple object such as a knife.[14] The purpose (or the end or the good—these terms tend to be used interchangeably) of a knife is to cut some material. To perform that function well it must be sharp, with a blade made of appropriate material and of sufficient length for the task, a handle that is appropriately shaped and made of a material which enables sufficient grip, the fixing between blade and handle should be strong, and the knife as a whole must be appropriately 'balanced'—not too heavy overall nor 'top-heavy' in one direction or the other. In addition, as well as these functional attributes, we might want to argue that a good knife should be one which is attractive to look at; that there is an aesthetic dimension to take into account as well.

While that places a number of demands on those who make knives, it is comparatively straightforward to determine a knife's purpose (allowing that different types of knife will be required for different functions), and to judge whether this or that particular knife is a good knife for its particular function. Even in this simple example, however, we should note that to do so will require that we see the knife in use over an extended period; if the fixing between the blade and handle were to break after a month or so, for example, we would be right in judging this not to be a good knife, one which is not fit for purpose, however sharp the blade may be or however aesthetically pleasing it may be to look at.

Starting from this example of a knife, it is clear that we could extend this reasonably easily to other more complicated objects such as a washing machine or a car. Does the washing machine clean clothes well and efficiently;

---

[12] Koehn (1995: 536).

[13] Aristotle (1955: 63, 1094a1–22). Note that references to Aristotle's work are both to the page number (e.g., 63) and to the original pages, columns (left or right, a or b) and lines of the Greek text (e.g. 1094a1–22).

[14] MacIntyre offers an equivalent example in considering what makes a good watch (2007: 57–9).

does the car get us from A to B safely, reliably, and economically? Do both perform their respective functions over an extended period of time? Do they fulfil their purpose?

What, then, of a person? Could we make the same kind of analysis and judgements as with a knife, washing machine, or car? Clearly, this is much more complicated—but not necessarily impossible. Indeed, it was a central feature of Aristotelian virtue ethics, as MacIntyre contends:

> moral arguments within the classical, Aristotelian tradition—whether in its Greek or its medieval versions—involve at least one central functional concept, the concept of *man* [sic] understood as having an essential nature and an essential purpose or function.[15]

The ancient Greeks even had a term for it; the ultimate purpose or good for an individual was, in Aristotle's terms, *eudaimonia*, and, although translation is not straightforward, MacIntyre suggests that it means something like, 'blessedness, happiness, prosperity. It is the state of being well and doing well, of a man's being well-favoured himself and in relation to the divine'.[16] So one's purpose in life is to become the sort of person who exists in this kind of state or condition.

Now this is a very broad definition, and necessarily so given the enormously wide range of lives, and life circumstances, which individuals lead and have. Within this broad definition, however, we might expect individuals to be able to define their understanding of their own purpose in life, and to be able to explain how it relates to some more general end or good. Some people might refer to this as their vocation or calling—perhaps to be a landscape painter, or musician, or doctor—although to cover the whole of one's life this would clearly need to extend beyond work to other activities and commitments, such as being a life partner or father. Purpose would, in that sense, have to become plural.

Could we then ask whether a particular individual is a good example of whatever it is which defines their purposes in life? Well yes, we probably could define in general terms what it means to be a good landscape painter, musician, doctor, life partner, father, and so on, and so make a judgement as to whether any particular individual meets those criteria. The Greeks had a word for this idea of purpose—they termed it *telos*, from which we get the idea that virtue ethics is a *teleological* theory of ethics. Using this terminology, we could say that an individual engages in a number of activities (later, we will call

---

[15] MacIntyre (2007: 58), emphasis in the original. MacIntyre's use of gendered language is common, but for simplicity's sake I do not comment further on it in individual quotations.

[16] MacIntyre (2007: 148). It should be noted that we will not be exploring the divine aspect in this book, interesting as it may be to some readers, although we will touch on it when considering churches as organizations in Chapter 9.

them practices) each of which has its own *telos* and which, in combination and in the ideal, lead to the individual's achievement of *eudaimonia*.

And what this also allows us to do is to arrive at an initial definition of the virtues. MacIntyre says:

> The virtues are precisely those qualities the possession of which will enable an individual to achieve *eudaimonia* and the lack of which will frustrate his movement toward that *telos*.[17]

Again, this is quite a broad definition, and says nothing about what individual virtues there might be; we will need to return to that below. But this definition does tie together the ideas of virtues being qualities of an individual which, together, form their character, and which then enable the individual to achieve their purposes in life. In other words, to be a good landscape painter, musician, doctor, life partner, father requires more than just a particular set of skills or capabilities; it also requires certain traits of character, certain virtues.

Virtue ethics, then, is actor- or person-oriented and to do with the development of character; it is associated with the idea of having a set of purposes in one's life which may be achieved partly through the possession and exercise of the virtues, leading to some overarching purpose, the achievement of *eudaimonia*. But let us, in moving on to the third component of virtue ethics, explore the relationship between skills and virtues a little further, in order both to clarify the distinction and to begin to understand what virtues look like.

For Elaine to become an architect required that she mastered a whole range of practical knowledge and technical skills. She needed to understand, for example, the properties of different materials, and the way in which these different materials might be combined to create a building, and the various working, leisure, and functional spaces within it. But, essential as those skills and knowledge are, it would not in the end make Elaine a *good* architect. For that, she had to learn to be patient with and attentive to clients in order to be sure that she understands their requirements. She needs to be diligent in her work to ensure that mistakes in design or in implementation do not occur. She may on occasion need to be courageous, but also courteous, in standing up for a particular aspect of her design, which she knows is necessary but costly, and which it may be difficult to explain to clients. In addition to the knowledge and skills she has gained (and which may very well need to be honed and updated over time), she will need certain qualities of character, certain virtues, to be a good architect. Patience, attentiveness, diligence, courage, and courteousness may well be some of these.

There are many lists of the virtues, and we will add others to the five we have identified as we go along. One ancient and helpful categorization, however, is

---

[17] Ibid.: 148.

the Platonic virtues of Temperance (self-control), Fortitude (courage), Justice, and Practical Wisdom. These are known as *cardinal* virtues (from the Greek for a hinge), in the sense that they provide a core set of virtues from which other sub-virtues might be derived. So, for example, honesty might be understood as a sub-virtue of justice, in that being honest is a way of being fair or just to others. Aristotle, however, included many other virtues such as wittiness, friendliness, modesty, and magnanimity (generosity of spirit) in his list of virtues.[18] Defining a specific set of virtues will not be a particular concern for us, although we will give some further consideration to individual virtues in Chapter 5, and to what we will call *corporate* virtues at the organization level in Chapter 7. Of more importance to us will be understanding the *concept* of virtue, rather than agreeing upon a definitive list of virtues.

A fourth component of virtue ethics follows from these first three. As we develop our characters, we exercise the virtues so that they become 'second nature' to us; they become, in other words, habitual. And this means that what we desire, and how we think and feel, all blend together, so that we generally desire good things and are able to act on those desires. Following this, MacIntyre offers an extension of his definition of virtue given above:

> Virtues are dispositions not only to act in particular ways but also to feel in particular ways. To act virtuously is not, as Kant was later to think, to act against inclination: it is to act from inclination formed by the cultivation of the virtues.[19]

Another commentator in the same tradition as MacIntyre describes the person of true virtue as being 'characterised by harmonious unanimity among her feelings, judgments and will'.[20] There is a sense here of a virtuous individual being 'at home' in him or herself, being what we might call an 'integrated' person who knows who he or she is, and is able to act accordingly. It also follows from this that, in the ideal, the truly virtuous individual will possess all of the virtues; there will be a sense of unity about them, a harmony such that their whole life is directed towards their *telos*, and this will occur, hard as it may be, only if all the virtues are possessed and exercised in concert.[21]

And this brings us to a fifth component of virtue ethics. We already noted in the description of a knife and its purpose that we could determine whether it really was or was not a good knife only by using it over an extended period of time. We have also seen that Elaine, in order to be judged a good architect, would need to possess and exercise a number of virtues in her job, and it is not difficult to appreciate that these take time to develop; character is not formed overnight. Indeed, character is something which we begin to develop early on in childhood as we learn from and imitate significant others including parents, older siblings, friends, teachers, and so on. On the opposite side, Elaine and

---

[18] Aristotle (1955: 104, 1107b18–20).     [19] MacIntyre (2007: 149).
[20] Porter (1994: 114).     [21] Ibid.: 121–3.

her husband Fred might worry that one of their children is 'getting in with the wrong crowd', and this is precisely a concern over the development of their character; perhaps their daughter is developing vices, such as being disrespectful, from her current group of friends.

We have also seen that virtue ethics is *teleological*, in other words that it has the sense of life being lived towards a series of purposes, and perhaps towards one overall purpose which we defined as *eudaimonia*. Taking this idea a stage further, the life of every human being could be described as being engaged in a *narrative quest*. The *quest* part of this is fairly self-evident—we are always searching for who we are, what our true purposes are in life, and striving towards these and towards our overall purpose. MacIntyre, in one of his more elliptical sayings, describes this as follows:

> The good life for man is the life spent in seeking for the good life for man, and the virtues necessary for the seeking are those which will enable us to understand what more and what else the good life for man is.[22]

This suggests that, as we set out in life, we have only a partial understanding of what a good life is,[23] and what the purposes which we might pursue within it might be, and that it is only in the living of it that we understand this more fully—'what more and what else' it might be. There are perhaps some similarities here with T. S. Eliot's famous line: 'We shall not cease from exploration, and the end of all our exploring will be to arrive where we started and know the place for the first time'.[24] Another way of describing this is to say that we can begin to tell the *story* of our lives, starting from some initially very preliminary idea of what a good life for us might be. But, over time, we may well become clearer on what projects and purposes we wish to pursue to become, in a phrase that is rather overused nowadays, what we were 'always meant to be'. It is in that sense that we can describe our lives as being on a *narrative quest*.

Following this idea, MacIntyre describes a human being as a 'story-telling animal';[25] we make sense of our lives through our individual and communal narratives and journeys through which we try to make sense of and to realize our own *telos*.[26] But it is, of course, possible that we do not achieve, or only partially achieve, our purposes in life. As MacIntyre says, 'Quests sometimes fail, are frustrated, abandoned or dissipated into distractions; and human lives may in all these ways also fail'.[27] Indeed, MacIntyre points to the tragedy of

---

[22] MacIntyre (2007: 219).

[23] But MacIntyre is clear that we must have *some* idea of what a good life is: 'without some at least partly determinate conception of the final *telos* there could not be any beginning to a quest' (2007: 219), and we learn this initial conception from significant others (role models), and from other sources including from books, films, and so on.

[24] Eliot (1969), from *Little Gidding* in *The Waste Land*.     [25] MacIntyre (2007: 216).

[26] See ibid.: 216–20.     [27] Ibid.: 219.

those who attempt or commit suicide, that they might complain, 'that his or her life is meaningless...that the narrative of their life has become unintelligible to them, that it lacks any point, any movement towards a climax or a *telos*'.[28] However, for most of us most of the time, we could reasonably describe ourselves as being on a narrative quest, even if this may not seem to proceed in any sense in a straight line. But this idea of the narrative quest in which we each engage enables MacIntyre to give yet another definition of the virtues:

> The virtues therefore are to be understood as those dispositions which will...
> sustain us in the relevant kind of quest for the good, by enabling us to overcome
> the harms, dangers, temptations and distractions which we encounter, and which
> will furnish us with increasing self-knowledge and increasing knowledge of the
> good.[29]

Up to this point, the discussion has been almost entirely at the individual level, about individuals and the development of the virtues, their exercise in pursuit of their *telos*, their narrative quest. But a sixth component of virtue ethics is that it does not just operate at the personal level; in addition, the community occupies a central part. In ancient Greece, for example, where the city (the *polis*, from which we get our words metropolis and politics) was both a residential and political community, 'the virtues find their place not just in the life of the individual, but in the life of the city and...the individual is indeed intelligible only as a [political animal]'.[30] Virtues, in other words, enable us to 'fit into' the various communities of which we are a part. Indeed it might even be argued that virtue ethics 'begins with the community as the ethical base rather than individuals existing in isolation. Within a community, people occupy recognised roles, and these roles in turn include ethical obligations. To fulfil such roles well, people need to develop virtues within themselves'.[31]

What this points to is the understanding that the individual, on his or her own narrative quest, cannot pursue this in isolation; we are very far here from any sense of a liberal, individualist understanding of society. There must be a link, if you like almost an intertwining, of the *telos* pursued by individuals and by their community in its shared sense of *telos*. Probably the best way of describing this is that the good for individuals and the *common good* must be interrelated. This idea of the common good, which was mentioned very briefly

---

[28] Ibid.: 217, emphasis in original.    [29] Ibid.: 219.    [30] Ibid.: 150.
[31] Horvath (1995: 505). It is for this reason that MacIntyre identifies different sets of virtues in different contexts. In the course of five chapters in *After Virtue* he explores the Homeric and Aristotelian virtues, together with sets of virtues found in the New Testament, Jane Austen, and Benjamin Franklin (see MacIntyre 2007: 182–3 for a summary). This also implies that virtue ethics is, in one sense, a relativist ethic, although the role of the community in defining what the appropriate virtues are means that this can never be an individualist understanding of relativism.

towards the end of Chapter 2, is an important concept and one which we will come back to in Chapters 4 and 7 when we think about the purpose of organizations and the ways in which they might make a contribution to the common good of society.

Probably the best definition of the common good can be found in Catholic Social Teaching which has had a long history of attempting to make connections between a faith perspective and social issues:[32]

> A society that wishes and intends to remain at the service of the human being at every level is a society that has the common good—the good of all people and of the whole person—as its primary goal. The human person cannot find fulfilment in himself, that is, apart from the fact that he exists 'with' others and 'for' others... The common good does not consist in the simple sum of the particular goods of each subject of a social entity. Belonging to everyone and to each person, it is and remains 'common', because it is indivisible and because only together is it possible to attain it, increase it and safeguard its effectiveness, with regard also to the future.[33]

Perhaps the most obvious example of a common good is the ecological climate. Following the definition given above, Pope Frances has written, 'The climate is a common good, belonging to all and meant for all. At the global level, it is a complex system linked to many of the essential conditions for human life'.[34] For obvious reasons, unless the common good of the climate is protected and maintained, the good of individuals and of all people cannot be sustained; the two 'levels' are essentially intertwined. Virtue ethics, then, is about both the individual and the community, and the interrelationship between the two.

Finally, let us consider the seventh component of virtue ethics. This follows on from all that has been said above and is simply that virtue ethics focuses on *excellence*. The Greek word *arête* can be translated either as virtue or as excellence, pointing to the fact that the two are essentially related. Although we do not use the word virtue much these days (except, perhaps in the sense of being chaste, and then only with reference to women), we do still refer to 'virtuosity' and to someone being a 'virtuoso', and we understand these as relating to something which, or someone who, displays outstanding abilities.

And this indicates the essentially positive nature of the virtues and of virtue ethics. It is about striving for excellence, about doing one's best both individually and for the benefit of the community. And it is through the pursuit of excellence in all the activities in which an individual engages that her character

---

[32] For a fuller exploration of Catholic Social Teaching, and the way in which MacIntyre's concepts explored here might inform it, see Moore, Beadle, & Rowlands (2014).

[33] Pontifical Council for Justice and Peace (2004: 165 and 164, respectively). Note that references are to the paragraphs, not pages, in the document.

[34] See the Encyclical Letter, *Laudato Si'* (2015: 18).

is developed, and she is enabled on her journey towards her own *telos* within a community which provides the social context of her life. Elaine, in trying to be an excellent architect, manager, daughter, wife, mother (and cellist and white-water rafter), is on her way (on her narrative quest) to fulfilling her purposes in life.

This has been a rather condensed exploration of virtue ethics so, before considering two criticisms of this approach, it may be helpful to summarize the seven components of virtue ethics which we have identified:

1. Virtue ethics is actor- or person-oriented and concerned about the development of character. But this does not mean that it is unconcerned about actions.

2. There is a very strong emphasis on the idea of purpose or *telos*; the virtues are the qualities of character which enable us in the pursuit of the projects and purposes, the ends and the good, in our lives.

3. Virtues are different from the knowledge and technical skills which we need to undertake particular roles so, while such knowledge and skills are essential to performing a role well, they are not enough. In addition, we need the virtues.

4. Virtues are deep-seated dispositions so that in possessing them there should be a harmony between our feelings, desires, thoughts, and actions. The person of true virtue possesses and exercises all the virtues in concert.

5. The *teleological* nature of virtue ethics means that we are on a narrative quest, continually attempting to understand what more and what else our purposes in life might be.

6. But this is not just an individual quest. We are also members of various communities and our good and the common good of these various communities are intertwined.

7. Virtue involves the pursuit of excellence in whatever it is that we undertake, benefiting both ourselves and the community or communities of which we are a part.


## TWO CRITICISMS OF VIRTUE ETHICS

Having outlined the key components of virtue ethics we need to acknowledge that, however convincing or otherwise the description above may be as a way of understanding ethics, and therefore as an approach to how we might live our lives, including our working lives, it is not without criticism. The first criticism, however, comes not from other ways of approaching ethics such as Kantianism or Utilitarianism, as might be expected, but from an entirely different discipline altogether—that of empirical social psychology. The argument is that the idea of virtue, and of individuals developing a character which will then have an impact upon how they will act in any given situation, is flawed. In practice, so the argument goes, actions are determined more by response to *situation* than by *character*. This is therefore sometimes known, for obvious reasons, as 'situationism'.[35] This argument depends on evidence from social psychology which suggests that, 'people . . . do not have broad and stable dispositions corresponding to the sorts of character and personality traits we normally suppose that people have'.[36]

However, there have been a number of stout defences of the virtues approach against this charge.[37] The first counter-argument is that situationism draws on experimental studies which tend to be one-off, and so do not give us a sense of character as something developed, and which we can judge, only over the long-term. In addition, what the situationist empirical data really reveals is not so much *lack* of character as *conflict* between different character traits; individuals have to choose between, for example, obedience to authority and well-being.[38]

To illustrate this, let us take one example which has been used repeatedly by the situationists. In the 'Samaritan Experiment',[39] students at Princeton Theological Seminary were given a questionnaire which asked about their religious and moral views, and were then required to walk to a different building on the campus to give a short talk. For some, the subject of the talk was the biblical 'Parable of the Good Samaritan'. As they were leaving the first building, they were told either that they were behind schedule and needed to hurry, or that they were on schedule, or that they had plenty of time and could relax. Between the two buildings, the students came across an individual apparently in some distress, slumped in an alleyway. What the students said in their answers to the questionnaire (which might be taken as evidence of their characters) made no difference to whether they stopped to help.[40] Nor did the subject they were asked to speak about (which, for those who were to speak on the Parable of the Good Samaritan, might have acted as a reminder of their moral commitments) make any difference. What did make a difference was how much of a hurry they were in. Of those in a hurry, only ten per cent

---

[35] Doris (2002: 23–6).     [36] Harman (2003: 92).

[37] See, for example, Solomon (2003), Weaver (2006) and Webber (2006).

[38] See Solomon (2003: 56) and Webber (2006: 204). For those who may be familiar with some or all of these studies, specious examples, according to Webber (2006: 195–201), include the Dime-in-the-slot Experiment and the Zimbardo Stanford Prison Experiment. The Milgram Obedience Experiment, the Bystander Experiment, and the Samaritan Experiment do not necessarily support the arguments propounded.

[39] See Darley & Batson (1973) for a detailed account of the experiment, and Webber (2006) for a summary and analysis along situationist versus character lines.

[40] The findings were statistically significant.

stopped to help; of those on schedule, 45 per cent stopped; and of those who
had plenty of time, 63 per cent (but only 63 per cent!) stopped.

Despite the virtues which one might think had been inculcated into them by
their faith and training, and despite the subject of the talk that some of them
held in their hands, for the majority the *situation* seemed to conquer their
*characters*; they were more concerned about completing the task in hand on
time than in helping an individual in distress. *Quod erat demonstrandum*!

But the response to this is firstly that it was a one-off experiment so told us
little about the real characters which these individuals had developed, and
secondly that they were caught by a *conflict* of virtues—compassion for the
unfortunate individual against deference to authority and a desire for punctuality which might be taken as a sign of consideration for others.

As so often with a critique, however, there is an element of truth here.
Clearly an individual's environment, the actual context which faces him or
her, will have an impact both on the development of character in the first
place, as well as on subsequent behaviour. But rather than take a particular
situation as determinative of the action which follows, virtue ethics holds
individuals responsible for how they exercise their virtues and how the virtues
they have are affected by the kinds of situations they experience.[41]

Quite likely, many of the students in the Samaritan Experiment did prioritize wrongly, or prioritized correctly but then did not go through with their
initial intention; in which case this is a situation from which they should have
learned, and which may then have been influential in the further formation of
their characters. Moreover, virtue ethics suggests that, where possible, being
proactive in the management of one's own environment to protect virtue is
also required—something which is sometimes called 'situation management'.[42] We will return to this point when we come back to organizational
virtue ethics in Chapter 7. But at least for the time being we can safely
conclude that situationism does not win the day and that the concept of
character survives this criticism, although with a slightly more nuanced
understanding concerning the influence of the environment than we had
previously.

The second criticism of virtue ethics is to do with actions. In the earlier
discussion about the components of virtue ethics we saw that, while virtue
ethics is actor-centred, actions are still important since they lead to us fulfilling
our projects and purposes in life (or not, if we get them wrong), and they
mould our characters in the right way (or, again, perhaps in the wrong way).
The criticism, however, is that virtue ethics is not sufficiently action-guiding.
That is, it is not at all clear what actions follow from a virtue ethics approach.
'What should I *do*?' does not seem to get a straightforward answer in virtue

---

[41] See Weaver (2006: 353).      [42] See Webber (2006: 194).

ethics since, 'there is no transcendental appeal or principle that virtue ethicists can invoke to evaluate appropriate action in any given setting'.[43]

Associated with this is the observation that virtue ethics is inherently circular. Consider the following two statements:

1. An act is virtuous if it is what would be done by a virtuous individual in this situation.
2. A virtuous individual is someone who has a disposition to carry out virtuous acts.

While both statements might seem to be true on their own, in combination they lead to a tautology. Substitute the definition of a virtuous individual from 2) into 1) and we find that an act is virtuous if it is what would be done by someone who has a disposition to carry out virtuous acts! This circularity, and the apparent lack of guidance on what action to take, has been a problem with virtue ethics since the time of Aristotle. But the answer lies in understanding more closely what Aristotle was really saying.

MacIntyre comments that there is 'a crucial distinction between what any particular individual at any particular time takes to be good for him and what is really good for him as a man',[44] and it is in the nature of virtue that it enables the individual to judge between these choices so as to determine what the truly virtuous act, in that particular situation, really is. MacIntyre, drawing directly from Aristotle, continues: 'Such choices demand judgment and the exercise of the virtues requires therefore a capacity to judge and to do the right thing in the right place at the right time and in the right way'.[45] Another commentator, drawing on a slightly different translation of Aristotle, says that, under virtue, one will act in a certain way 'when one should, towards the things one should, in relation to the people one should, for the reasons one should, and in the way one should'.[46] In other words, the virtuous individual, drawing on all of her practical experience and practical wisdom, seeks to make a judgement which, in that particular situation, is consistent with her overall judgement as to what is truly good for her as a person, as well as for others and for the community, and acts appropriately on that judgement.

It is apparent from this that decision-making under virtue ethics is likely to be a complex process of deliberation. In line with this, and with the earlier discussion about virtue ethics being about a disposition to act, so that in possessing virtues there is a harmony between our feelings, desires, thoughts, and actions, another commentator has argued that there are four dimensions to virtue: an *intellectual* dimension enabling careful and wise deliberation; an *emotional* dimension which links the intellectual dimension with feelings;

---

[43] Morrell & Brammer (2016: 385).     [44] MacIntyre (2007: 151).
[45] Ibid.: 150. (For the reference to Aristotle see, 1955: 101, 1106b21–3 and 128–9, 1115b1–19).
[46] Webber (2006: 206), quoting from Aristotle (1955: 1106b21–3).

a *motivational* dimension which enables the individual not to be swayed by inappropriate influences so that she does things for the right reasons; and a *behavioural* dimension which finally enables an appropriate action in response.[47] This helps in making it evident that in virtue ethics there is no direct link from virtue to action; we cannot say that the courageous individual, for example, will always act in a particular way, or even in a particular way in a specific situation, because there are always so many other considerations to be taken into account before an action is decided upon.

Having said all that, virtue ethics also suggests that, by developing our characters consistently over time, in many instances we will know instinctively what the right or good thing to do is, so that a long process of deliberation is not necessarily required. And linked to this, virtue ethics also suggests that it is often possible to tell whether someone is virtuous or not by their instinctive *reaction* to a particular situation (consider the students in the Samaritan Experiment), rather than once he or she has had time to deliberate. Associated with this, it has been argued that virtue does indeed offer quite considerable action guidance in that it says very clearly, 'Be (generally and in this particular situation) honest, charitable, generous', and, since vice represents an equivalent prohibition, 'Do not be (generally and in this particular situation) dishonest, uncharitable, mean'.[48]

But even with this obvious but helpful point, it is clear that virtue ethics offers a nuanced answer to the link between virtue and action, and we can see why it might be criticized for not being sufficiently action-guiding. Virtue ethics' response is that there are many aspects to any morally complex decision which need to be weighed before an action which will lead to the substantial good can be determined. And formation of character is key in being able to so decide.

## BEING ABLE TO PROVIDE REASONS FOR ACTION

Despite the complexity involved in decision-making from a virtue ethics perspective, one thing that is clear is the link to the good, in other words to good ends and purposes. We saw this in the earlier discussion about the components of virtue ethics, but it is worth some further exploration at this point. We will then see, by way of an example, how all this might work out in practice.

---

[47] Alzola (2015: 293).

[48] See Hursthouse (2001: 36) and the chapter on 'Right Action' (25–42) for a more general discussion about virtue ethics and its action-guiding qualities versus Utilitarianism and deontology.

Aristotle, as we saw above, held that every rational activity should aim at some end or good, in other words that it should have some purpose to it. Following from this, MacIntyre, in a book published later than *After Virtue*, offered an account of how we might justify any particular action. He argued for the idea of 'a chain of "for the sake of" relationships',[49] and therefore for our being able to provide reasons for our actions. Rational action, he argued, ought to be accountable in such a way that, if asked, 'Why did you act in that way?',[50] the individual should be able to respond by recounting perhaps a series of deliberations (some of which may very well have been implicit at the time of the action itself), in which she moved from what she believed was her true good, to what may be a series of judgements about which actions best moved her towards that goal. Ultimately, this should lead to an ability to justify any particular action in such a way as to explain how this action is for the sake of its own good, or towards some other good, and in such a way that it is, in the end, a constitutive part of the individual's, and perhaps the community's, *telos*. In other words, there ought to be a clear line of reasoning from the question, 'Why did you act in that way?' to the good end which is being aimed at.

Let us consider further, by way of an example, Fred's dilemma over whether to separate from Elaine with a view to divorce. This is clearly a major, life-changing decision. Fred is a reasonably virtuous individual, and he has some idea (as good as any of us are ever likely to have) as to who he is and what goals (ends, goods, or purposes) he should therefore be aspiring to in his life. These have led him to pursue various projects and purposes, among them a career as a secondary school teacher (he teaches physics), family life with Elaine and their three children, and landscape painting (he is rather good). However, while family life has generally been a happy set of relationships for many years, he is acutely aware that his relationship with Elaine has been under severe strain more recently, and that this has led to a poor relationship not only with her but also with the children, such that the atmosphere in the house feels almost permanently poisonous. Despite trying all kinds of ways to improve the situation, Fred has reached a point at which he thinks it might be best for him, and for them, if he were to move out.

It would seem that Fred might well be able to give a reason for this particular action, tragic as it is, which he could ultimately justify in terms of his own purposes in life—'what is really good for him as a man'. But this would also involve a detailed consideration of what is in the best interests of Elaine (including for her work, which he knows is suffering as a result of the unhappiness in their marriage), and the children, enabling them to better pursue their own goals and projects. This might well involve not just an

---

[49] MacIntyre (1988: 131).    [50] Ibid.: 131.

extended intellectual deliberation, but one which draws upon his emotions, and tests his motivations before reaching a decision. And Fred is not so stupid as to think that he can work out for himself 'what is really good for him as a man', which he is why he has been trying to engage Elaine in discussion about their situation, has been to relationship counselling himself, and has tried to persuade Elaine to come too. As we saw, it is in the nature of virtue that it enables the individual to judge between sometimes difficult choices so as to determine what the truly virtuous act, in this particular situation, really is— that is, what will lead to the substantial good for all? Fred is perhaps intuitively aware that the exercise of the virtues requires a capacity to judge and to act in a certain way when he should, towards the things he should, in relation to the people he should, for the reasons he should, and in the way he should. He is, at least, trying.

We will have to leave Fred (and Elaine and the children) there for the time being. But what this story illustrates is the complexity of the process through which a virtuous individual will need (and want) to go in order to reach a decision, and a decision on which he will act. It is not that virtue ethics does not lead to action, but that in any situation which involves some degree of moral complexity, such action cannot be easily predicted. There are no principles (such as the Kantian promise- and duty-based ones) which are ultimately decisive, even though such principles may well be one factor in the process. So, returning to statement 2) above—that a virtuous individual is someone who has a disposition to carry out virtuous acts—we can see that this is true, but that it is far more nuanced in terms of working out what the virtuous act actually is than it might at first seem.

## VIRTUE ETHICS AT THE ORGANIZATIONAL LEVEL

There is one final issue which we need to consider in this chapter before we are in a position to move on. Up to this point, we have considered virtue ethics from an almost entirely individual point of view, although we have also noted the important interrelationship between the individual's good and that of the community in its pursuit of the common good. However, in Chapter 4 we will begin to consider how all of this might apply at the organizational level. But this raises a question as to whether we can legitimately extend these ideas from the individual level to aggregations of individuals such as groups and organizations.

Recall that in Chapter 2 we defined a formal organization as 'a purposive aggregation of individuals who exert concerted effort toward a common and explicitly recognized goal'. As individuals, it is straightforward to talk in the way that we have done about virtues and character. And in doing so, we are implicitly acknowledging that we are moral agents, responsible for our own actions, and liable to be blamed and possibly punished for getting things wrong, or praised and possibly rewarded for getting things right. But can the same ideas apply when we are dealing with aggregations of individuals, typically as groups (teams as they are usually referred to in organizations) and as organizations themselves? Is the anthropomorphization of groups and organizations not a category error? In other words, is it transforming what is really an object into a subject and then giving it human-like characteristics such as virtues?

There has been a long-standing debate in the business ethics literature about what is generally known as 'corporate moral agency', in other words whether entities like corporations (but by extension organizations in general) can be regarded as moral agents in the same way as with individuals. One view is that organizations cannot be regarded as moral agents in the same way as individuals, but they can be regarded as having agency in a restricted sense.

To understand this, it is helpful to distinguish between *moral, causal,* and *compensatory* responsibilities.[51] If, for example, an individual deliberately felled a tree such that it crashed onto a person's house, and caused damage and an injury to the homeowner, we would rightly say that the individual was responsible in all three senses—*morally*, because he decided to fell the tree and then did so, *causally* because doing so then caused the damage and injury, and in a *compensatory* sense because he should pay for the damage and injury so caused (albeit, perhaps, via an insurance policy). But if the wind blew the tree over with the same result, we would attribute only *causal* responsibility; the wind *caused* the tree to fall, but we could not sensibly apply either moral or compensatory responsibility to the wind.

Suppose, however, that the act was occasioned by a tree-felling company. Then we might want to attribute both *causal* and *compensatory* responsibility to the company, but not *moral* responsibility—that would remain with the individual who carried out the felling who, whatever the company may have instructed him to do, should have refused and pointed out the danger involved.

In this way, organizations can be regarded as having agency in this restricted *causal* and *compensatory* sense. In other words, we can legitimately attribute intentional causal and compensatory agency to the corporate body because its members carry out acts which they believe are what the corporate body 'wants' them to do, and if those acts then cause harm it is the corporate body which should pay.[52] This does not mean that moral, and quite possibly causal and even compensatory responsibility should be taken away from individuals—no one should be able to hide behind the corporate 'veil' and

---

[51] Velasquez (2003).     [52] See ibid.: 557.

say, in effect, 'I only did what I was told'. But it does allow us both meaningfully and efficiently[53] to say, for example, 'the organization was to blame'.

We are familiar with this way of speaking about organizations, even if we do not often stop to analyse what we mean by saying that an organization is to blame. The language we usually use for this is that of corporate or organizational culture, and it is common to hear of organizations as having, for example, a 'malign' culture (Barclays Bank was described like this for its involvement in Payment Protection Insurance mis-selling, and the LIBOR fixing scandal, for example).[54] Culture, on this basis, is often apparently to blame for ethical problems in organizations, and restoring a 'good' culture is often presented as a solution to such problems.

The way in which culture operates is by being shared in such a way that it generates joint commitments on behalf of organizational members to share certain values (organizational profitability over customer service in the case of Barclays, for example), which then subsequently and *causally* affect the actions of the same and other organizational members.[55] Organizations, in this sense, have cultures. But we should always remember that when we speak like this of organizations we are still using metaphor—organizations are *like* this in that they appear to have a 'malign' (or possibly praiseworthy) culture. But we should also acknowledge that culture is a metaphor-with-teeth. In other words, organizational culture really does affect the way in which organizational members see and understand the organization, and really does have an impact on their subsequent actions. Perhaps this impact is not always completely effective since individuals retain their own agency, and so may be able to resist malign cultures although, as we know, this is not easy. But that culture affects behaviour is not in doubt.

If we turn from these arguments about the nature of agency, responsibility, and culture and think about this in terms of virtues and character at the organizational level, it will be apparent that the same kinds of arguments can be applied. One approach might be to say that an organization is ontologically no different (no different in essence) from an individual and so possesses virtues and vices, and has a character. But, just as with the idea of corporate moral agency, we can dismiss this immediately; organizations and humans clearly *are* different kinds of entities. The alternative is to take the metaphorical approach, just as we have done with culture and much as we discussed in Chapter 2 when we considered theory-as-metaphor. On this understanding, we would say that organizations are *like* people in that we can describe them as having virtues and vices, and summarize this by way of talking about

---

[53] In relation to efficiency, Hasnas (2012: 194) makes the point that, 'One might say that the language of corporate moral responsibility reduces communicative transaction costs'.
[54] This case is discussed in Dempsey (2015).
[55] See Dempsey (2015).

organizational character. We know that, in reality, they are *not* like this, just as Elaine is *not* a brick, but it is helpful to describe them that way because, as we have seen, it helps us to see and understand organizations in a particular, and sometimes particularly helpful, way. MacIntyre himself seems to accept this position when he says that 'the modern corporation presents itself as a moral being'[56]—implying that it is not, in fact, a moral being but nonetheless seems to be, and considers itself to be, as though it were an entity with moral agency.

If we follow this approach, we can say the following about an organization, that it 'is not merely a passive container that holds the virtues of its members, but rather it provides a more generative (or perhaps deleterious) context in which organizational members interact in ways that prompt, enable and/or enhance (or perhaps diminish or inhibit) virtue'.[57]

If we accept this, we can understand virtues at the organizational level as being 'features of the organization that engender virtuousness on the part of members'.[58] Again, this is a metaphor-with-teeth since it is saying that organizational character, based on the aggregation of the virtues and vices an organization 'possesses', impacts upon organizational members and their actions. And on this basis we could combine the virtues and vices which an organization displays into a description of its character. In Chapter 7 we will do just this and explore a definition of organizational character which incorporates some of MacIntyre's terms. For now, it is worth noting that the argument in this book is that organizational character and organizational culture are both important metaphors of organizations, that both are metaphors-with-teeth, but also that they are different from each other and that, in our understanding of organizations, we will be better served by understanding and employing them both.[59] Again, we will come back to this in Chapter 7.

## SUMMARY

In this chapter we have set virtue ethics in context, looked at seven components of virtue ethics, and considered two criticisms of this approach—the 'situationist' critique, and an argument that virtue ethics is insufficiently action-guiding. We then explored why, within a virtue ethics approach, we should be able to give reasons for our actions as being constitutive of our purposes in life. Having reached this level of understanding at the individual

---

[56] MacIntyre (1979: 124).     [57] Bright, Winn, & Kanov (2014: 456).
[58] Cameron, Bright, & Caza (2004: 768).
[59] For a more detailed exploration of corporate culture and character than is possible here, see Moore (2005a).

level, and of the relationship between the individual and social levels, we moved to consider whether and how we could apply these ideas at the organizational level and argued that, so long as they continue to be understood as a metaphor (albeit a metaphor-with-teeth), virtue, vice, and character can be applied at this level.

This now sets the scene so that we are ready to move on and consider how all of this might apply to organizations and management, and to a more detailed understanding of MacIntyre's ideas in this respect.

# 4

## A MacIntyrean Approach to Organizations and Organizational Ethics

### INTRODUCTION

We have arrived at what is undoubtedly a key chapter in this book. We have already come to understand what formal organizations are, why they exist, some of the problems at both individual and communal levels which are associated with them, and why conventional approaches to organizational ethics have their limitations (Chapter 2). We have then begun to explore what virtue ethics is all about, mostly at the individual level, and seen that it is also possible to apply concepts such as virtue, vice, and character at the organizational level (Chapter 3). We have come across MacIntyre at various points as a key contributor to the virtue ethics approach. Now we need to explore in detail how, taking some of his central concepts, we might apply these to organizations and, by implication, to management in organizations.

### DIFFERENT KINDS OF GOODS

The first thing we need to do, however, is to develop the discussion in Chapter 3 about purpose (*telos*), and other words which we have used pretty much synonymously—ends and goods. Inherent in virtue ethics, as we have seen, is the idea that we have various projects and purposes in our lives which lead us, via our narrative quest, to understand what more and what else the good life for us might be, in pursuit of our true end (*eudaimonia*). We have also noted that, in our pursuit of this, the community or communities of which we are a part play an important role, and hence we developed an understanding of the idea of the *common good*.

So, we have some idea of *the* good to which we aim, accepting that this is always under development both for us as individuals and for communities. What virtue ethics then adds to this is the idea that there are particular *goods* (in the plural) which we pursue which help us on this journey. And following Aristotle,[1] MacIntyre makes a crucial distinction between two different kinds of goods. The first kind is *internal goods*, the second *external goods*. What are they, and what is the difference between them?

To illustrate this, MacIntyre gives the example of a 'highly intelligent seven-year-old child whom I wish to teach to play chess, although the child has no particular desire to learn the game. The child does however have a very strong desire for candy and little chance of obtaining it'.[2] In effect, by bribing the child with little incentives, including the incentive to win by playing chess with her in such a way as to make it difficult but not impossible for the child to win, she will learn to play chess. However, teaching her to play in this way carries with it the danger that the only reason she learns to play chess is for the candy; that she never comes to love chess for the sake of chess. It also carries with it the danger that she will cheat in order to win, so that she obtains the candy; why wouldn't she if the only point of playing chess is to get more candy? MacIntyre continues:

> But, so we may hope, there will come a time when the child will find in those goods specific to chess, in the achievement of a certain highly particular kind of analytical skill, strategic imagination and competitive intensity, a new set of reasons, reasons now not just for winning on a particular occasion, but for trying to excel in whatever way the game of chess demands. Now if the child cheats, she will be defeating not me, but herself.[3]

Within this description, we can see the two kinds of goods which MacIntyre refers to. *Internal goods* are those specifically to do with chess, to do with a particular kind of analytical skill, strategic imagination, and competitive intensity. *External goods* are, in this case, candy. Now we might immediately react to this by saying that candy is actually *bad* for the girl, so that it cannot be a good in the sense intended. MacIntyre was writing at a time before concerns over the sugar content of food and childhood obesity became prevalent, but even so we might suspect that he used the example deliberately to emphasize the point that we often mistake which kinds of good we should aim for, and that external goods, while highly desirable in one sense, can be bad for us if we seek too much of them. We will come back to this point below.

MacIntyre makes two further points about internal goods: they are internal because we can specify them only in the terms of the activity of which they are a part—chess in this instance—and because it is only by taking part in the practice of chess that we can really appreciate what these internal goods actually are. The external observer of a chess match, who has not played

---

[1] Aristotle actually makes a distinction between three different kinds of goods: external, of the soul, and of the body (1955: 78, 1098b11).

[2] MacIntyre (2007: 188).          [3] Ibid.: 188.

chess himself, really has no idea what it is actually like to play, and hence has no 'feel' for the internal goods associated with the playing of chess. The child who learns to play chess well, who really 'gets into' playing it, who begins to understand what it means to be an excellent chess player, does come to understand these things. And, so we might hope, she might eventually spurn the candy—she will play for the joy of playing, as well as perhaps for the competitive excitement of winning, and she will play irrespective of the rewards, candy or otherwise.

There has been some discussion as to whether MacIntyre is entirely correct in saying that only those who have played chess (or whatever other example we might wish to take), can really appreciate its internal goods. In a commercial context, for example, it has been argued that discerning customers are good judges of the quality and craftsmanship involved in, say, a beautiful piece of furniture or a fine wine, even if they have never been involved in the making of them.[4] This may be true to a certain extent, but it is surely the case that participation in the relevant practice does make a difference. Elaine, you may recall, is a cellist and plays in a local orchestra, and she appreciates a live classical concert in a way that Fred does not. The tables are turned when they go to an art gallery, however, where Fred's experience of landscape painting enables him to appreciate the art in a way that Elaine cannot (and besides, Elaine's architect's eyes are often on the building rather than the pictures).

But this also allows us to say something else about internal goods. In commenting on internal goods in relation to what he calls 'productive crafts' (which is about as close to 'business' as he gets), MacIntyre says:

> The aim internal to such productive crafts, when they are in good order, is never only to catch fish, or to produce beef or milk, or to build houses. It is to do so in a manner consonant with the excellences of the craft, so that there is not only a good product, but the craftsperson is perfected through and in her or his activity.[5]

This indicates that internal goods are of two kinds. First, there is the good product or, we may add in an organizational context, the good service. The internal good of the practice of architecture in which Elaine is engaged is the provision of excellent buildings: fit for purpose, aesthetically pleasing, congenial to their surroundings, and as ecologically sustainable as possible. Second, however, there is the internal good which involves the perfection of the practitioners engaged in the craft or practice. Now 'perfection' may seem to be a rather strong term, and we might more naturally think of this as to do with the development and flourishing of individuals. The point, however, is that it is by pursuing excellence in the products or services that, *in that very process*, individual practitioners are also developed as people. In that sense,

---

[4] This argument can be found in Keat (2000: 128–9).
[5] MacIntyre (1994: 284), see also MacIntyre (2007: 189–90).

production (using the term broadly to include providing services) 'is simultaneously an instrumental and moral-practical activity'.[6] Elaine is not just designing excellent buildings; as she does so, she is being changed and developed as an individual in the process. As we noted in Chapter 3, it is through the pursuit of excellence that an individual's character is developed, and she is enabled on her journey towards her own *telos*; it is part of her narrative quest. For Elaine, this is precisely what is going on (or, at least, what we might hope is going on) in the context of her job.

What, then, about external goods? As we have seen, candy is one example, but more generally external goods are such things as fame, reputation, money, and, in a business context, profit. Perhaps most generically we can characterize external goods as involving *success* in some way or other, whereas internal goods involve the pursuit of *excellence*—the chess-playing child, we may hope, will come to have reasons for 'trying to excel in whatever way the game of chess demands'. So she may learn to love the game and to play it well, and she may play it just for the love of the game and the social and personal benefits which she obtains from it (the internal goods). But it is possible that she might be good enough to play seriously, and develop a reputation, first at school, then later within the community, and perhaps eventually even as a grandmaster both nationally and internationally. As such, the external goods which she obtains from chess may extend beyond candy, fame, and reputation and may also include financial rewards; playing chess might result in an income, perhaps even *the* income on which she depends.

But this points to some further differences between internal and external goods. First, while internal goods can be achieved only by participating in the relevant practice, external goods can be achieved in any number of ways: one can become famous, obtain money, and generally be regarded as successful by engaging in any number of a very wide range of activities. That is why MacIntyre calls them *external* goods; they are external to the practice of, for example, chess. Second, external goods always belong to someone in a way which excludes others from them. Someone's fame or reputation is at the expense of another who is not quite as talented. Someone gets the managing director's position and the salary which goes with it (and other perquisites including some degree of fame within the organization and perhaps also outside of it), while the other candidates do not. There is, in other words, competition for external goods in which some will win out over others. With internal goods, however, while there is competition in a sense, this is always competition to excel, and the pursuit of excellence is always a good for the practice as a whole.[7] The chess-playing child, if she were to become an internationally recognized grandmaster, might develop new strategies which

---

[6] Breen (2012: 623).      [7] MacIntyre (2007: 190–1).

take the game of chess to another level; following her, all serious chess players would need to aspire to a new standard of excellence. Competition would have led to a yet greater level of sophistication in the practice of chess from which all chess players could benefit.

It is probably already apparent from the discussion so far that there is an implicit prioritization between the two kinds of goods as MacIntyre defines them. Internal goods are goods which we should pursue *for their own sake*. That is to say, internal goods are those which are a constituent part of *the* good for any individual; they are part and parcel of the ends we should pursue in order to realize our projects and purposes in life, our *telos*. External goods, on the other hand, are those which we should pursue *for the sake of some other good*. This is not to say, however, that they are not goods in and of themselves, a point which MacIntyre makes explicitly:

> I need to emphasize at this point that external goods genuinely are goods. Not only are they characteristic objects of human desire, whose allocation is what gives point to the virtues of justice and of generosity, but no one can despise them altogether without a certain hypocrisy.[8]

But, if we pursue fame, reputation, wealth, success, and so on *for their own sake*, then we have missed the point about them, and about the projects and purposes in our lives, our true end, and in the process probably misunderstood what internal goods are all about. Recall that Elaine earns a good salary from her employer DesignCo. This is an external good from her engagement in the practice of architecture. But she puts that external good to use mostly in other areas of her life, contributing to the family income in such a way that, as well as the functional aspects of life—house, food, car, and so on—the money allows her and the family to do other things—in her case, to play the cello and to go white-water rafting. These, as well as being an architect, are actually the priorities in her life from which she derives the internal goods which enable her to pursue her own *telos* in life. The external good of her salary does not have any point in and of itself; it serves only to facilitate these other activities. And if Elaine really is concerned about the level of her salary by way of a status symbol, we might well think less of her.

The point, therefore, is that there is an *ordering* involved here, in that internal goods are ultimately more important than external goods because it is only internal goods which enable us to achieve our *telos* in life. But we could also say that we need to get the *balance* right in pursuing these two different kinds of goods. We need external goods—we quite literally could not live without them—so we will need to spend time and energy pursuing them. But we need to remember that we are pursuing these external goods only, and only in so far as, we can then realize internal goods. Spending all our time and

---

[8] Ibid.: 196.

energy on the pursuit of external goods would mean that we had got the balance in our lives wrong.

We will come back later in this chapter to explore the relationship between internal and external goods a little further. But, armed with this understanding, we can move on to consider another (and perhaps *the* central) part of MacIntyre's framework for understanding virtue ethics and organizational ethics from a virtues perspective.

## PRACTICES AND INSTITUTIONS

At various points reference has been made to practices—most notably chess and the practice of architecture in which Elaine is engaged, but also family life and, in an academic context, research and scholarship as other practices. In a sense, we might say that these are just various activities in our lives in which we might engage, but MacIntyre takes this further by defining practices in a very specific way, such that his idea of a practice is central to his argument. So, while it is somewhat lengthy and complicated, it is worth citing his definition in full:

> By a 'practice' I am going to mean any coherent and complex form of socially established cooperative human activity through which goods internal to that form of activity are realized in the course of trying to achieve those standards of excellence which are appropriate to, and partially definitive of, that form of activity, with the result that human powers to achieve excellence, and human conceptions of the ends and goods involved, are systematically extended.[9]

Despite the complexity (and the whole definition being contained in a single sentence!), we can already see quite a number of terms and ideas with which we are familiar. First, it speaks of 'goods internal to that form of activity', and these are obviously the internal goods which we have already come across. Second, it speaks of 'standards of excellence' and of 'human powers to achieve excellence', and again we have come across this both in the components of virtue ethics which we explored in Chapter 3, where the pursuit of excellence was the seventh component characteristic of virtue ethics, and in the discussion above about internal goods, where we saw that internal goods involve competition, but competition to excel in order to raise standards. Third, MacIntyre's definition of a practice speaks of 'ends and goods' and how, in and through practices, our ideas of what these may be are 'systematically extended'. And again, this links back to our previous discussions about narrative quests and the pursuit of purpose in our lives, and how we are always seeking to discover 'what more and what else' the good life involves.

[9] Ibid.: 187.

But there are a few new ideas in this definition as well. First, and most notably, practices are 'coherent and complex forms of socially established cooperative human activity'. Up to now, we have considered virtue ethics from the individual perspective and linked this to the community level and its pursuit of the common good. But now we have an *intermediate* level between the individual and the community. Practices are, under MacIntyre's definition, social activities, so they are things which we do together in groups or teams; sometimes, practices are referred to as *social* practices in order to remind us of this. Practices, therefore, involve collaboration with others, and this collaboration is in the common pursuit of the internal goods which are the key outcome of practices. But in addition to this, practices are not just any old activity which we might collaborate in together. They have to be sufficiently 'coherent and complex' if they are to justify being designated as practices. In order to emphasize this, MacIntyre gives a number of examples and counter-examples:

> throwing a football with skill [is not a practice]; but the game of football is, and so is chess. Bricklaying is not a practice; architecture is. Planting turnips is not a practice; farming is. So are the enquiries of physics, chemistry and biology, and so is the work of the historian, and so are painting and music. In the ancient and medieval worlds the creation and sustaining of human communities—of households, cities, nations—is generally taken to be a practice in the sense which I have defined it. Thus the range of practices is wide: arts, sciences, games, politics in the Aristotelian sense, the making and sustaining of family life, all fall under the concept.[10]

So while the idea of a practice applies to a very wide range of human activities, it has to be sufficiently 'coherent and complex' to warrant the description, which is why limited activities, such as throwing a football or planting turnips, are not in themselves a practice.

Taking this idea of a practice and the examples which we already have, we can see how it can be applied to most of the major activities in our lives. In a sense, we live our lives, and certainly the most important aspects of our lives, in practices under MacIntyre's definition. Consider Elaine and Fred again. Elaine is engaged at least in the practices of architecture, family life, and music. Quite whether reading thrillers, white-water rafting, and doing zany deals on eBay (some of the other activities she engages with, as we learned in Chapter 1) constitute practices we will leave for now, although it is worth reinforcing the point that *not everything* is a practice—a point to which we will return particularly in Chapter 8. Fred, as well as being engaged in the practice of family life with Elaine, teaches physics and does landscape painting and, again, is quite likely to be engaged in other practices besides. Elaine and Fred, in other words, live their lives, and certainly the most significant parts of their lives, by engaging in practices.

---

[10] Ibid.: 187–8.

Before moving on, however, it is worth noting that in Fred's case it is *physics* (as in MacIntyre's examples above), which is the practice in which he engages as a school teacher, not *teaching* itself. This might seem to be counter-intuitive, and there was quite a dispute over this point when MacIntyre originally made it. But it is an important point so, not just for the benefit of school teachers but also for understanding what management is all about when we come to that below, it is worth exploring further. MacIntyre argued as follows:

> Teaching itself is not a practice, but a set of skills and habits put to the service of a variety of practices. The teacher should think of her or himself as a mathematician, a reader of poetry, an historian or whatever, engaged in communicating craft and knowledge to apprentices. . . . It is part of my claim that teaching is never more than a means, that it has no point and purpose except for the point and purpose of the activities to which it introduces students. All teaching is for the sake of something else and so teaching does not have its own goods.[11]

MacIntyre's point, to return to the example of physics, is that Fred as a physics school teacher is himself engaged in the practice of physics which is, in a sense, a lot 'bigger' than simply what goes on in the school classroom. Physics also, of course, takes place in university departments where not only is existing knowledge transmitted to students, but experimental and theoretical work takes place to extend the boundaries of that knowledge. In addition, the application of physics takes place in commercial, military, and other settings. Taken all together, this is the practice of physics. And what Fred does is to engage in that practice by 'communicating craft and knowledge to apprentices', in other words to those who are just setting out in understanding what physics is all about. Fred's role is to encourage them to explore and understand at least parts of this particular practice and, perhaps for some, to inspire them to make it one of the significant practices in their own lives—to go on and make a career out of it, for example. This also, of course, implies that Fred should remain connected to the wider practice, maintaining contact with others engaged in the practice, reading to keep his own knowledge up to date, and so on. He is, in other words, first and foremost a *physician* (in its original rather than medical sense), and is only secondarily a teacher of physics. Similarly, as MacIntyre indicates above, other teachers are primarily mathematicians, poets, or historians and only secondarily teachers of these same subjects.[12]

But this also points to two other aspects of practices. First, while all practices clearly involve technical skills and knowledge, these serve the purpose only of enabling the practice in its pursuit of its own goals and the internal goods

---

[11] MacIntyre & Dunne (2002: 5 and 9).

[12] Primary school teachers are obviously an exception to this, and have to be polymaths if only at a very basic level. It is, therefore, not quite clear which practice(s) they engage in while at work, although it may be the case that their original degree subject is the one to which they feel greatest allegiance.

associated with them 'with the result that human powers to achieve excellence, and human conceptions of the ends and goods involved, are systematically extended'. So in architecture, which MacIntyre also gives as a specific example of a practice, the technical skills and knowledge which Elaine has gained are always being put to the ends and goals of architecture. And these ends and goals are always under the process of development; 'practices never have a goal or goals fixed for all time',[13] so that architecture, as with other practices, is also engaged in a kind of quest to do with 'what more and what else' it is all about.

And this points to the second further aspect of practices, which is that practices have histories.[14] In other words, when we begin to engage with any particular practice, we are always joining an existing 'coherent and complex form of socially established cooperative human activity', and as a result we should regard ourselves as beginners (apprentices) in that activity and learn from those who are already engaged in it, and from those 'giants' of its past who have defined its present standards of excellence. Elaine started this process when she began her university architecture course, although even then she had already been inspired by others—teachers, parents, and including an ancient great aunt who had herself been an architect—who had first fostered her interest in architecture. She continued that process by being employed by architectural firms and engaging in various architectural projects, and continuing to learn from other, more experienced architects—including her boss at DesignCo, even though he seems to have lost the passion for architecture that he once had (recall that he is now fixated on 'the numbers'). In addition she would need to have learned about and come to appreciate the history of this practice, its twists and turns through Renaissance, Baroque, Neoclassical, and even Brutalist styles, in order to understand and 'locate' the practice of architecture as she currently experiences it. Elaine has been apprenticed into and become a fully engaged member of the practice of architecture which has its own history to which she is subject.

Before moving on, there is one final point to be made in relation to practices at this stage, and this is to consider the place of the virtues within them. We saw in Chapter 3 various definitions of virtue which MacIntyre offers. It might be helpful to repeat these here:

> The virtues are precisely those qualities the possession of which will enable an individual to achieve *eudaimonia* and the lack of which will frustrate his movement toward that *telos*.[15]

> Virtues are dispositions not only to act in particular ways but also to feel in particular ways. To act virtuously is not . . . to act against inclination: it is to act from inclination formed by the cultivation of the virtues.[16]

---

[13] MacIntyre (2007: 193).  [14] Ibid.: 194.  [15] Ibid.: 148.  [16] Ibid.: 149.

The virtues therefore are to be understood as those dispositions which will ... sustain us in the relevant kind of quest for the good, by enabling us to overcome the harms, dangers, temptations and distractions which we encounter, and which will furnish us with increasing self-knowledge and increasing knowledge of the good.[17]

But now that MacIntyre has given us the concept of a practice, he is able to provide a further definition of a virtue:

A virtue is an acquired human quality the possession and exercise of which tends to enable us to achieve those goods which are internal to practices and the lack of which effectively prevents us from achieving any such goods.[18]

In other words, virtues find their home particularly in practices, and it is through the possession and exercise of the virtues, over and above the technical skills and knowledge involved, that we can achieve the internal goods of practices. Recall that for Elaine such things as patience, attentiveness, diligence, courage, and courteousness, over and above the technical skills and knowledge she possesses, were some of the virtues which she required to be a good architect. We can now see that all of these—technical skills, knowledge, and virtues—are part and parcel of what are needed to engage in practices well, and so to realize the internal goods of practices. And *vice-versa*—as MacIntyre warns, not having the virtues effectively prevents us from realizing the internal goods of practices.

There will be more to say about practices, but with this understanding we can move on to consider the second major part of the framework which MacIntyre gives us for understanding virtue ethics and organizational ethics from a virtues perspective. In addition to practices, MacIntyre gives a very specific definition of what he terms institutions. And again, it is worth giving the full definition which he provides:

Institutions are characteristically and necessarily concerned with what I have called external goods. They are involved in acquiring money and other material goods; they are structured in terms of power and status, and they distribute money, power and status as rewards. Nor could they do otherwise if they are to sustain not only themselves, but also the practices of which they are the bearers. For no practices can survive for any length of time unsustained by institutions. Indeed so intimate is the relationship of practices to institutions—and consequently of the goods external to the goods internal to the practices in question—that institutions and practices characteristically form a single causal order in which the ideals and the creativity of the practice are always vulnerable to the acquisitiveness of the institution, in which the cooperative care for common goods of the practice is always vulnerable to the competitiveness of the institution. In this context the essential feature of the

---

[17] Ibid.: 219.
[18] Ibid.: 191. It is worth noting that I am not strictly following the order of *After Virtue* in my exposition of MacIntyre's ideas.

virtues is clear. Without them, without justice, courage and truthfulness, practices could not resist the corrupting power of institutions.[19]

As with MacIntyre's definition of practices, there are some aspects which are already familiar to us in this definition. First, and most obviously, this is where external goods find their place in MacIntyre's framework, and he reinforces here what we have already seen about external goods—that they are things like money, other material goods, power, and status. But while external goods are, as we have seen, genuinely goods, we also see here something of a concern associated with them when they are themselves associated with institutions. There is a certain acquisitiveness and competitiveness associated with institutions, and while this is a necessary feature of them if they are to sustain themselves, it does lead to some suspicion; they might become overly focused on external goods and this might have an effect upon the practices which are 'housed' within institutions. We will need to explore this further in a moment. But this brings us to the second aspect which is already familiar to us, but which now also needs further exploration.

We might have thought, from the earlier discussion of practices, that they simply exist by themselves. But what MacIntyre is arguing is that this cannot be the case, at least not for 'any length of time'. So institutions become the 'bearers' of practices or, to put it the other way round, practices have to be 'institution-alized' if they are to survive. Consider again the practice of chess which we looked at earlier. Even in the discussion there we saw the possibility that the seven-year-old girl might develop a reputation for playing chess, first at school, then later within the community, and perhaps eventually as a grandmaster both nationally and internationally. But that assumed that there were chess clubs at school and in the community, and that there was some kind of national and international organization which had determined, and continued to oversee, the standards required for someone to become a grandmaster. In other words, there is an institutional structure associated with chess, and without it chess could not survive as anything other than a game played by enthusiasts similar to other board and card games (though not bridge which, like chess, has similar practice and institutional features). MacIntyre reinforces this point when he says that, 'Chess, physics and medicine are practices; chess clubs, laboratories, universities and hospitals are institutions'.[20]

But it is also important to note that, while practices and institutions are different, they are very closely connected—there is an 'intimate relationship' between the two such that they form 'a single causal order'. If we were to visit a chess club, we probably would not instinctively make a distinction between the practice and the institution—we would simply see people playing chess together. But give only a little thought to it, and we would see easily enough that there is, in fact, a distinction. The chess club has a structure to it, a

---

[19] Ibid.: 194.    [20] Ibid.: 194.

committee which decides such things as membership criteria and fee structure (it has to balance the books, after all), and which also decides who will represent the club in which teams, and which leagues the teams will play in. And yet, this is all about chess or, at least, provided individuals are not playing out their desires for power or status via the chess club, it should be. There should be schemes to encourage young players to join, and to enable them to learn the game (possibly without bribing them with candy), and indeed to learn to love chess for itself. There should be intense satisfaction in the club as young players learn to become good players, and some kind of celebration when, eventually, one of them beats one of the club's leading players. There should be similar satisfaction if one of the club's players went on to great things—not just for the enhanced reputation which the club might achieve, but for the sheer pleasure of seeing someone achieve the standards of excellence associated with chess. There is, in other words, a 'single causal order' between the practice of chess and the institution of the chess club; the two should work together and primarily in support of the practice of chess. When in good order, the 'join' between the practice and the institution should be almost invisible.

But MacIntyre's definition of an institution and its relationship with the practice of which it is the 'bearer' also points, as we saw above, to the potential for *tension* between the two. Indeed, on MacIntyre's analysis, such tension is *inherent*; it is built into the relationship between them. Institutions must pursue external goods for their own survival, and because institutions and external goods support practices and the attainment of internal goods which is what, ultimately, it should be all about. But in the process, institutions are *inevitably* acquisitive and competitive. Since, as we saw, external goods are always objects of competition in which there will be losers as well as winners, the institution has to pursue these in the competitive environment in which it is situated. Recall from Chapter 1 that Elaine was concerned about DesignCo, but also about architectural firms more generally, that they were becoming more utilitarian; was it really about the architecture or about the numbers and the money, with architecture merely as a means to an end? Elaine was experiencing precisely the tension which MacIntyre identifies between practices and institutions. It is probably not unreasonable to suggest that most of us who have worked in organizations have had similar experiences.


## ORGANIZATIONS AS PRACTICE-INSTITUTION COMBINATIONS

This understanding of practices and institutions, and the way in which they interrelate, suggests that we might begin to think of organizations in a rather

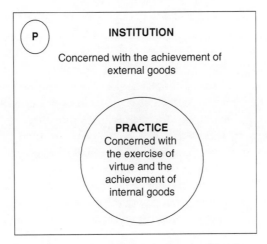

**Figure 4.1.** An organization as a practice-institution combination

*Source*: This diagram first appeared in Moore (2002), but without the smaller circle with the 'P' inside, and subsequently in its full form in Moore (2005a). These are both copyright Cambridge University Press and are reprinted here with permission

different way. In other words, we might conceive of them as practice-institution combinations. And it might be helpful to represent this diagrammatically as shown in Figure 4.1.

The practice is represented as a circle because this suggests a rounded, satisfying environment within which practitioners can exercise the virtues (as well as the necessary technical skills and knowledge) in pursuit of the achievement of the internal goods which are the outcome of the particular practice. The institution, on the other hand, is represented as a rectangle with straight lines and sharp corners because this suggests the rather 'harder' environment associated with the pursuit of external goods. The main point, however, is that the idea of an organization as a practice-institution combination provides a way of thinking about organizations. It is another metaphor (as discussed in Chapter 2) which offers a particular way of 'seeing' and therefore of understanding organizations.

MacIntyre implies this way of thinking about organizations in the examples he gives: 'chess, physics and medicine are practices; chess clubs, laboratories, universities and hospitals are institutions', as cited above. But he does not really explore the implications of this way of thinking about organizations;[21] that has been left to those of us who have picked up on his ideas and felt that they have something which is both insightful and important to say to our understanding of organizations.

---

[21] Apart from the examples given here, probably the closest MacIntyre comes is in his celebrated example of two types of fishing crews in MacIntyre (1994).

The diagrammatic representation in Figure 4.1 also allows us to say several other things about organizations. First, this is a way of thinking about most if not all organizations. This is a representation of DesignCo Ltd, the architectural firm for which Elaine works, as well as a representation of a chess club or a hospital. Indeed, so long as the particular activity can be genuinely recognized as a practice (and we noted above that not everything fits MacIntyre's definition), and so long as the practice is institutionalized (which it would have to be if it is to survive for any length of time), then this is a *generic* representation of organizations. In other words, it can be applied to business organizations as well as to those in the statutory and voluntary sectors. In Chapters 8 and 9, as a way of evidencing this, we will look at a number of examples of how MacIntyre's framework of practices, institutions, goods, and virtues has been applied to a wide variety of occupations, organizations, and organizational types.

Second, although Figure 4.1 represents a single practice 'housed' within a single institution, this may be an oversimplification. Think, for example, of a university. Here it is possible to identify a whole range of practices associated with all the different subjects which are taught and researched there. And, as we noted above in the discussion of teaching, each of those practices is not coterminous with the institution in which they are 'housed', but extends beyond the bounds of the institution—architecture is an obvious example, with its practical application in architectural firms and professional bodies outside of a university. Equally, in complex organizations, while the boundaries of the institution may be clear (Unilever plc, for example), the range of practices in which it engages may be very wide indeed. And the institutional form itself, with any number of subsidiary companies, may itself be quite complex. So, like any representation, we need to remember that there may be practical complexities with which we would have to grapple if we wished to apply it.

Nonetheless (and third), like any model, the simplification which the practice-institution combination represents draws our attention to something rather important. If an organization can be genuinely identified as having a practice or practices at its core, with the implications this has for the possession and exercise of the virtues and the pursuit of internal goods (good products or services and the 'perfection' of the practitioners in the process), then organizations are by definition '*essentially* moral spaces'.[22] We noted in Chapter 2 that organizations might be either systemically or opportunistically corrupt, but what we can draw from this way of thinking about organizations is that when they pursue a good purpose (of which more below), and are in good order (of which more in Chapter 7), then organizations are places in which individuals can together pursue excellence and develop their characters,

---

[22] Beadle & Moore (2011: 103), emphasis in original.

as well as engage in their narrative quest towards their true *telos*, while also contributing to the common good of the community through the excellence of the goods and services which the organization provides. That makes organizations a location for moral projects, a moral space, included in which is the potential for the 'perfection' of the practitioners in the process.

Finally, this way of representing organizations also allows us to locate management and begin to give some idea of its role. In Figure 4.1, as well as what we might call the core practice in the larger circle, there is another practice represented by the smaller circle with the 'P' within it, located in the top left of the figure. This follows something which MacIntyre commented upon in relation to institutions:

> Yet if institutions do have corrupting power, the making and sustaining of forms of human community—*and therefore of institutions*—itself has all the characteristics of a practice, and moreover of a practice which stands in a peculiarly close relationship to the exercise of the virtues.[23]

In other words, the point which MacIntyre is making is that the making and sustaining of institutions is itself a practice. By definition, this is directed precisely at those individuals who occupy managerial roles, and hence we are able to locate management and managers within this framework, and to give an outline definition of the role of management—which is to make and sustain the institution, and therefore to be concerned with the pursuit and distribution of external goods. We will come back and explore this idea of management and managers much more fully in Chapter 6, but for now it is worth noting two things.

First, the making and sustaining of institutions is a *secondary* practice; the primary or core practice is whatever the organization is really all about— architecture in the case of DesignCo. This does not mean that the secondary practice is not important, but just as with the idea that there is an order implicit in internal and external goods, with internal goods taking precedence, so there is an order implicit in the core or primary practice at the heart of the organization and the secondary practice of making and sustaining its institutional form; management's primary role is to serve the core practice.

Second, however, the making and sustaining of the institution is still a practice and, as MacIntyre says, one which 'stands in a peculiarly close relationship to the exercise of the virtues'. It is not entirely clear what MacIntyre meant by this, and given his general concerns about the modern executive caught up inside bureaucratic organizations (of which more in Chapter 6), it seems unlikely that he had management specifically in mind. Nonetheless, it does intuitively make sense that management could be described as a practice (although in Chapter 6 we will qualify this and clarify that this really means a

---

[23] MacIntyre (2007: 194), emphasis added.

domain-relative practice), particularly if its role is conceived primarily as maintaining the institution such that it nurtures the primary practice at the core of the organization, and that the pursuit of external goods (one of the key roles of the institution and therefore of management) is always subservient to this task. But if this is the case, then managers have an opportunity, just as do the practitioners in the core practice, to possess and exercise the virtues in pursuit of the internal goods of the secondary practice of making and sustaining the institution. Hence, even those who are employed solely at this 'level' in an organization can be engaged in a practice which enables their development and flourishing as individuals on their narrative quest towards their own *telos*. We will come back to this in more detail in Chapter 6.


## ORGANIZATIONAL PURPOSE AND MAPPING THE VIRTUOUS ORGANIZATION

At various points above, we have spoken of internal goods and the way in which, both in the production or offering of the products or services which the organization provides, and in the 'perfection' of individual practitioners in the process, there is the potential for these internal goods of the practice to contribute to the common good of the community. This means that we might be able to make some kind of judgement as to the 'goodness of purpose' of any particular organization in terms of the extent to which the internal goods of the practice at the core of the organization contribute to the overriding good of the community.[24] This is clearly not the kind of exercise which could be conducted in a strictly quantitative way but, in line with the idea that it is the practitioners collectively within a practice who are able to determine the appropriate standards of excellence of the internal goods, so this kind of judgement at the community level would need to be taken collectively. As MacIntyre comments, 'In contemporary societies our common goods can only be determined in concrete and particular terms through widespread, grassroots, shared, rational deliberation'.[25]

In relation to DesignCo, we might make some kind of judgement as to the organization's purpose, and how good it is, initially by considering the kinds of buildings which it has designed over recent years. DesignCo, as described in Chapter 1, designs office buildings often for city centre locations. Many of these are utilitarian although even with these we might expect buildings of good quality, which fit harmoniously into their environment, and so on.

---

[24] Moore (2012a: 367); see this paper also for the original discussion of the virtuous organizational mapping.
[25] MacIntyre (2010).

The occasional corporate headquarters which DesignCo designs offers more scope by way of allowing the architects, including Elaine, to express themselves, and to realize the potential of their practice. Generally, however, we might be able to make some kind of initial assessment that DesignCo's purpose is a reasonably good one; the community needs such buildings for it to function well and thereby satisfy the reasonable requirements of its citizens, and DesignCo meets that need.

We would also, however, need to make some kind of judgement as to how well DesignCo looks after its staff, not just in terms of their salaries and career development, but in relation to their development as architects, administrators, and so on, and as people. If we were to find that DesignCo carried on its business while exploiting its employees, we would necessarily want to qualify our judgement about how good the organization's overall purpose was.

This point about the development of practitioners is worth developing somewhat. Instinctively, we might think that the contribution an organization makes to the common good is related entirely to the goods and services it provides.[26] But MacIntyre's idea of a practice, and the 'perfection' of practitioners in the process, demands that this contribution to the common good is extended beyond this. And if we think about it, this makes perfect sense. A fundamental part of the common good is having virtuous individuals making good decisions, and carrying out good actions on behalf of themselves, their families, and the various organizations which make up a community, including the political organizations of government. How do these individuals become virtuous in the first place? Well, as we saw in Chapter 3, virtue and character are developed from a very young age. But our character development continues through our education and on into our adult lives, and particularly through the practices in which we engage. And while family, friends, community, religion, and so on may well be important in these contexts, so too are the organizations with which we engage, and particularly those in which we work and the practices in which we thereby take part.

There has been a long-standing argument as to whether capitalism and capitalist organizations generate or deplete virtue in individuals,[27] but either way the influence of organizations on our moral lives is not something we should underestimate. Expecting organizations to engage with the flourishing and moral development of their members may seem to place an undue burden on them,[28] but the point is that *they are doing this anyway*. It is just (though

---

[26] This is the approach which Conscious Capitalism takes, for example—see footnote 61 in Chapter 2.

[27] See Hirschman (1982).

[28] Catholic Social Teaching, which was mentioned in Chapter 3 in relation to the notion of the common good, seems to prioritize the development of people over the goods or services which an organization provides. This seems to get this out of proportion—see Moore (2016), in which I argue against this.

this is, admittedly, a big 'just') a matter of whether they are doing this well or not. We will come back to this point in subsequent chapters because it impacts on the way individuals understand their working lives (Chapter 5), how managers conceive their task (Chapter 6), and how organizations organize themselves to achieve this (Chapter 7).

Assuming, then, that we could arrive at some kind of judgement about how good the purpose of an organization is both in relation to its products or services and the development of its people, we might think of this as representing one dimension of the organization. Another dimension would then be the extent to which the organization pursued external goods, and most generically success, versus the extent to which it pursued internal goods, and most generically excellence; in other words, the extent to which it prioritized external over internal goods, the institution over the practice, or *vice-versa*. It would be possible to conceive of an organization that, as perhaps with DesignCo, overall had a good purpose (the design of buildings for office use and the appropriate development of its people in the process), but nonetheless did so in such a way which prioritized external goods such as profit over internal goods, success over excellence, to an inordinate degree.

In making a judgement about DesignCo's pursuit of success, we might begin by inspecting its accounts and see how its gross and net margins compared with other architects' firms over a number of years. Larger than normal margins might be evidence of efficiency, but they might also be evidence of exploitation of employees or suppliers, for example, and a general desire to return a high level of profitability irrespective of its effects on others or the practice of architecture at its core.

In considering its pursuit of excellence, we would want to make a judgement on how excellent the buildings were which DesignCo designed, how fit for purpose, how aesthetically pleasing, how congenial to their surroundings, and how ecologically sustainable they were. Of course, because many of these are subjective judgements, there may not be universal agreement. But by asking planning officers from the local authority, those who work in the buildings (recall that Elaine had already discovered that occupants found them generally uninspiring), those who work in similar buildings designed by different architects, as well as passers-by, together with other architects, it would be possible to come to some kind of general assessment of the extent to which DesignCo pursued excellence in its designs, while recognizing the budgetary constraints within which it was working. If indeed, as Elaine felt, DesignCo's designs seemed to be becoming more utilitarian, the same old designs fitted into spaces which don't quite 'work' with them, then we would justifiably have some concerns about its pursuit of excellence.

We might also want to ask DesignCo's employees overall about its pursuit of success and excellence and the extent to which they felt it was pursuing success over excellence or the other way round, or whether it had the balance

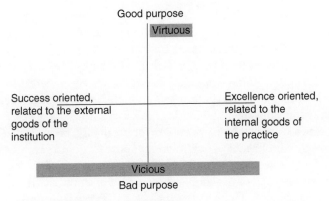

**Figure 4.2.** Mapping the virtuous organization

*Source*: This diagram first appeared in Moore (2012a) and was adapted from Crockett & Anderson (2008). It is copyright Sage Publications and is reproduced here with permission

about right.[29] We might then be able to combine these views together with the other data to come to some overall judgement on DesignCo's position in relation to the pursuit of success and excellence.

Collecting this kind of data, recognizing its subjective and qualitative nature, might nonetheless allow us to create a kind of mapping of an organization, as shown in Figure 4.2. This suggests that the goodness (or otherwise) of the purpose of an organization can be mapped as one dimension, while the extent to which it pursues success or excellence can be mapped on the other dimension. This implies that these two dimensions are conceptually different from one another. It would, for example, be possible to imagine a charitable organization involved with the relief of poverty in developing countries, and which took good care of and sought to develop its employees, and hence had an excellent purpose, but which nonetheless seemed to have got the balance between the pursuit of success and excellence wrong, seeking to enhance its reputation and increasing the salaries of its top employees, while paying insufficient attention to the provision of the services it actually provided on the ground.

Working with the mapping in Figure 4.2, it might be thought that the virtuous organization would be located at the top right of the diagram—obviously with a good purpose, but pursuing excellence over success. However, as we discussed above, external goods are also goods, and they are needed to enable the organization, both the core practice and the institution, to survive and develop. Thus, it is a question of getting the balance between the pursuit of these two kinds of goods right—which is why the virtuous organization is shown as being roughly in the middle, though just on the side of excellence.

---

[29] This has been done in some of the empirical work which has been conducted using MacIntyre's framework; we will come back to this in Chapter 8.

Figure 4.2 also locates vicious organizations anywhere along the bottom of the mapping. 'Vicious' is used since vice is the opposite of virtue, and while we might expect vicious organizations not only to have a bad purpose, but also to pursue success over excellence, it is possible to conceive of a vicious organization (a concentration camp, for example) which nonetheless pursued 'excellence' in its operations in terms of both efficiency and the development of its staff, while conveniently ignoring why it existed.

One of the advantages of this way of mapping organizations is that it can be used for organizational analysis, both in mapping the journey an organization may have taken over recent years (DesignCo's journey could be mapped, for example), and by way of explaining where it is currently and the direction it seems to be taking, and comparing these with the ideal—in other words in comparison with the virtuous position shown in Figure 4.2. This may also offer the opportunity for organizations to reconsider their direction of travel, and hence lead to organizational change. This has already been done with a number of organizational examples, and we will revisit this mapping and consider these findings in Chapter 8, when we look at practical illustrations of the virtues approach in business organizations.

## SUMMARY

In this chapter, we have explored the key concepts which MacIntyre offers us—internal and external goods, practices and institutions, and their relationships to virtue. We have seen how organizations might be understood as practice-institution combinations, pursuing both internal and external goods, and seen that this gives us a powerful metaphor for the reconceiving of organizations. It explains a tension inherent in organizations, between the practice and the institution and the pursuit of internal versus external goods, as well as helping us to see that organizations are essentially moral spaces. Both the products or services which an organization provides, and the development of its members, can then be seen as contributing to the common good. And this idea of the 'goodness of purpose' of an organization, coupled with whether it is getting the ordering and balance right between its pursuit of internal and external goods, enabled us to explore a mapping of a virtuous organization.

This then completes Part I, where we have explored the virtues approach and put together a conceptual framework for understanding organizations from a virtue ethics perspective. With this in place, we are now in a position to go on to Part II, which explores the implications of this approach for individuals, managers, and organizations.

# Part II

# Implications for Individuals, Managers, and Organizations

# 5

---

# Implications for Individuals

## INTRODUCTION

Having set out a framework for considering virtue ethics, mostly from a MacIntyrean perspective, and seen how it might begin to apply to individuals, managers, and organizations, Part II explores all of this in greater detail. We begin here by considering the implications of this approach for individuals both in their lives in general, but then specifically in their working lives in organizations. In Chapter 6 we will then explore the implications for managers and management, about which we have said relatively little so far, before Chapter 7 returns to working out what all of this means for organizations.

## ENDS, NARRATIVE QUESTS, PRACTICES, GOODS, AND VIRTUES—MACINTYREAN VIRTUE ETHICS FOR INDIVIDUALS

Let us begin with a brief reprise of what we have said so far about the virtues approach which we have explored particularly in Chapters 3 and 4, and how this applies to individuals. But in doing so, we will also take the opportunity to extend the discussion at various points.

Ethics at the individual level can be thought of as, in general, asking and seeking to answer the question, 'How, then, should I (or we) live?' The 'then' in this question implies that we have already gone some way towards answering the question, in the sense that we have some idea of the principles or values by which we might choose to live. Virtue ethics has its own particular way of conceiving of an answer to this question, and its 'then' encourages us to think of life as having something to do with the ends or purposes which we might, or perhaps even should, pursue if we are to realize our true *telos*. MacIntyre termed this the good life which we might pursue, not in an individualistic, hedonistic sense, but in relation to our overall sense of who we are, what abilities we possess, and how we might use these creatively for our own and the community's good. This gave rise to thinking in terms of having purpose or purposes (*telos*) in our lives, and of this being summarized in terms of some ultimate purpose or indeed state to which we might aspire. Aristotle termed this *eudaimonia* which MacIntyre, as we saw previously, defined as 'blessedness, happiness, prosperity. It is the state of being well and doing well, of a man's being well-favoured himself and in relation to the divine'.[1]

Another way of putting this, MacIntyre suggests, is that we need to be transformed from 'human-nature-as-it-happens-to-be (human nature in its untutored state)...by the instruction of practical reason and experience into human-nature-as-it-could-be-if-it-realized-its-*telos*'.[2] But in order to pursue our *telos* and the ultimate aim of *eudaimonia*, we find ourselves engaged in a narrative quest. That is, we are both involved in the story of our own lives and in the quest to discover 'what more and what else'[3] the good life for us consists of. This is about as far as we got to in Chapter 3 in considering the various components of virtue ethics. But we now need to develop this particular set of ideas somewhat.

It is fairly obvious that if we were to begin to tell the story of our lives we would need to go back to before we were born, to our parents and quite possibly their parents, and to wider family, and to their friends and acquaintances, and also to the social context into which we were born, and to the ways in which all these shaped us. In other words, our story is part of a narrative which began before we did, and will continue after we die, and involves not just our own narrative but also an 'interlocking set of narratives'.[4] MacIntyre extends this point in the following way:

> I am someone's son or daughter, someone else's cousin or uncle; I am a citizen of this or that city; a member of this or that guild or profession; I belong to this clan, that tribe, this nation. Hence what is good for me has to be the good for one who inhabits these roles. As such, I inherit from the past of my family, my city, my tribe, my nation, a variety of debts, inheritances, rightful expectations and obligations. These constitute the given of my life, my moral starting point. This is in part what gives my life its own moral particularity.[5]

Now, of course, it is just about possible, in the individualistic age in which we live, to deny certainly most, and perhaps all, of these prior connections and commitments; someone could emigrate and cut off all ties to family, friends, and former organizations such as school, university, workplaces (and possibly even the tax authorities!). Even then, unless the person were to live as a hermit, she would begin to accumulate such connections and commitments afresh

---

[1] MacIntyre (2007: 148).　　[2] Ibid.: 53.　　[3] Ibid.: 219.
[4] Ibid.: 218.　　[5] Ibid.: 220.

wherever she then chose to live; she would simply construct another, even if entirely different, set of relationships.

Most of us, however, do not take this somewhat drastic step, but live more or less happily within the network of prior connections and commitments, the 'interlocking set of narratives' which form our 'moral starting point'. However, we will, of course, add to this interlocking set of narratives as we make our own friends, perhaps find a life partner, and engage with other social activities and organizations and the people within them. In other words, as we grow up we move on from the 'given' of our moral starting point to engage in our own narrative quest, while not denying the ties to our past.

Elaine, as we know, is married to Fred and they have three teenage children. But Elaine is also, of course, a daughter to her parents who live some distance away. It turns out that she is an only child, and that her father, to whom she is particularly close, is seriously unwell. Her mother is somewhat younger than her father and was planning to work for a few more years before joining her husband in retirement. But with his illness, she has decided to give up work and to become his carer—a nearly full-time occupation, at least for the time being. This situation has had knock-on effects for Elaine, who is trying to balance all the other parts of her busy life with support for her parents, and for her mother in particular. Persuading her mother to make alternative arrangements for her father, so that she can take time off to recharge her own batteries, and being herself a part of those alternative arrangements, has not proved easy. But once a month her mother goes to her own sister for a long weekend, and Elaine and professional carers look after her father.

Elaine is, in these respects, typical of someone who acknowledges her moral connections and commitments to the wider and interlocking set of narratives of her life. But it is also putting a further strain on her relationship with Fred and it creates stresses with her children when mother is not around. Fred is supportive of this arrangement, but he finds the weekends when Elaine is barely present particularly difficult. It is one other factor in his deliberations about whether it would be better to separate from Elaine, though, if anything, it is a 'pull' factor, keeping him committed to the relationship. Fred, in that sense, also recognizes the wider commitments, to Elaine's family, that his marriage to Elaine entails, one moral particularity of his own life.

The more general point from this is that our narrative quest towards our own *telos*, and the projects which we might pursue in support of this, are not simply ones which we can choose entirely for ourselves. We could look on these other connections and commitments as constraints on our otherwise free choice to pursue our own lives and projects, but a more constructive way of thinking about them is to see them as part and parcel of our narrative quest towards our own *telos*. The example here is of the practice (under MacIntyre's definition) of family life, and is indicative of the commitments to other 'practitioners' (parents, spouse, children, and other family members) which arise through our engagement in that practice. But this is merely one example, and the same kind of commitments, albeit generally without the blood ties, would arise in other practices, as we will see in a number of real-life examples in Chapters 8 and 9.

What MacIntyre's approach to virtue ethics suggests is that the most important of the various activities in which we engage can be described as practices under his definition. Family life, as we have seen, is one of these, but so are chess, architecture, physics, medicine, and so on. MacIntyre encourages us to see our lives, or at least the key parts of them, as lived inside practices. And, as we saw, it is by exercising the virtues and pursuing excellence in each practice that we can, together with other practitioners, attain the internal goods of that practice. And these internal goods, together with those from the other practices in which we engage, lead to *the* good for ourselves and hence to us fulfilling our own purposes in life—though recognizing that it is in the nature of a narrative quest that we are always likely to be considering 'what more and what else' there is to discover about ourselves and our purposes.

We will need to explore further this idea of life lived inside practices in a moment. But this understanding also allows us to consider two virtues which MacIntyre considers to be particularly important. We have already come across virtues such as patience, diligence, and courteousness, as well as the four cardinal virtues of temperance (self-control), fortitude (courage), justice, and practical wisdom. But since we are engaged in a narrative quest towards our true *telos*, one key virtue which we need to add to these is constancy. MacIntyre defines it in the following way:

> Constancy requires that those who possess it pursue the same goods through extended periods of time, not allowing the requirements of changing social contexts to distract them from their commitments or to redirect them.[6]

It is, perhaps, this particular virtue which Elaine is demonstrating towards her parents at this point in their lives; remaining committed to this most funda-mental relationship between parent and child, even though the tables are now turned, and she is supporting them rather than the other way round. And it is, perhaps, this particular virtue which Fred is struggling with, knowing that he wants to remain committed to Elaine and to supporting her in these other commitments which she has at this particular time, while also knowing the pain which their own relationship is causing both of them.

But, while this situation, and the virtue of constancy which it demands, may be particularly important in Fred and Elaine's lives at present, there is a second virtue which we need to consider. If lives are lived mostly in practices, and if virtue ethics is about realizing our true *telos*, forming our character in such a

---

[6] MacIntyre (1999b: 318).

way that we can pursue good purposes both for ourselves and for the common good of the community, then one of the key virtues we will need is integrity. Integrity is one of those words which we find bandied about in discussions about ethics (in statements like the UK's 'Seven principles of public life',[7] for example), as well as in corporate mission and values statements where it usually means something related to uprightness and honesty. MacIntyre, however, defines integrity in the following way:

> To have integrity is to refuse to be, to have educated oneself so that one is no longer able to be, one kind of person in one social context, while quite another in other contexts. It is to have set inflexible limits to one's adaptability to the roles that one may be called upon to play... [to] exhibit the same moral character in different social contexts.[8]

The implication of possessing and exercising this virtue is that the character we have developed is revealed consistently in every practice in which we engage; we are the same person at work as we are at home, as we are when we are engaging with a practice like medicine (as a patient if not as a nurse, doctor, or consultant). This does not mean that we would not appropriately emphasize particular aspects of our character in particular circumstances—we are likely to be more efficient at work and more relaxed at home, for example. But, if we possess integrity, we would be no less just, no less caring, no less patient at work as at home.

MacIntyre is particularly exercised about this in relation to managerial work in modern corporations. Based on some empirical work in which he was himself involved, he comments, 'when the executive shifts from the sphere of the family to that of the corporation he or she necessarily shifts moral perspective',[9] and he develops this into a dramatic metaphor, insisting on:

> the importance of seeing contemporary social life as a theatre with a set of adjoining stages upon which a number of very different moral philosophical dramas are being acted out, the actors being required to switch from stage to stage, from character to character, often with astonishing rapidity.[10]

And he concludes his concerns by saying:

> The outcome is the creation of more than one self. The agent has to fabricate distinct characters... until quite recently, character was taken to be fixed and

---

[7] Here, integrity is defined as follows: 'Holders of public office must avoid placing themselves under any obligation to people or organisations that might try inappropriately to influence them in their work. They should not act or take decisions in order to gain financial or other material benefits for themselves, their family, or their friends. They must declare and resolve any interests and relationships'. This is, of course, a rather narrow definition, aligned to conflicts of interest. See https://www.gov.uk/government/publications/the-7-principles-of-public-life/the-7-principles-of-public-life-2, accessed 19 September 2016.
[8] MacIntyre (1999b: 317–18).    [9] MacIntyre (1979: 127).    [10] Ibid.: 127–8.

largely unchanging in an agent; types of character were limited and each agent's character was of a determinate type. But now in the modern corporate organisation character has become more like a mask or a suit of clothing; an agent may have to possess more than one.[11]

This is a concern directed at corporate life, although it may also apply more generally. But, if this is a reasonable description of the reality of everyday life as many of us experience it, and if as a result we struggle with the virtue of integrity, how, then, might we begin to frame some sort of response to this?

## PRACTICES AND THE UNITY
## OF AN INDIVIDUAL LIFE

We have already seen that, in pursuing the good of our lives through the projects and purposes in which we engage, we do so most particularly within practices. And we have already seen that this is practices in the plural—we are always likely to be taking part in a variety of practices at any one stage in our lives. MacIntyre describes this as follows, and then extends this rather obvious point in a new direction while also taking us back to the idea of the 'everyday plain person' which we met in Chapter 1:

> no individual lives her or his life wholly within the confines of any one practice. She or he always pursues the goods of more than one practice, as well as goods external to all practices, and so cannot escape posing and answering the question, even if only by the way in which he or she lives, of how these goods are to be ordered, of which part each is to play within the structures of a whole life.
>
> Characteristically, the plain person responds ... not so much through explicit arguments, although these may always play a part, as by shaping his or her life in one way rather than another. When from time to time, the plain person retrospectively examines what her or his life amounts to as a whole, often enough with a view to choice between alternative futures, characteristically what he or she is in effect asking is "To what conception of my overall good have I so far committed myself? And do I now have reason to put it in question?"[12]

There is, of course, a link here back to the idea of 'reasons for action' which we saw in Chapter 3 (that we should be able to explain why we carried out such and such an action by providing a link from it to what we understand to be our true good), and to the question discussed there about what might lead to the substantial good for all. The point is simply that, in living lives mostly inside practices, and pursuing the goods of practices, we will also need to consider the ordering, or the relative priority, of each of these practices in our lives, and

---

[11] Ibid.: 125.     [12] MacIntyre (1992: 7–8).

how these lead to the overall good of our lives. And we will, therefore, need to consider life as a whole, not just as a series of unrelated practices, and to review it on occasions, as the second part of the quotation above indicates.

For Elaine, the circumstances with her parents, and the potential break-down of her relationship with Fred, are inevitably forcing such a consideration and review, even if she has relatively little time for the kind of measured reflection which might be desirable. How do the key practices in which she is engaged—family life including taking her commitments to her ageing parents seriously, while also being a wife and a mother; architecture and her working life in general; playing the cello—fit together? Does she need to give greater priority to some rather than others, at least for the time being? What alterna-tive futures can she envisage and how do they fit with who she herself is and has become? She is, in effect, asking precisely the questions at the end of the quotation above: 'To what conception of my overall good have I so far committed myself? And do I now have reason to put it in question?'

We also saw in Chapter 3 that there was a direct link between virtues at the individual level and the idea of the common good of society—that we are not just on an individual narrative quest, but that we are also members of a community, and our good and the common good of the community are intertwined. So it is worth at this stage making a broader connection to this idea of the ordering of practices and of the goods associated with them. Some commentators on MacIntyre's work have put this helpfully in the following way:

> the normative character of MacIntyre's definition of a social practice . . . is secured within a larger account of the moral life as a whole. There must be some *telos* to human life, a vision anticipating the moral unity of life, given in the form of a narrative history that has meaning within a particular community's traditions; otherwise the various internal goods generated by the range of social practices will remain disordered and potentially subversive of one another. Without a commu-nity's shared sense of *telos*, there will be no way of signifying 'the overriding good' by which various internal goods may be ranked and evaluated.[13]

The point here is that not only do we as individuals need to review our lives as a whole, and to consider which practices, and the relative priority of such practices in our lives, we wish to give attention to, but that the same kind of process needs to take place at the level of the community. We have already noted this in Chapter 4 together with MacIntyre's point that, 'In contempor-ary societies our common goods can only be determined in concrete and particular terms through widespread, grassroots, shared, rational deliber-ation'.[14] And again, as we have noted before, this is some way from a liberal,

---

[13] McCann & Brownsberger (1990: 227–8).    [14] MacIntyre (2010).

individualist conception of society where the role of the state is not to provide opportunities for such debate, let alone to reach conclusions, but simply to provide conditions where individuals can pursue their own projects. MacIntyre would argue that not only is this impossible in practice, but also that it is highly undesirable.

## VIRTUE AT WORK

This provides a link to what we need to consider next: what does all this mean for the practice or practices in which we engage at work in organizations? Clearly, from all we have said so far, the practice we engage with at work—architecture for Elaine, physics for Fred—is only one of the practices in our lives at any given moment. But equally clearly, it is likely to be one of the most significant practices given the amount of time and energy which it often demands. And equally clearly, it is likely to be significant for the contribution we can make to the common good: the products or services which we are involved in supplying, and the way in which our engagement in the practice develops us as people.

Recall from Chapter 4 that MacIntyre talks about the perfection of practitioners as one of the internal goods arising out of a practice. While, as we said there, we might more naturally think of this as being about human flourishing and moral development, the point is that engaging in practices, including those at work, makes a difference (for good or ill) to us. And in the ideal, we should find that our involvement in our work practice develops us as people, enabling us to realize our true *telos*.

Elaine and Fred's eldest child, Jason, has just finished school and, in between school and university, has decided to work for a year. All of a sudden, it appears that he is able to get himself up on time, dress smartly making sure that there is a clean, ironed (*his* ironing!) shirt ready for tomorrow before he goes early to bed. He seems to be able to respond appropriately and pleasantly to those in authority over him, and generally to take a critical interest in what the organization he is working for does (his job is in the back office of a private-sector care home). Elaine and Fred are surprised at this almost instantaneous transformation from the scruffy, monosyllabic, and rather surly teenager they thought they had raised. But they shouldn't be—all that is happening is that the organization, and the discipline inherent in the efficiency of its operations, is drawing out and developing parts of their son's character which they had helped to form. Organizations do that. And while most organizations would not go so far as establishing an 'Institute for the Formation of Character', as Robert Owen did at his mill in New Lanark, Scotland in the early nineteenth century,[15] in practice organizations are, by their very nature, institutions for the formation of character, as we saw in Chapter 4.

This, however, implies two things. First, that unemployment is a very significant social ill because it deprives individuals of this opportunity for the development of their characters through this activity, as well as of the sense of making some contribution to the common good, and of earning their way in the world. Structural unemployment, particularly youth unemployment, is significantly deleterious to the common good, and can hardly be thought of as a price worth paying for controlling inflation, as was once claimed by a UK chancellor of the exchequer.[16]

But second, it implies a very high view of work, and therefore of organizations which supply that work. On this understanding, we as individuals should take very seriously the opportunities our work in organizations offers for our flourishing and moral development, including a critical awareness that this may not always be for our good. And we should expect, and perhaps even demand, that organizations offer work which is rewarding in this respect, while recognizing that this requires just as much of an input from our side as from the organization's. Jason, Elaine and Fred's son, is already learning that what he gets out of his employment, in more than monetary terms, depends partly on what he puts in.

This understanding of what we might, at its best, contribute to and expect from our employment in organizations is usually referred to as 'meaningful work', and it is helpful to consider how this has been characterized and the implications this holds for us as individuals, but also for organizations and for managers within them.

## MEANINGFUL WORK

We spent some time in Chapter 2 looking at how work had been characterized in the early industrial period, particularly through the literature of that time. Work then, at least for the masses, was often soulless and dispiriting, and many of those commenting upon it railed against the effect on ordinary

[15] See http://infed.org/mobi/education-in-robert-owens-new-society-the-new-lanark-institutes-and-schools/, accessed 19 September 2016. The military may be an exception in this respect, although the form of conditioning which takes place, which encourages inductees to partially subordinate their individuality for the good of the unit, is a rather extreme form of character development.
[16] This was an infamous statement by Norman Lamont, as chancellor of the exchequer, made in the UK Parliament in May 1991. See Department of the Official Report (Hansard), House of Commons, Westminster, http://www.publications.parliament.uk/pa/cm199091/cmhansrd/1991-05-16/Orals-1.html, accessed 19 September 2016.

workers. They were holding out a much higher vision of what work should be about. As it has been put more recently:

> Working is about the search for daily meaning as well as daily bread, for recognition as well as cash, for astonishment rather than torpor; in short for a sort of life rather than a Monday through Friday sort of dying.[17]

It has been claimed that this idea of searching for meaning in our lives is 'a universal human motivation which addresses a fundamental need for a sense that one's life is worth living',[18] and it is clear how this fits well with the virtues approach which we have been exploring in relation to the idea of pursuing goods, ends, goals, and purposes in our life. More broadly, meaningfulness is related to several important dimensions in our lives: a sense of being connected to something which is 'bigger' than we are and which is objectively worthwhile; a sense that we are not alone but somehow belong or have a place in the world; and hence meaningfulness answers what has been termed our need for 'existential security'.[19]

And it has been argued that work makes a very important contribution to this wider sense of meaningfulness. This is not to say that we cannot obtain meaning from other activities (practices) in which we engage outside of work—clearly we can and should. But there is something about work which makes it particularly significant to our wider search for meaning. Work somehow furthers our life story[20] (the idea of the narrative quest which we explored in Chapter 3 and above), it helps us to make our home in the world,[21] and in that sense work is a critical element in the living of a good life.

But obviously those claims can be realized only if the work in which we engage is, itself, meaningful. Boring, mundane, monotonous, or, as above, soulless and dispiriting work might well have the opposite effect, leading to meaninglessness rather than meaningfulness. Following this, meaningful work has been defined as 'the way we express the meaning of our lives through the activities (work) that comprise most of our waking hours', or 'that which gives essence to what we do and...brings a sense of fulfilment to our lives'.[22]

Meaningful work has been characterized as having two dimensions: the objective and the subjective.[23] The objective dimension relates to the idea that whatever we do through our work must have some importance which is readily recognized by others. This links directly to the ideas which we have already considered—that the internal goods of practices, the product or service and the perfection of the practitioners in the process, should make a contribution to the common good of the community. Without that, the work we engage in is clearly not meaningful. MacIntyre comments that, 'objective

---

[17] Terkel (1975: 1).      [18] Yeoman (2014: 240).      [19] Ibid.: 241.
[20] Ibid.: 243.      [21] Ibid.: 246.      [22] Chalofsky (2003: 73–4).
[23] See Yeoman (2014: 244–9).

activity is activity in which the end or aim of the activity is such that by making that end their own individuals are able to achieve something of universal worth',[24] and this neatly links the objective and subjective dimensions of meaningful work. The subjective dimension, then, is that the work should be meaningful to the individual who carries it out. Hence, meaningful work is 'work that the subject finds fulfilling, and which contributes to or connects positively with something the value of which has its source outside the subject'.[25]

We can probably think fairly readily of instances which would fail to meet one or both of these criteria. One such example is of the character of Sisyphus in Greek mythology who was punished by the god Zeus by making him roll a large boulder up a steep hill.[26] But the boulder always rolled away before Sisyphus got it to the top, so that he was condemned to carrying out this purposeless task endlessly. Clearly, this example fails on both dimensions of meaningful work. But suppose Sisyphus was then given a drug which made him think that rolling stones endlessly uphill was fun, and so gave meaning to his life. Would this make it meaningful work? Obviously not, for objectively we can see that it is still a meaningless activity, even if subjectively Sisyphus was convinced, albeit in his drugged state, that it was meaningful.

But that leads us to consider one difficulty with the concept of meaningful work. This is that the experience of work varies very widely, so that some jobs which are objectively meaningful, and so satisfy that dimension, are not experienced that way by workers (perhaps because they feel the job is 'beneath' them), and so fail to satisfy the subjective dimension. And *vice-versa*, some jobs which might be considered relatively meaningless (cleaning, catering, and what is known as 'dirty work' such as emptying dustbins) are experienced as meaningful by those who undertake them.[27] Both of these issues relate to the subjective dimension of meaningful work and to something which we will need to say more about in a moment. However, the objective aspect of meaningful work and the potential problems with it—how would we get consensus on whether a particular job is meaningful or not?—is something we have already considered in Chapter 4 and above in relation to the extent to which the internal goods of any practice contribute to the common good. In the same way, while we could probably agree, or anticipate agreement, on the meaningfulness of many jobs, we would need widespread deliberation about whether particular jobs did contribute to the common good or not.

An example here might be whether those who work in the tobacco industry can genuinely be involved in meaningful work; would this not fail the objective

---

[24] MacIntyre (1998: 225).
[25] This is an adaptation of a quote cited in Yeoman (2014: 244) where it refers to a meaningful life rather than just work.
[26] This story is related in Yeoman (2014: 244) where she is also drawing on other sources.
[27] Beadle & Knight (2012: 441).

dimension test given the harmful nature of the products the industry produces?[28] How do such products contribute to the common good? But how would we collectively decide, other than by a gradual change in society which might lead eventually to the activity being ostracized or perhaps made illegal (with all the problems which making a substance illegal tends to lead to)? Considering how the political dimension associated with these kinds of decisions (political not in the party sense, but in the Aristotelian sense of deciding for the common good), is largely beyond the scope of this book. But we do need to acknowledge the need for appropriate deliberative structures which enable these kinds of conversations and decisions.

## ORDERING OUR DESIRES

Let us return to the subjective dimension of meaningful work. One of the difficulties we face in growing up is to reflect upon and order our desires in such a way that we develop into what MacIntyre calls 'independent practical reasoners'.[29] MacIntyre describes this as follows:

> To have learned how to stand back in some measure from our present desires, so as to be able to evaluate them, is a necessary condition for engaging in sound reasoning about our reasons for action. Here one danger is that those who have failed to become sufficiently detached from their own immediate desires, for whom desire for their and the good has not become to a sufficient degree overriding, are unlikely to recognise this fact about themselves. And so what they present to themselves as a desire for their own good or for *the* good may in fact and often enough is some unacknowledged form of infantile desire that has been protected from evaluative criticism.[30]

The point here is that we may not learn to evaluate our desires sufficiently, so that these desires remain *disordered*. Consider this in relation to one common way in which work has been characterized. This approach to what is known as 'work orientation' divides work into three types: job, career, and calling.[31] Those who have a job-work orientation value it only as a means to an end; work is valuable to them only in so far as it enables them to 'earn a living'. Using the terminology we developed earlier, work is valued only for the external goods which it leads to (wages or salary), not for the internal goods related to the work itself. Another common way of expressing this is that the motivation to work is *extrinsic*, in other words that it is outside of oneself.

---

[28] See, for example, http://www.tobaccofreeportfolios.org/facts/, accessed 19 September 2016.
[29] MacIntyre (1999a).      [30] Ibid.: 72–3, emphasis in original.
[31] See, for example, Beadle & Knight (2012: 442), although this is a very common distinction which can be found in multiple sources.

A career-work orientation values work for things like increased pay, the possibility of promotion, and the prestige which may go with seniority in an organization. Again, it is obvious that the primary motivation here is for external goods and is therefore similarly extrinsic. We talk of people having 'climbed the career ladder', and while we might thereby express some admiration (but possibly also a certain degree of envy), we really ought to ask which ladder it is they have been climbing and whether that is, in itself, a good career to follow—how does it contribute to the common good?

The third work orientation is a calling and those who have this orientation value work primarily for the fulfilment which it offers. In that sense, it is to do with what we have come to call internal goods or, in contrast to the extrinsic motivation identified above, entails an *intrinsic* motivation. Obvious examples here include priests, doctors, nurses, teachers, and those who work on the ground for development agencies sometimes in conditions which might affect their own well-being or even, in the extreme, their lives. In each case, we would expect that the primary motivation for choosing to train and work in these areas is because of the good—the contribution to the common good—which the work offers, together with the meaning that this holds for the individual. In other words, it meets both the objective and subjective criteria of meaningful work.

All of this is not to say, of course, that external goods are not also required and sought. Unless this is a voluntary activity (which would require that the individual is able to draw on external goods obtained by them previously, or provided from some other source), the individuals would expect and need to be paid for what they do. And in some cases they might be paid very well—doctors, for example. But we would be surprised and disappointed if a doctor said that he went into medicine for the monetary rewards alone, or that it looked like a good career to pursue (the job and career work orientations). We would hope that the primary motivation was about the promotion of health among members of the community so that they were enabled to lead more fulfilling lives. We would, in other words, hope that a sense of calling was the main reason the doctor chose that occupation, and that intrinsic motivation overshadowed extrinsic motivation.

But this then leads us into another potentially problematic issue for the idea of meaningful work. Is meaningful work only for the few? There are only so many jobs as priests, doctors, nurses, teachers, and development workers to go round, and the level of education and training required for each of these is high. Does this condemn the rest of us to work which is not meaningful? Well, this is partly about how we see our work and how we can connect it to its wider significance. The story of the three workers in a quarry who, when asked what they were about, replied in one case, 'earning some money', in another, 'quarrying stone', and in the third, 'building a cathedral', illustrates this point. Most of us, even if we would not consider that we have a vocation as such, could connect what we do to its wider significance in relation to the contribution which the goods and services we are involved with make a contribution to the common good. However, in doing so, we would do well not to protect ourselves from 'evaluative criticism' in undertaking such a reflection—as might workers in the tobacco industry example above. But even if we can think of ways in which our and our organization's contribution to the common good might be improved upon, most of us can probably connect our work to the objective dimension of meaningful work—that it does make some positive contribution to the world— and thereby find meaningfulness in that.

The difficulty, however, is that both because of the nature of much modern work, and perhaps because of our own disordered desires (desires for money and status, for example), we might opt for work as job or career, and not seek meaningfulness in it. In other words, work becomes principally about its extrinsic motivation, about earning enough to do interesting things in the other parts of our lives or in retirement, in pursuing a career and taking satisfaction, and achieving status, in having climbed the ladder, without particularly asking which ladder and what the point was.

From the virtue ethics perspective which we have been developing, it should be clear that accepting second best in this most important area (practice) of our lives is not good enough. We should seek meaningful work, meaning in our work, partly because it contributes to the common good (the objective dimension) and partly because it contributes to our development as people and the realization of our *telos*, our purpose in life (the subjective dimension). We will consider more of how this can be done in a moment, but it is first worth reflecting on the effects on us of not engaging in meaningful work.

Extensive research has been carried out in this area and shows that non-meaningful work harms us. It limits us in the formation of the capabilities we need to fully participate in significant activities over the course of our lives. For example, if we experience lack of autonomy (which is crucial for our moral development) at work, it is likely to affect our ability to lead autonomous lives more generally—it is not something which can easily be 'made up' in other parts of our lives. Non-meaningful work can also lead to physical, mental, and psychological deterioration, with one study showing an increase in heart disease in office workers who experienced lack of control over their work environment, for example.[32] As one commentator has put it:

> Specifically, the harms of non-meaningful work undermine an individual's ability to participate in the work of social cooperation over a lifetime by: stunting the development of her capabilities for free and autonomous action; undermining her sense of self-esteem and self-worth, of her standing in relation to others; and

---

[32] The examples here are taken from Yeoman (2014: 239), and citing Bosma, Marmot, Hemingway, Nicholson, Brunner, & Stansfield (1997) for the heart disease example.

thwarting her sense of efficacy, of being able to act with others upon the world. Together, these harms to capabilities, status and efficacy reduce a person's ability to build the practical identity necessary to securing a sense that her life has meaning.[33]

If, then, we wish to order our desires appropriately, we will need to become 'valuers' by developing our 'capabilities for objective valuation and subjective attachment', so that 'we learn to appreciate which objects have value, and to generate the relevant orientations towards those objects'.[34] In this way work would not be just about a job or a career, but would have a sense of calling to it. But how, then, can work be made meaningful?

## MAKING WORK MEANINGFUL

From all that has been said, it will be apparent that the first requirement for meaningful work is to do with its objective value in making a contribution to the common good. Without this, while we might do all we can to make our work subjectively meaningful, it will ultimately fail the test of meaningful work. That, of course, may well have implications for the kind of organization we wish to work for. For if we cannot say with some certainty what the purpose of the organization we work for is, and how it contributes to the common good, we would have good reason to question our continued employment there.

For Elaine and Fred, this may not be too hard. Architecture, as a practice in general and in the particular kinds of office buildings which her employer DesignCo designs, has the potential to contribute to the common good by the way in which it enhances the built environment, and provides good spaces for people to work in. While Elaine's concerns about the way DesignCo is going (the buildings becoming more utilitarian, and the focus more on internal cost cutting and profit), might provide evidence that the practice of architecture, as realized in DesignCo, is not pursuing excellence in a way which is objectively satisfying, Elaine still holds onto the ideal of the practice of architecture as it could be. And she still desires that her own creative side might be given more expression because of the contribution to the common good this might make. In other words, she still holds to the objective meaningfulness of architecture.

In a similar way, Fred can make a strong case for the objective meaningfulness of the teaching of physics, the practice in which he is engaged at work. The contribution which physics makes to the quality of our lives, goods such as the use of lasers in optical operations, is not hard to observe. And, in addition, since Fred is involved in the education and general development of

[33] Yeoman (2014: 239).  [34] Ibid.: 245, emphasis removed from original.

school pupils at a formative stage in their lives, he can easily make the case for the contribution this makes to the common good.

But despite being able to satisfy the objective criteria of meaningful work, it can, as we observed above, be experienced as subjectively meaningless. What, then, contributes to subjective meaningfulness? The most common approach to this is in what is known as 'job design', and from research done in this area the intrinsically rewarding characteristics of work comprise: skill variety (the number of skills used by workers); task identity (the extent to which workers perform a job from start to finish); task significance (the extent of the impact of the work); autonomy (the degree of decision making residing with the worker); and feedback (the extent of communicated job recognition).[35]

In addition to this, it has been observed that direct contact with the beneficiaries of their work can make work more meaningful to employees.[36] Interestingly, workers experiencing such 'flow' in relation to their work report 'total absorption in tasks... enjoyment, concentration or immersion in tasks, including a distorted experience of time and levels of intrinsic motivation that eclipse considerations of external reward'.[37] In other words, attention to, and the satisfaction inherent in the pursuit of excellence in internal goods, seems to override the desire for external goods such as pay and status. Another interesting feature of those with calling-work orientations is that they have been found to engage in 'job crafting' through which 'they attempt to improve their experience of tasks and engage in extra-role behaviour that improves their experience of work'.[38] An example is cleaners attempting to improve their work through increasing their interaction with clients.[39]

This idea of job crafting is something which is worth developing. In relation to what we might call, following MacIntyre, *practice-based work*, as a means of thinking about meaningful work, a way of characterizing it might be to describe it as being involved in a craft. Being a craftsperson might then be a good way of encapsulating how someone might best approach work if the notions of virtue, practice, narrative quest, and *telos*, as we have described them, are seen to provide a convincing and perhaps attractive way of 'coming at' moral philosophy.[40] But what would this involve?

There are four main implications for individuals if they were to become or, perhaps, rediscover being a craftsperson. First, as we have already said, individuals would need to focus on the *intrinsic* value or, in MacIntyre's terms, the internal goods of their work rather than its *instrumental* value. This would not entirely exclude consideration of external goods such as pay

---

[35] This originates in work by Hackman and Oldham (1975). See Beadle & Knight (2012: 439–40) for a discussion.

[36] Michaelson, Pratt, Grant, & Dunn (2014: 80).

[37] Beadle & Knight (2012: 440).     [38] Ibid.: 442.     [39] Ibid.: 442.

[40] This section on craft and the craftsperson is based on Moore (2005b).

and status (they are goods, after all), but it would be to get the ordering of these correct (internal over external goods) in a balanced pursuit of both. This may not be easy, particularly in organizations which encourage individuals to think in terms of instrumental rewards such as pay and career enhancement (and thereby, implicitly at least, do not give due consideration to providing meaningful work), and it may be difficult for individuals not to collude with the organization in this regard. But, of course, that is precisely why the virtues are needed, to enable us to 'sustain practices and enable us to achieve the goods internal to practices, [and] sustain us in the relevant kind of quest for the good'.[41]

Recalling that, as we noted in Chapter 3, the Greek word *arête* can be translated both as virtue and excellence helps us to realize that, in practical terms, this would mean that the individual should endeavour to produce the best of which he or she is capable. Thus, Elaine should continue to try to produce the best and most creative architectural designs possible, despite the constraints at DesignCo. And this would involve not just a design which was conceptually and creatively excellent, but also one that would 'deliver' as far as her employer DesignCo was concerned, even if others there failed to recognize it.

The second implication is that we should not underestimate the corrupting power of institutions over practices. And this means taking seriously the need to exercise the virtues in order not just to achieve internal goods but also to sustain the practice. MacIntyre makes a general point about this when he says, as we saw in Chapter 4, that the essential feature of the virtues is clear: 'without them, without justice, courage and truthfulness, practices could not resist the corrupting power of institutions'.[42] So within those who engage directly in the practice at the core of the organization there needs to be a commitment to exercise the virtues, potentially against the institution which houses the practice, if and when it becomes too focused on external goods, which is actually to the detriment of both the practice and the institution. MacIntyre states this explicitly:

> For the ability of a practice to retain its integrity will depend on the way in which the virtues can be and are exercised in sustaining the institutional forms which are the social bearers of the practice. The integrity of a practice causally requires the exercise of the virtues by at least some of the individuals who embody it in their activities; and conversely the corruption of institutions is always in part at least an effect of the vices.[43]

This second implication leads directly on to the third since it is probably clear that this will involve practitioners working together. No one is likely to be able to resist the power of the institution alone. Hence, individuals should see part of their task at work as to do with building community. This happens in any

---

[41] MacIntyre (2007: 219).    [42] Ibid.: 194.    [43] Ibid.: 195.

case since being a craftsperson, by its very nature, requires working with other craftspeople in pursuit of the common task of seeking excellence in the achievement of internal goods. And, perhaps not surprisingly, this idea of building community and creating social 'space', is also part of what makes work meaningful. Friendly places to work, where opportunities for interaction and socializing amongst employees are built in, enable this building of community and make work subjectively more meaningful.[44] While recognizing the benefits of 'new blood' to organizations, this is also likely to mean that craftspeople will tend to stay with the organization for considerable periods— for how else could loyalty, stability, a sense of community, and of 'interlocking narratives' be established?

Fourth, it is obviously appropriate to think about which particular virtues would be needed if we, as individuals in a working community, were to make this way of conceptualizing work a reality. We noted earlier that constancy and integrity would be required, and we see from the quotation above that justice, courage, and truthfulness are those which MacIntyre thinks are particularly important. In general, it would probably be appropriate to return largely, though not exclusively, to the cardinal virtues which we met in Chapter 3. So, in addition to courage and justice which have already been mentioned, we would look for temperance (self-control) and practical wisdom in individuals as craftspeople.

In addition, however, there might be two other virtues which we should consider in this context. One is trust, which we should interpret as a virtue which both offers trust to others and is about being trustworthy oneself. And, perhaps particularly in relation to the building of community, magnanimity (benevolence, altruism) would seem to be required. MacIntyre develops the virtue of 'just generosity',[45] as he calls it, in relation to very different kinds of communities than those we might experience at work in organizations, but it may well be this which is required of individuals at work if the communal nature of work is to be realized.

## DO MANAGERS, ORGANIZATIONS, AND GOVERNMENTS HAVE A RESPONSIBILITY TO PROVIDE MEANINGFUL WORK?

The implications of what we have covered are that we as individuals should seek work which is both objectively and subjectively meaningful. But that leaves a rather big question as to whether those who provide employment—managers

---

[44] Cartwright & Holmes (2006: 203).    [45] MacIntyre (1999a: 119–22).

and organizations—and those who oversee employment in general—the state— have a responsibility to provide it.

As we have noted on more than one occasion, while this book is set at the individual, managerial, and organizational levels, there are implications for the state. And we have observed that the approach here is some way from any sense of a liberal, individualist society: governments do have a role, which they simply cannot escape even if they were to try, in interpreting and seeking the achievement of the common good. While, in relation to work, governments might most naturally think of this in terms of reducing unemployment, or in seeking to control the worst effects of a capitalist system in relation to zero-hours contracts, for example,[46] the implications of the above discussion are that governments also have a role in promoting 'the social and economic conditions for widespread meaningful work'.[47] And while this is principally a normative argument (in other words, that governments *should* do this), there are instrumental reasons, such as improved health and capabilities, which support the idea that meaningful work is 'a good whose just distribution should be an object of common concern'.[48]

In a similar manner, there are instrumental reasons for why organizations and managers should be involved in promoting meaningful work. When individuals find that performance is everything, they can lose any sense of meaning in their work, and this can affect their attitude, behaviour, and mental health.[49] And on the other side, meaningful work can lead to increased job performance, organization citizenship behaviour (willingness to go beyond one's job description), and customer satisfaction,[50] as well as to greater organizational commitment and engagement, the retention of key employees, the effective management of organizational change, and hence overall improvement in organizational performance.[51] With such a range of benefits, managers could also be expected to seek to provide meaningful work for their subordinates, and not see it as a trade-off between meaningfulness and performance.[52] And while this might seem to be making an argument from

---

[46] Figures from the April to June 2016 Labour Force Survey in the UK show 903,000 people are employed on a 'zero-hours contract' in their main job. This represents 2.9 per cent of all people in employment, an increase of 0.5 per cent from the same period in 2015. People on a zero-hours contract are 'more likely to be young, part-time, women, or in full-time education when compared with other people in employment'. On average, they work twenty-five hours a week. See https:// www.ons.gov.uk/employmentandlabourmarket/peopleinwork/earningsandworkinghours/articles/ contractsthatdonotguaranteeaminimumnumberofhours/september2016, accessed 19 September 2016.

[47] Yeoman (2014: 235). The argument made in Yeoman's paper is for a 'liberal perfectionist framework' from which she develops 'a normative justification for making meaningful work the object of political action' (235).

[48] Beadle & Knight (2012: 445).   [49] Chalofsky (2003: 80).

[50] Michaelson et al. (2014: 78).   [51] Cartwright & Holmes (2006: 201).

[52] Michaelson et al. (2014: 86).

consequentialist principles, it is quite often the case with virtue ethics that what seems to be the right thing to do anyway can, if done from genuine motivation, also have beneficial effects.

## SUMMARY

In this chapter we have considered what the particular approach to virtue ethics which we are exploring in this book means for individuals, both in their lives in general and in their working lives in particular. We have seen how we live the most important parts of our lives in practices, as MacIntyre defines them, and how the pursuit of excellence in seeking to obtain the internal goods of practices—the good product or service and the 'perfection' or flourishing of the individual in the process—leads to the achievement of our *telos*, or purpose in life. We have seen how this involves a complex network of connections and commitments, and how these imply commitments to other practitioners whether these are within our family, our workplace, or in other settings. We then developed what all this meant for us in one of the most significant practices in our lives—our work. We explored the substantial notion of meaningful work and how we, as individuals, should take this idea seriously. But this also has quite serious implications for managers and for organizations. And it is to the implications of the virtue ethics approach for these that we turn next.

# 6

---

# Implications for Managers

## INTRODUCTION

So far, we have said relatively little about managers and management. This chapter sets out to make good that deficit and to explore what the MacIntyrean framework which we have developed implies for managers. We begin, however, by drawing a distinction between managers and management. Following that, we explore what MacIntyre himself has said about managers—which turns out to be quite a lot, almost all of it negative. We will then look at various critiques of his position before, somewhat paradoxically, using the framework MacIntyre provides to characterize managers and management within a virtue ethics approach, and to consider which virtues are required to be a virtuous manager.

## MANAGERS AND MANAGEMENT: WHAT'S THE DIFFERENCE?

Consider the example of a professional string quartet. Their repertoire is broad and they play in a variety of locations around the country, though not yet internationally. They have become reasonably well known, have three albums to their name, and are on the road most weeks. They can fit all of their instruments and equipment into a small van they have purchased, which all of them can drive. So all they need to do, when working away from home, is to book somewhere to stay, meet at some pre-arranged location, and off they go. When not away, they rehearse and plan future concerts, do occasional recording sessions at a professional studio, spend time with their families, and so on. Because they do not live that close to each other, they meet at one of their member's large house for rehearsals, and the other three can stay over there if need be.

Two things are probably already apparent from this description. The first is that they do not have a manager; the operation is sufficiently small-scale, and its level of complexity sufficiently limited, for them not to need to employ someone else. But second, aside from actually playing together, there is a lot of organizing and coordinating which needs to be done. Which bookings to accept; what programme to offer; where will they stay and what travel arrangements need to be made; when will they fit in time to rehearse; and what new pieces might they add to their repertoire? All of this, and more, has to be decided. So there is a lot of what we would typically call 'management' to be done, and they have to share this out between them.

But were they to become even better known, their schedule more complex, the need to deal with large professional locations become commonplace, international engagements to start to come in, and the need to deal with the marketing of the quartet, and consequently with the media, begin to make increasing demands, they would quite likely have to revisit this. And while they could employ someone relatively junior just to organize all the practicalities, it might make more sense to engage someone who could act, in effect, as both their agent and coordinator, someone with oversight of what they are doing now and, perhaps, what they might aspire to in the future. In other words, they might need to employ someone who begins to 'manage' their affairs. This person would, quite obviously, need to understand enough of the musical world to be able to do that effectively, without, of course, needing to play any kind of musical instrument, let alone a violin, viola, or cello.

One point which emerges from this scenario is that *managers*, as those who are 'professional' organizers and coordinators, are distinct from *management*,[1] in the sense of the kinds of organizing and coordinating which everyone, including managers of course, have to do some of, and which goes on all the time in a whole variety of different ways, beginning with 'self-management' at the individual level. But it is those who spend most or all of their time organizing and coordinating activities and other people, who we typically refer to as managers.

Another point which emerges is that such professional managers are always managing *something*, be it a string quartet or the building of a new corporate headquarters, one designed by Elaine's employer DesignCo, for example. This is an important point to which we will return later. But for now we might note that, in the MacIntyrean terminology which we have developed, there is a difference between the practice of music making, for example, and the organization associated with it—the formal organization required to be a successful string quartet, for example. While some of the organizing is closely associated with the practice, and probably needs to be decided by the practitioners (which programme to offer for a particular concert, for example), some of it is very different from the practice (sorting out travel arrangements and making

---

[1] I am indebted to Ron Beadle for helping me to see this distinction and its implications.

bookings for accommodation, for example). And the latter could be done by anyone with the requisite knowledge and skills, and without any need to engage with the practice itself. Another way of expressing this, again drawing on the MacIntyrean terminology we have developed, is to say that the primary concern of the practice is with internal goods—the excellence of the music, in this case, as well as the 'perfection' of the practitioners—while the primary concern of managers is with external goods, including handling practicalities efficiently and, ultimately, in ensuring financial sustainability.

MacIntyre, as we noted earlier, had a rather negative attitude to those who had become professional managers, those who had, in a sense, lost direct contact with the practice and simply organized and coordinated things to do with it. It was to these, professional managers as a type, to which MacIntyre's critique was directed. But to see why, we need to begin somewhat further back in his argument.

## WHY DOES MACINTYRE HAVE SUCH A NEGATIVE VIEW OF MANAGERS?

The key book which we have been drawing on is MacIntyre's *After Virtue*, originally published in 1981.[2] Although it is now in its third edition, the 2007 version we have been citing still contains the original text. In that book, as was mentioned briefly towards the beginning of Chapter 3, MacIntyre argued that modern-day morality is based on what he called 'emotivism'. As was said there, emotivism 'is the doctrine that all evaluative judgments and more specifically all moral judgments are *nothing but* expressions of preference, expressions of attitude or feeling, insofar as they are moral or evaluative in character'.[3] The implication of this is that our society is based on attempts to make others comply with our wishes—'others' become merely a means to our ends, and as a result all social relations become manipulative. MacIntyre argued that emotivism was the result of what he saw as the inevitable failure of the Enlightenment project and its associated principle-based ethics, which we also touched on briefly in Chapter 3.

From this starting point, however, MacIntyre made an interesting move. He suggested that there are what could be described as particular 'characters' in society, and it is these characters which 'are the masks worn by moral philosophies'.[4] In other words, if we want to understand what a particular moral philosophy looks like in practice, we have only to identify the particular

---

[2] This section and, indeed, most of the remainder of the argument in this chapter is taken from Moore (2008).

[3] MacIntyre (2007: 11–12), emphasis in original.          [4] Ibid.: 28.

characters who embody it. And while MacIntyre included therapists and aesthetes in his critique,[5] the particular character which he singled out, as the embodiment of emotivism, was the manager, 'that dominant figure of the contemporary scene'.[6] In other words, MacIntyre was arguing that managers who, like organizations, have become ubiquitous in the modern world, are engaged in manipulative relationships which turn others into means to whichever end a particular manager might be seeking to achieve. But why is this so?

MacIntyre located the managers he was talking about within bureaucratic organizations (we will need to revisit the concept of bureaucracy later), in which 'the manager treats ends as given, as outside his scope; his concern is with technique, with effectiveness in transforming raw materials into final products, unskilled labor into skilled labor, investment into profits'.[7] MacIntyre has been consistent throughout his career with regard to this point. He had, for example, previously written, 'in his capacity of corporate executive, the manager not only has no need to take account of, but *must* not take account of certain types of considerations which he might feel obliged to recognize were he acting as parent, as consumer, or as citizen'.[8] And in an article written later than the original publication of *After Virtue*, MacIntyre gave the example of power company executives unable to consider enabling a reduction in levels of power consumption despite the fact that, as parents and citizens in other walks of life (and particularly nowadays with the increased concern for the ecological environment), they might well regard this as a desirable outcome.[9] Managers, on this account, neither do, nor are able:

> to engage in moral debate. They are seen by themselves, and by those who see them with the same eyes as their own, as uncontested figures, who purport to restrict themselves to the realms in which rational agreement is possible—that is, of course, from their point of view to the realm of fact, the realm of means, the realm of measurable effectiveness.[10]

There may well be a link here to corporate governance which, at least in its Anglo-American form, imposes upon corporations listed on stock markets the 'discipline' of the financial markets to align managers' interests with those of shareholders via such things as share options.[11] Ends are, in that sense, given even to senior managers. Similarly, according to MacIntyre, managers are morally neutral achievers of pre-determined ends, skilled at being effective irrespective of whatever ends are being sought, and unconcerned with what those ends might be. And it is 'by appeal to such effectiveness in this respect

[5] Ibid.: 30.      [6] Ibid.: 74.      [7] Ibid.: 30.
[8] MacIntyre (1979: 126), emphasis in original.      [9] MacIntyre (1999b: 322).
[10] MacIntyre (2007: 30).
[11] See, for example, Froud, Johal, & Williams (2002), O'Sullivan (2003), and Williams (2000).

that the manager claims his authority within the manipulative mode'.[12] In other words, managers allow themselves, and are allowed, to manipulate others simply because this is the most effective way to get things done: the ends justify the means. However, MacIntyre continued his argument by observing that, for this to be the case, managers must possess two types of knowledge:

the claim that the manager makes to effectiveness rests of course on the further claim to possess a stock of knowledge by means of which organizations and social structures can be moulded...[together with knowledge of] a set of law-like generalizations which would enable the manager to predict that, if an event or state of affairs of a certain type were to occur or be brought about, some other event or state of affairs of some specific kind would result.[13]

MacIntyre was, in effect, arguing that managers act as though they are operating in a world characterized by the kind of cause-and-effect relationships with which we are familiar in the natural sciences—drop an apple and it will fall, for example. But via a lengthy argument for which we do not have the space here,[14] he demonstrated that in the social sciences generalizations were few and far between, and that they generally lacked predictive power. He concluded in characteristic fashion that, 'the salient fact about those sciences is the absence of the discovery of any law-like generalizations whatsoever'.[15]

An example might help to illustrate this point. How might DesignCo seek to increase its profits? A very simple general rule might be to increase its revenues and reduce its costs. Indeed, so simple but also powerful is this formula that we might argue that it is, in effect, a law-like generalization, and its predictive power absolute. But, of course, increasing revenues might lead to overtrading and, if care is not exercised and sufficient financial resources put in place, DesignCo might go out of business for lack of cash. Or cutting costs, perhaps by making some of its architects redundant, might lead to DesignCo being unable to fulfil some of its projects on time so incurring penalties, and hence reducing rather than increasing its profits. We would clearly have to specify a very large number of conditions under which increasing revenues and/or reducing costs would lead to increased profits, and these might well need to include the unpredictability which arises from competitive reactions to any course of action an organization might take.[16]

Hence, as far as managers are concerned, MacIntyre argued,

the expert's claim to status and reward is fatally undermined when we recognise that he possesses no sound stock of law-like generalizations and when we realise

---

[12] MacIntyre (2007: 74).      [13] Ibid.: 77.
[14] Ibid.: 79–106.      [15] Ibid.: 88.
[16] This is one of four sources of systematic unpredictability which MacIntyre draws on to make his point in this regard. See MacIntyre (2007: 93–100).

how weak the predictive power available to him is. The concept of managerial effectiveness is after all one more contemporary moral fiction and perhaps the most important of them all...the realm of managerial expertise is one in which what purport to be objectively-grounded claims function in fact as expressions of arbitrary, but disguised, will and preference.[17]

In other words, we are back to emotivism and the manager as, in effect, acting out emotivism in his or her daily activities. We have already seen in Chapter 5 how MacIntyre uses a dramatic metaphor in which we might see 'contemporary social life as a theatre with a set of adjoining stages'.[18] And in this respect he continued with that metaphor arguing that, 'it is histrionic success which gives power and authority in our culture. The most effective bureaucrat is the best actor'.[19] And he concluded:

> that another moral fiction—and perhaps the most culturally powerful of them all—is embodied in the claims to effectiveness and hence to authority made by that central character of the modern social drama, the bureaucratic manager. To a disturbing extent our morality will be disclosed as a theatre of illusions.[20]

As is very evident, this is potentially a very damning critique of managers and the role they play in modern organizations, and in society in general. But it also links to MacIntyre's concerns about institutions and the unbridled pursuit of external goods. It is managers whose primary responsibility seems to be to pursue these, and as a result managers can be seen as 'cultivators of consumptive acquisitiveness',[21] or as proponents of the vice of *pleonexia*, 'the drive to have more and more'[22] which, in modern societies, has become a virtue rather than a vice, or so MacIntyre has argued. And, developing MacIntyre's thought somewhat, it has also been argued that managers, in pursuing external goods such as profit, and hence the scale economies which enable these, become destroyers of small-scale communities of virtue.[23]

Does MacIntyre have anything positive to say about managers? Well, perhaps not so much something positive, but there does seem to be at least a touch of sympathy for them in his approach. We explored the virtue of integrity in Chapter 5, and an associated concern was that our integrity—our ability to be the same person in different situations—was particularly challenged in the modern world where we are required 'to switch from stage to stage, from character to character, often with astonishing rapidity'.[24] And that general concern was expressed particularly in relation to those who work in modern corporations. MacIntyre developed this concern referring to it as 'compartmentalization' in which:

---

[17] Ibid.: 107.     [18] MacIntyre (1979: 127).     [19] MacIntyre (2007: 107).
[20] Ibid.: 76–7.     [21] Beabout (2013: 107).     [22] MacIntyre (1995: xiii).
[23] Beabout (2013: 109–10).     [24] MacIntyre (2007: 128).

each distinct sphere of social activity comes to have its own role structure governed by its own specific norms in relative independence of other such spheres. Within each sphere those norms dictate which kinds of consideration are to be treated as relevant to decision-making and which are to be excluded.[25]

Managers, on this account, live in at least two social spheres. In one, as a member of a family and community, for example, there may well be certain moral norms which tend to dominate and, within these, discussions about ends and means are perfectly allowable. In the other, as a manager within a bureaucratic organization, he is not allowed to engage in a debate about ends, because these have been, as we have seen, pre-determined. And hence relationships tend to become manipulative because the manager's role is to achieve the given ends as efficiently as possible. The manager is, on this account, at best, an amoral agent. But MacIntyre's sympathy is, in a sense, with such managers who we might think of as 'locked up' inside such bureaucratic organizations and into such pre-defined roles. MacIntyre notes that, 'every society of course has invited individuals to inhabit roles with different requirements. But difference has not entailed the kind of separation, the kind of partitioning which is peculiar to corporate modernity.'[26] But equally, MacIntyre thinks that it may just be possible to resist this compartmentalized kind of life, although the first step in such resistance would be for the manager to recognize the 'radically imperfect social world'[27] which he or she inhabits. We will return to this slightly more hopeful prospect shortly. But first, we need to question whether MacIntyre is, in fact, correct in his very serious set of concerns which we have laid out.

## IS MACINTYRE RIGHT ABOUT MANAGERS?

Does the way in which MacIntyre characterizes managers chime with our view of people we know who are managers (including, perhaps, our own bosses past and present), or with ourselves if we are managers in the kind of context MacIntyre describes? Well, to some extent we may have to answer 'yes' it does chime. But it is equally likely that we would want to answer 'no', at least in some respects.

Consider Elaine again. We saw that Elaine is a middle manager in a medium-sized company. She manages a small team which consists of both architects and clerical assistants. Among the team is the recently recruited junior architect, whom she has already had to warn about poor performance. And as the pressure within the business has mounted, and the designs have

---

[25] MacIntyre (1999b: 322).      [26] MacIntyre (1979: 132).
[27] MacIntyre (1982: 357).

become even more utilitarian, Elaine has attempted to have conversations with her boss, raising questions as to what DesignCo is all about, only to get a knowing nod in reply. Elaine might well feel that her direct boss, who used to have a real love for architecture, and from whom, as we saw, she had learned a lot in her early days at the company, has 'sold out' and has become a typical example of the kind of manager which MacIntyre has described. But Elaine is not willing to go the same way, and one of the ways in which she demonstrates that is in the very essence of her questioning, which is all to do with the ends of the organization; she will not take these simply as given.

Nonetheless, DesignCo is a bureaucracy, though not in the sense we usually think of—bureaucracy as a noun which describes the very nature of the organization, as is often (but perhaps unkindly) used in relation to public-sector organizations. DesignCo is, however, 'bureaucratic', used as an adjective describing a style of organizing which might apply to any organization.[28] In other words, DesignCo, like all organizations of any size, has systems for all kinds of things, from quality-control procedures for approving architectural designs to strategic planning and budgeting systems. It maintains these kinds of bureaucratic controls because they are necessary to the proper functioning of the organization. And one of the effects of this is that Elaine, like all others in the organization, is expected to abide by the systems. In other words, her *agency*—her ability to decide things for herself—is constrained. And that applies just as much to the ends of the organization, which are largely determined by the senior management and the board of directors on behalf of the shareholders, as to anything else. The new managing director as perhaps the key decision maker in this regard has, as we saw, been the one who has been applying the pressure to cut costs in an attempt to maintain margins in otherwise difficult trading conditions. And Elaine is not sure she can see herself standing up to him despite the strength of her feelings about the way in which DesignCo, and architecture in general, seem to be going.

In that sense, Elaine is like the managers who MacIntyre describes, 'locked up' inside a bureaucratic organization with little opportunity to exercise her own agency. But she is determined to resist, at least in so far as she is able. And so, in an area where she does have more agency, she goes beyond what DesignCo expects in terms of staff appraisal and development (another bureaucratic system which many of the other managers in DesignCo see in minimalist terms). She is trying to develop her small team of architects so that they each become the very best possible architect of which they are capable. She is trying hard to ensure that she and they do not lose their love of architecture. And just occasionally, they come up with a really creative design which works so well that they are all delighted—and all the more so when they

---

[28] Hoggett (2004: 168).

slip it past the senior architect who signs off for quality-control purposes without apparently noticing either the brilliance of the design or the slight extra costs it will involve (though Elaine suspects that he spots both, and is really on 'their' side). And recently she has noticed that the junior architect is taking a real interest in his work, wants to check out his ideas with her, and is bringing some of the knowledge he gained while on his architectural degree to the team, to everyone's benefit. He is, at last, really engaged and Elaine finds the fact that she has turned this situation around, and has helped to inspire in him a love of architecture, enormously rewarding.

And so she should, for she is acting with integrity—in other words, in this respect at least, she is being the same person at work as she is at home, where she tries to do exactly the same with her three children. But, despite these quite significant 'wins', Elaine knows that she still lives a somewhat 'compartmentalized' life. There are some aspects of her role where she simply has to buckle down and get on with whatever the organization demands of her, like it or not. And, in relation to the ends of the organization, she recognizes how difficult it would be to step out of line, and that perhaps her only option here is 'exit' rather than 'voice'.[29] For the time being at least, and given her need for the salary and, if she was honest, the status which the managerial position offers, and given all the other pressures in her life at present, she acknowledges that she is prepared to compromise rather than resist or leave.

Elaine had, in anticipation of and in preparation for the promotion which led to her current managerial position, undertaken various training courses offered by her local college. She became aware, as a result, of some general managerial knowledge and techniques which helped her to develop her managerial competence and style. She was particularly impressed by a young lecturer who kept stressing the contingent nature of the knowledge he was passing on. This contingency, he stated, was in two parts. One was that anything which appeared to be a rule which could be used in any situation and whose outcome was predictable, should be viewed with suspicion; so much depended on the context in which it was applied, and there were so many things which were unpredictable.

An example he gave was of a hugely successful chief executive who had inherited an organization tuned close to perfection by her predecessor and at a time when the market was rising steadily. The question which should have been asked at the end of her tenure was not what general rules of management she had applied to be so outstandingly successful, but whether she had left the organization ready to meet the downturn in the market which happened to occur next, and was anticipated by many commentators. Management was contingent on circumstances and chance, the lecturer stressed.

---

[29] This is a very common distinction used to indicate the choices people have when confronted by situations with which they disagree. It originates in Hirschman (1970).

The second part of contingency was that managerial knowledge had to be applied to the particular, not just learnt in the abstract. Management in a medium-sized architectural practice bore some relation to management in a large mineral extraction company, but there were also significant differences. In that sense, management, the lecturer stressed, was an art, not a science.[30]

We can summarize Elaine's situation and, at the same time, respond to MacIntyre's critique of managers as follows.[31] Yes, she may well be operating in a context characterized by emotivism, but not all social relations, including those in her work organization, are manipulative. She may experience the managing director as operating in that mode, but while her agency may be constrained, she does seek, as far as possible, not to operate as a manager in a manipulative mode herself, and this is particularly evident in the way she deals with the members of her team and in the way in which they respond to this approach. She is aware that she operates within a bureaucratic organization and that ends are largely given, but she is still very willing to question those ends, even if she is aware that she is unlikely to be able to influence the ultimate ends of the organization to any great degree.

She is also aware of managerial knowledge and techniques, and appreciates and uses these, but she does so without expecting them to provide her with law-like generalizations. And she is very aware of the unpredictability of social life and the inability of managerial knowledge and techniques to provide cast-iron predictions of the future. She also recognizes that her life is, to a degree, compartmentalized, and that she is required to operate to different moral norms in different contexts, and even to apply different moral norms at different times within the same organizational context. But again, her agency is not so constrained that she cannot seek to exercise the virtue of integrity, while recognizing that there are areas in which she fails to be entirely consistent.

Is Elaine-as-manager a better description of most managers than MacIntyre's characterization? If so, it would point to the accuracy of MacIntyre's character-ization in terms of its origins and component parts, but it would also suggest that he is overly pessimistic in his assessment of these. Managers are not necessarily villains, demons, or agents in the service of power, who have to operate a Faustian bargain 'accepting the material goods of money, power and prestige while trading away what is more worthwhile: the pursuit of an excellent, integrated human life ordered towards meaningful and worthwhile common goods'.[32]

---

[30] The lecturer had, of course, read MacIntyre's *After Virtue*.

[31] This response to MacIntyre's critique is set out in more detail in Moore (2008), where references can be found to other sources used in this argument.

[32] Nash (1995: 231) characterizes or, perhaps better, caricatures MacIntyre's view of man-agers as demonic. Hine (2007: 360) refers to MacIntyre's unsympathetic characterization of the manager as implying 'a determinism of managerial purpose and agency in the service of power'. Beabout (2013: 62) refers to MacIntyre's treatment of the manager as a 'villainous stock character'. The quotation is from Beabout (2013: 71).

But if it is the case that Elaine-as-manager is a better description of most managers—that most managers are not simply morally neutral efficient achievers of pre-determined ends—then perhaps what we require is an organizational framework which allows us to locate and characterize what virtuous managers are all about. And, as we noted, it may therefore be something of a paradox that we turn back to the framework which MacIntyre offers for thinking about organizations to see if this may help us to think more creatively about managers and the tasks of management, and perhaps even to reimagine it.[33] We have already touched on this in Chapter 4 where we considered that framework in its entirety, but it is now time to explore the managerial implications of this in more detail.

## LOCATING MANAGERS WITHIN MACINTYRE'S FRAMEWORK

As we saw in Chapter 4, we can characterize organizations, within the framework which MacIntyre offers, as practice-institution combinations. But within the diagram which we used to represent this (Figure 4.1), there were actually two practices. There was the core practice—architecture, or whatever—housed within the institution. But also within the institution there was another practice which, to repeat the point made in Chapter 4, originated in the following comment by MacIntyre:

> Yet if institutions do have corrupting power, the making and sustaining of forms of human community—*and therefore of institutions*—itself has all the characteristics of a practice, and moreover of a practice which stands in a peculiarly close relationship to the exercise of the virtues.[34]

What we inferred from this was that management could be redescribed in MacIntyrean terms as the practice of 'making and sustaining the institution'. Two things followed immediately from this, the first being that this was a *secondary* practice. The most important practice in any organization is the practice at its core, and we might say that the secondary practice of making and sustaining the institution is there to serve this primary practice. In other words, there is an ordering here which follows from the ordering which we saw in relation to internal and external goods. The second thing which followed was that professional managers, those whose primary task is the making and sustaining of the institution, also have an opportunity to engage in

---

[33] 'Re-imagining the morality of management' is part of the title of my paper on which this chapter is based. See Moore (2008).
[34] MacIntyre (2007: 194), emphasis added.

a practice, albeit a rather different one from the core practice. In that sense, they have the opportunity to exercise the virtues in the pursuit of internal goods, though again rather different internal goods from those of the core practice, and to be 'perfected' in the process. On this account, then, managers are moral agents, even if that agency is constrained, and should be in a position to draw on the internal goods from this particular practice in their lives in their narrative quest towards their own *telos*.

It is worth spending a little more time on this issue of management as a practice. There were early attempts to apply MacIntyre's work where it was argued that management was a practice in that it could be regarded as a 'coherent and complex form of socially established cooperative human activity' (the first part of MacIntyre's definition).[35] However, just as MacIntyre argued that teaching was not, in itself, a practice (as we saw in Chapter 4), and similarly just as he has argued that 'employment' is not a practice but a feature of the lives of certain types of institution or organization,[36] so we need to stress that management is not simply a practice, but that managers are engaged in the practice of making and sustaining the institution. However, even that somewhat subtle distinction needs to be qualified. Again, as we noted with teaching, teachers are teachers of something. And we have made the same point already in relation to managers—they are managers not in the abstract, but in relation to some particular practice, be it the manager the string quartet may need to employ or Elaine-as-manager in relation to architecture. Of course, there are generic features of management, a general body of knowledge and techniques, as we have seen above. But managers need to be aware that the institution they are engaged in making and sustaining has at its heart a core practice, and they need to appreciate that this is both the focal point and part of the context in which they carry out their craft.

Following this, it has been argued that we should refer to management, as carried out by professional managers, as a 'domain-relative' practice.[37] This implies both that management possesses its own internal standards of excellence recognizable to practitioners, and that the activities in which managers engage are always related to another particular domain—music-making, architecture, or whatever. There is, therefore, no 'management in general' but only 'management in the particular'.[38]

It is worth developing this point further by considering Figure 6.1. The first point to note about this diagram is that it simply reinforces what we have seen before: that there are two practices. The second point is that managers at all levels are engaged with both practices—note that the diagonal line across the

[35] Brewer (1997), for example.
[36] This is based on personal correspondence between MacIntyre and Ron Beadle, cited in Beadle (2002: 52).
[37] See Beabout (2012, 2013).     [38] See Beabout (2013: 188–9).

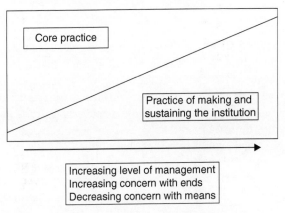

**Figure 6.1.** Management and its relationship to two practices

*Source*: This diagram first appeared in Moore (2008). This is copyright Cambridge University Press and is reprinted here with permission. Note, however, that this has been changed slightly, referring to the 'practice of making', whereas the original called this the 'Institutional practice'

diagram does *not* run between the two corners, but starts a little above the bottom left-hand corner and finishes a little below the top right-hand one. At the left-hand side of this diagram we have what we might characterize as first-line supervisors. These are people who spend most of their time directly involved with the core practice, but in their supervisory role they are engaged in 'the making and sustaining of the institution' even if this is only to a limited degree. At the right-hand side of the diagram we have senior managers who are mostly involved in making and sustaining the institution. But senior managers should recognize that they also need to remain engaged with the core practice, even if to only a limited degree. And it is worth noting that, on this account, many people will actually engage in these two practices when at work and so will have the possibility of obtaining the internal goods from both.

Elaine, for example, is a classic middle manager, and so would be located somewhere near the centre of Figure 6.1. She is still engaged in the core practice of architecture, and spends about half her time working in that capacity on various projects. But she is also a manager, and so spends the other half of her time on managerial activities including, as we have seen, managing and developing the members of her team. She may not be typical in this respect to all managers in that she continues to 'practice' her original craft, although she is no different in this regard to other professionals—engineers, accountants, lawyers, and so on—and to others such as academics who continue to engage directly in their core practice almost irrespective of how 'high' in the organization they reach. A sales manager who continues selling as well as managing a team of other salespeople would be in the same position.

## CHARACTERIZING VIRTUOUS MANAGERS

Now that we have located managers within MacIntyre's framework, and have a clear idea what the role of managers is (engaging in the domain-relative practice of making and sustaining the institution), and the relationship of managers to the core practice of the organization, we can begin to explore what it is that would characterize virtuous managers. And the first characteristic follows from the means-end debate which we discussed earlier. That is, the virtuous manager would be concerned about the ends the organization serves, and the extent to which both its products or services and the 'perfection' of its members (the internal goods of the core practice but also, in the latter case, of the secondary practice of making and sustaining the institution itself) contribute to the common good. That is, in shorthand, that the virtuous manager would be concerned for the *good purpose* of the organization.

We have recognized, both in describing Elaine's situation in some detail and in Figure 6.1, that the ability to engage in and influence the ends of an organization depends on level. That is, the further 'up' an organization a person goes, the greater the concern the person should have about this, coupled with a greater level of influence. But this does not relieve even those at the most junior end of management from a concern with purpose. The defence, 'I was only following orders', while potentially admissible in a court of law, is clearly not admissible morally.[39] But at the top end of the organization, as we have seen, this will require that senior managers engage in a debate both internally (in a board of directors or as trustees, for example) and in the community, about what the internal goods of the practice are, and the way they contribute to the common good. Recall again MacIntyre's claim that, 'In contemporary societies our common goods can only be determined in concrete and particular terms through widespread, grassroots, shared, rational deliberation'.[40] It is the role of senior managers in particular to engage in that deliberation, and to put in place appropriate structures to facilitate it.

The second characteristic of a virtuous manager follows from all that we have said so far about the framework which MacIntyre offers us. Managers should be concerned about the core practice of the organization and about

---

[39] The classic case is that of Adolf Eichmann, one of the most prominent Nazis to use this defence at his Nuremberg trial in Israel in 1961: 'I cannot recognize the verdict of guilty....It was my misfortune to become entangled in these atrocities. But these misdeeds did not happen according to my wishes. It was not my wish to slay people....Once again I would stress that I am guilty of having been obedient, having subordinated myself to my official duties and the obligations of war service and my oath of allegiance and my oath of office, and in addition, once the war started, there was also martial law....I did not persecute Jews with avidity and passion. That is what the government did....At that time obedience was demanded, just as in the future it will also be demanded of the subordinate.' See, for example, http://rationalwiki.org/wiki/Nuremberg_Defense, accessed 19 September 2016.

[40] MacIntyre (2010).

those who practice their craft there. This is for several fairly obvious reasons. First, the organization as a practice-institution combination depends on the core practice—without it, there quite simply is no organization. Thus, there is an instrumental reason for maintaining this concern for the core practice. And this continued engagement with and concern for the core practice may be fairly easy for someone like Elaine who has grown up with the practice and continues to be involved directly with it. It may be less easy, but certainly not impossible, for someone who becomes a 'professional' manager and moves between practices.

For example, in my early industrial career, working for a large multinational manufacturing group with various interests, I reported to a director of operations who had recently moved to our company which was engaged in paint manufacture, from another company in the group involved in textiles. I discovered that, prior to the move, he had spent a day at another paint company in the group personally making a batch of paint. He seemed to understand something of the need to have a 'feel' for this new core practice if he was to be able to manage it well, even though he would not have expressed it in these terms. The point is that managers' engagement with the core practice is both necessary and possible.

The second reason for being concerned about the core practice, and a somewhat 'higher' reason than the instrumental one given above, is that it is the internal goods of the core practice, the goods or services it produces or provides, which have the potential to contribute to the common good. The virtuous manager, concerned about the ends of the organization, would seek to ensure excellence in the core practice since this is what leads to internal goods which have the potential to make a contribution to the common good.

The third reason for being concerned about the core practice is also to do with internal goods, but in this case it is the internal good of the 'perfection' of the practitioners in the process. As we saw in Chapter 4, a fundamental part of the common good is having virtuous individuals making good decisions and carrying out good actions on behalf of themselves, their families, and the various organizations which make up a community, including the political organizations of government. And the organizations in which we work, and the practices in which we thereby take part, have an important contribution to make to this. Elaine seems to have understood this judging by the way she seeks to develop members of her team—their flourishing, at least as architects, is an important concern for her.

And this leads directly to the third characteristic of the virtuous manager, which is that this concern for the 'perfection' of practitioners should lead to an attempt to provide meaningful work for them. This follows from the discussion in Chapter 5, where we noted that there were instrumental reasons for providing meaningful work—both because of the negative implications of not providing it, as well as the positive implications of doing so. But the virtuous manager, concerned for the flourishing and moral development of those for whom she is responsible, and aware of the potential contribution to the common good to which this may lead, would want to provide meaningful work in any case. And one other implication of this is that the virtuous manager would be on the lookout for new recruits who might be seeking, explicitly or otherwise, for this kind of work and who would be amenable to it—in other words, recruits who see work as more than just a job or a career.

Having established these first three characteristics of the virtuous manager (a concern for ends, and for the core practice of the organization and those who practise their craft there, and hence for the provision of meaningful work), we turn to consider a fourth characteristic. The manager's role is to do with the making and sustaining of the institution, and institutions, as we have seen, are characteristically and necessarily concerned with external goods—money, other material goods, power, status, and, perhaps most generically, success. It follows, therefore, that managers should also be concerned about such things. That the organization has sufficient amounts of these external goods is clearly essential to its survival and development. In that sense, making a profit as far as a business is concerned, or running a surplus as far as not-for-profit organizations in the public and voluntary sectors are concerned, is unproblematic. But it is unproblematic only in so far as it enables the survival and development of the core practice. Recall that external goods are not goods which we should pursue for their own sake, but for the sake of the internal goods of practices to which they can lead. As far as the virtuous manager is concerned, the appropriate pursuit of external goods may also lead to the need to resist those inside or outside the organization who promote the achievement of external goods to too great an extent. Elaine, for example, is struggling with her managing director in just this regard.

The fifth characteristic of the virtuous manager is to do with something we might call the 'mode of institutionalization' of the organization.[41] This is not something we have come across before, and we will have more to say about it in Chapter 7, but for now it is probably easiest to explain this concept by way of an example. DesignCo is a limited company, now 'owned'[42] by a number of private shareholders, among them the managing director and a few of the senior members of staff who used to be partners in the previous arrangement, but also including several external shareholders.[43] The previous arrangement

[41] See Moore & Beadle (2006: 377–8).

[42] It should be noted that shareholders actually own only shares in a company, and these shares give them rights only to the residual profit once all other liabilities are met. However, because of the control rights which share ownership also gives, including the rights to vote for directors and for or against a takeover, it is commonly held that companies are shareholder-owned, even though this is technically a misnomer. See Haldane (2015) for a broader discussion of this point and its implications.

[43] Note that in the UK at least, architect practices can choose to become a limited liability company or a limited liability partnership. See http://www.arb.org.uk/company-formations, accessed 19 September 2016.

took the legal form of a partnership which, while giving the protection of limited liability, did not easily allow for additional capital to be introduced into the organization other than by way of bank loans.

But this change of the 'mode of institutionalization' has had other impacts, not least the pressure to maintain margins in the challenging economic conditions which prevail. This pressure is, as we have seen, exerted principally by the managing director, but he also finds himself on the sharp end of pressure from one of the external shareholders who, as well as the dividends which will come his way as a result, sees the potential for DesignCo to be primed ready for a takeover in which he may realize several times the value of his original shareholding.[44]

We might ask which mode of institutionalization of DesignCo (a partnership or a limited company) is likely to be most conducive to organizational virtue. And while not at all wishing to preclude virtuous shareholder-owned companies, the point, in relation to being a virtuous manager, is that the mode of institutionalization should be a concern. Not that, in many cases and certainly at 'lower' levels, this is something which a manager may be able to influence directly. But that does not mean that a virtuous manager can simply ignore this aspect of organizations. The mode of institutionalization, which can sometimes be thought of simply in terms of the legal form but is actually somewhat more complex than that,[45] can have a major impact on the managerial task, and the ability to do all the other things which we have already identified the virtuous manager should be aiming at.

Moving on, the sixth characteristic of a virtuous manager is to do with the environment in which the organization operates.[46] It is probably obvious by now that not only is the 'internal' environment (the mode of institutionalization which we have already considered and the character of the organization which we will come to shortly) important to the virtuous manager. In addition, the external environment (the regulatory environment provided by government, the market environment of firms and consumers, the labour environment of workers and their pursuit, or otherwise, of meaningful work, and the financial market environment and the extent to which this is focused on external goods), is bound to affect the extent to which an organization can pursue virtue, and hence the extent to which managers within the organization can do so. A hostile environment is clearly problematic. Indeed, as MacIntyre has commented, 'We should therefore expect that, if in a particular society the

---

[44] Although takeovers of architectural practices may not hit the headlines, the *Architects' Journal* reported in April 2013 that one in five UK practices were 'ripe for takeover'. See https://www. architectsjournal.co.uk/home/one-in-five-practices-ripe-for-takeover/www.architectsjournal.co.uk/home/one-in-five-practices-ripe-for-takeover/8645006.article, accessed 26 September 2016.

[45] We will explore this further in Chapter 8, particularly when looking at the Volvo case.

[46] See Moore & Beadle (2006: 378–80).

pursuit of external goods were to become dominant, the concept of the virtues might suffer first attrition and then perhaps something near total effacement, although simulacra might abound'.[47]

MacIntyre here is clearly targeting both consumer society and financial markets, and suggesting that what we take to be virtues may actually be things which only look like virtues. But what has that to do with the virtuous manager? And the answer lies in the fact that managers, and the organizations they represent, are both parts of that environment and help to create and re-create it. And this may, therefore, lead to a requirement for the virtuous manager to resist the environment, just as he may have to resist his own compartmentalization, to resist inappropriate constraints on his agency, and to resist those inside the organization who promote the achievement of external goods to too great an extent. Resistance, it seems, may be required in a number of areas of virtuous managerial activity—a point to which we will return shortly.

The seventh characteristic of the virtuous manager is that she will be engaged in developing what we might call the character of the organization. We explored this very briefly in Chapter 3, where we began to distinguish between organizational culture and character, and we will have more to say about this in Chapter 7. Hence for now we will simply note and park this idea here.

Finally, there is a rather obvious characteristic of the virtuous manager about which we have so far been silent. Clearly, the virtuous manager needs to be competent as a manager. And while this is implicit in many of the other seven characteristics, it is worth making it explicit. In order to be competent, the virtuous manager, assuming that she has come up through the 'ranks' of the core practice, will have needed to demonstrate competence there—Elaine would find it hard to be a manager, let alone a virtuous one, if she did not have the respect of those she is managing, and of those to whom she reports as a good architect in her own right. In addition, however, there is managerial competence. In other words, there is the need to have absorbed the general knowledge and techniques associated with the practice of management, and to be able to apply these appropriately in context—competent, domain-relative management, in other words.

## WHICH VIRTUES WILL MANAGERS NEED?

This sets a demanding agenda for those who would aspire to be virtuous managers. And so it raises the question as to which virtues are needed to do the role well. As we have noted previously, it is not a particular concern of this

---

[47] MacIntyre (2007: 196).

book to attempt to produce a definitive list of virtues, whether for individuals, managers, or, as we shall come to in Chapter 7, for organizations. One of the potential problems with virtues is that almost anything might be considered to be one, and so this can lead to lengthy lists which may not be very helpful. One such list, specifically related to managers, contains thirty-one virtues (including punctuality and clarity in expression) and adds three possible traits (toughness, ambition, and cunning) to these.[48] Since it would require significant mental effort just to remember the list, it seems unlikely that someone would be able to consciously possess and exercise them all.

We have, however, so far referred mainly to a rather smaller number of virtues: constancy and integrity; the four cardinal virtues of justice, courage, temperance, and practical wisdom; being trusting and trustworthy; and just generosity in relation to building a community of practitioners. For the virtuous manager this would seem to offer a pretty good starting point although, as we have noted before, there may be sub-virtues (honesty as a sub-virtue of justice, for example) which might be important on specific occasions (for Elaine in having to tell the junior architect that he wasn't matching up to the demands of the role, for example).

Given all that we have said about the characteristics of the virtuous manager, however, there may be two of these virtues which we would want to emphasize. We noted that resistance may be required in a number of areas of managerial activity. Which virtue or virtues are most likely to be needed for resistance to be put into effect appropriately? Perhaps most obviously this will require courage to stand up to those people, and those wider forces in society, which have a tendency to push organizations and managers within them towards an inordinate pursuit of external goods, and so to corrupt practices. (Recall that enabling the pursuit of excellence in the core practice is one of the primary characteristics of the virtuous manager.) This is not to say that virtuous managers are necessarily objectionable people, always challenging, often critical. Virtuous managers should also be fun, creative, witty, generous, and so on, and know how to make their point without necessarily causing offence. But it is to take seriously a point which MacIntyre has made about practices and their relationship with institutions and virtues, a point which we noted already in relation to individuals engaged in practices, but which bears repeating in this context:

> For the ability of a practice to retain its integrity will depend on the way in which the virtues can be and are exercised in sustaining the institutional forms which are the social bearers of the practice. The integrity of a practice causally requires the exercise of the virtues by at least some of the individuals who embody it in their activities; and conversely the corruption of institutions is always in part at least an effect of the vices.[49]

---

[48] Beabout (2013: 180). Beabout's book is written from a specifically MacIntyrean perspective and is generally excellent. And, as we will see below, it actually focuses on wisdom as the key virtue.
[49] MacIntyre (2007: 195).

And it is probably clear that managers are the key agents in this respect, operating as they do within, and at the intersection of, both the core practice and the institution.

But this will also require, in particular, a second virtue—that of practical wisdom. This virtue is sometimes considered to be the 'highest' of the four cardinal virtues. It has also been referred to as the 'nurse'[50] of all other virtues in that it 'may be said to regulate the other virtues by directing them towards their true end'.[51] Practical wisdom, then, is usually considered to be the key intellectual virtue. But practical wisdom also plays another role in that it 'directs the activities of the individual *toward the common good of his community*'.[52] So practical wisdom helps us to see what the common good is, and since the pursuit of the common good is one of the concerns of the virtuous manager, so she needs practical wisdom to help in determining, with others, just what that might be. Virtuous managers have, following this, been called 'wise stewards'.[53]

Before concluding, there is one other point which needs to be reinforced. Being a virtuous manager is clearly a very challenging role. It may even, on occasion, lead to the need to make oneself unpopular by challenging others inside the organization (whatever their position) or outside of it. But, as we have said, management is a domain-relative *practice*. As such, it has its own internal goods which are to do with the making and sustaining of a virtuous institution, an institution which has as its principle objective the support of its core practice and the pursuit of excellence within it, enabling the common good and including the 'perfection' of its practitioners. And the exercise of virtue towards the excellent achievement of those internal goods will also enable the individual on the narrative quest towards his or her own *telos*. In other words, there is the potential for managers to be 'perfected' in the process of being managers. Management, in that sense is, or at least has the potential to be, a highly rewarding practice. Indeed, provided that the internal goods of the core practice make a contribution to the common good (so fulfilling the objective criterion), being a manager should be meaningful work in its own right.[54] In other words, and against MacIntyre, being a manager has the potential to be a morally significant practice.

---

[50] This was said by John Dewey, an American philosopher, psychologist, and educational reformer. See Westbrook (1991: 161).

[51] Porter (1994: 155), see also Beabout (2012: 420).

[52] Porter (1994: 164), emphasis added.     [53] Beabout (2013).

[54] It is also worth adding that, as a practice, management must also be 'institutionalized'. This is rather different from the organizational-level institutionalization we have been considering here, and would include those organizations who apprentice practitioners into the practice (business schools, for example), and bodies which support it (in the UK, the Chartered Management Institute, http://www.managers.org.uk/, for example). I am not at all convinced, however that management is a profession, mainly due to the ubiquity of the practice and the inability to define and control entry and standards which are the pre-requisites of a profession. But that is an argument for another time.

## SUMMARY

In this chapter we have explored the difference between management as a set of activities and 'professional' managers as a role. We looked at MacIntyre's critique of professional managers, and developed a more nuanced understanding of what the managerial role actually entails. We then located managers and management within the practice-institution combination framework which MacIntyre offers before identifying eight characteristics of the virtuous manager. We considered which virtues might be necessary to be a virtuous manager, noting particularly the need for courage and practical wisdom, and concluded that, by engaging in this domain-relative practice, managers should be able to realize its internal goods, and that this should enable the manager towards his or her own *telos*.

In all of this, however, the context for managerial activity has been the organization. What implications, then, does MacIntyre's framework have at the organizational level? It is to this that we turn next.

# 7

## Implications for Organizations

### INTRODUCTION

We developed in Chapter 4 the virtue ethics framework for organizations which MacIntyre's work offers. That is, a framework of internal and external goods, virtues, practices, and institutions, where we came to understand organizations as practice-institution combinations. We then explored in Chapters 5 the implications for individuals particularly, though not exclusively, when at work, and in Chapter 6 for managers. This chapter, the last in Part II, looks at the implications of all of this for organizations. It begins with a discussion of the characteristics of a virtuous organization before proposing a taxonomy of organizational-level virtues, exploring the concept of organizational character and contrasting this with organizational culture. It then discusses how organizations might 'crowd in' virtue through appropriate organizational design and governance approaches.

### THE CHARACTERISTICS OF A VIRTUOUS ORGANIZATION

As we saw in Chapter 6, the role of managers, based on the MacIntyrean virtue ethics approach we have been following, is to make and sustain the institution which houses the core practice of the organization, enabling excellence in the pursuit of the internal goods of that core practice, while pursuing sufficient external goods to ensure, at the very least, the core practice's survival and development. Organizations, as we have seen, can then be redescribed as practice-institution combinations, a metaphor for organizations which, as should already be reasonably clear, helps us to see certain key aspects of organizations, even if, like all metaphors, it may hide others.

Given this, it is not surprising that the characteristics of a virtuous organization follow directly from, and to a large extent mirror, those which virtuous managers should be trying to achieve. As a result, we can summarize some of these characteristics reasonably succinctly, although with others we will take the opportunity to extend the previous discussion.

First, then, the virtuous organization would have at its core a practice the internal goods of which (the excellence of the product or service and the 'perfection' of the practitioners) would make a contribution to the common good of the community. In Chapter 4 we described this as the 'goodness of purpose' of the organization and, as we saw there, it formed one dimension of the mapping of virtuous organizations which was presented in Figure 4.2. This diagram is reproduced in this chapter as Figure 7.1, and we will come back to it when we have considered some of the other characteristics of a virtuous organization. We will also think more about how an organization might judge and develop its understanding of its 'goodness of purpose' when we look at mechanisms for 'crowding in' virtue.

The second characteristic is that a virtuous organization would understand that its primary function is to focus on the core practice, to ensure excellence in the pursuit of the internal goods of that practice. The success-excellence dimension in Figure 7.1 relates to this, and we have already said a good deal about the pursuit of excellence so that it does not need to be repeated here. But there is one point which is worth exploring further. It might be reasonably clear, though we have not stated this explicitly so far, that practices are reasonably self-contained. That is, the practitioners are, to some extent, best left to organize themselves, since they know what the practice involves, what are the standards of excellence to which they should aspire, and they are (or, at least, should be) good at pursuing these, and apprenticing others into them. While, as we know from MacIntyre's framework, practices need institutions (recall that practices cannot exist for any length of time without them and together they form a single causal order), nonetheless there was a tension inherent in this arrangement, focused around the fact that the practice and institution aim at different types of goods. Hence, we saw that practices might well be corrupted by the institutional pursuit of external goods, and they might need to resist them in this regard. It was that kind of tension which we saw being played out in DesignCo, with Elaine and the managing director perhaps epitomizing the two sides, and with Elaine's immediate boss apparently sitting rather tamely in the middle.

But there is also the opposite danger, which is that the practice might become somewhat self-satisfied and complacent, and so no longer pursue 'best practice'. This is likely to be because of individual practitioners no longer exercising the virtues, and it may therefore be difficult for those same practitioners to realize that this has come about. It may then be the role of the institution, which should be aware of best practice elsewhere, to call the practice back to the pursuit of excellence, partly because that is what it should do anyway, and partly to protect the external goods which derive from the excellence of the internal goods. In other words, the practice-institution combination should be a self-correcting mechanism in this regard.

The third characteristic of a virtuous organization relates to the 'perfection' of practitioners, and therefore links back to the discussions of the flourishing and moral development of organizational members in Chapter 4, and of meaningful work in Chapters 5 and 6. We raised the question in Chapter 5 as to whether it was simply the responsibility of individuals to seek out meaningful work or whether, in addition, managers and organizations had a responsibility to provide it. We noted there and in Chapter 6 that there were instrumental reasons in favour of meaningful work, but also that virtuous managers would want to try to provide this in any case. But, as with so much else which we discussed in Chapter 6, managers' agency may be constrained in this respect. While Elaine was able to make some progress in this regard with the members of her own team, it would be much more difficult for a manager in, for example, a car manufacturer with a major technological and capital commitment to assembly-line production, to do much to change the job design of workers, other than perhaps by way of job rotation, in order to make their work more meaningful. But the virtuous organization would at least seek to take steps in such a direction. We will come back and look at examples of the provision of meaningful work in Chapter 8, including in car manufacturing, so for now we simply note the principle that this is something a virtuous organization would seek to provide as its way of contributing to the 'perfection' of its members.

The fourth characteristic of a virtuous organization takes us in a rather different direction. While the pursuit of a good purpose, the focus on the core practice, and the provision of meaningful work in enabling the flourishing and moral development of organizational members are all fairly obvious, if challenging, characteristics of a virtuous organization, it is also the role of the institution to focus on external goods. We have noted previously that such things as fame, reputation, wealth, profit, and, perhaps most generically, success are goods (not 'bads') and that, as MacIntyre pointed out, 'no one can despise them altogether without a certain hypocrisy'.[1] So the institutional focus on securing external goods is entirely necessary and a good thing. But, as we have stressed repeatedly, it is not a good thing in and of itself. Recall that external goods are not goods which we should pursue for their own sake, but for the way in which they sustain practices and so enable the internal goods of the practice (which are goods that we should pursue for their own sake) to be realized.

This is why we have referred to the need for the correct ordering of these goods (internal goods should take precedence over external goods), and the balanced pursuit of both. It is why, as we see in Figure 7.1, the virtuous organization is located just on the side of excellence on the success-excellence axis; it orders its goods correctly and pursues both, but in a balanced way.

[1] MacIntyre (2007: 196).

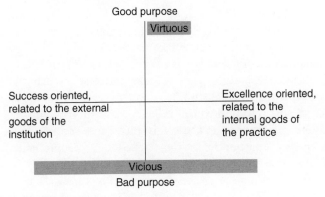

**Figure 7.1.** Mapping the virtuous organization
*Source*: See the copyright acknowledgement notice in Figure 4.2

It is, however, worth developing the relationship between internal and external goods further at this point, even though this will take us on something of a digression from the characteristics of a virtuous organization. Clearly, as far as an organization is concerned, the internal goods of the practice—the excellence of the product or service—lead directly to the achievement of external goods. Products are sold, services provided, and in return the organization receives payment—an external good. But, of course, the products could not have been made, or the services provided, without some external goods to begin with—there must have been some capital investment and working capital, for example, to get the practice off the ground. It doesn't particularly matter, in a kind of 'chicken or egg' dilemma, which came first. The point is that there is an 'essential but complex circularity between internal goods and external goods'.[2] The circularity of the relationship is obvious—internal goods lead to external goods lead to internal goods and so on. The complexity stems from recognizing that this relationship between internal and external goods can occur both *inside* and *outside* of a particular practice-institution combination.[3]

Let us take the example of DesignCo. As an architectural practice, we would typically say that it offers a 'design service' to its clients. The end result of this design service is a physical building, together with all the services, fixtures, fittings, furnishings, colour schemes, landscaping, and so forth, which go with it. DesignCo's internal goods are the designs it provides, and it is these for which it gets paid—and which therefore represent the most obvious external goods it attains, besides its reputation and so forth. And, obviously, it needs to generate sufficient external goods in the form of money to pay its employees, maintain its offices, advertise its services, and so forth—in other words, to

---

[2] Moore (2012a: 380), emphasis removed.      [3] Ibid.: 380.

sustain both itself and the practice at its core. As a result, as we have seen, internal and external goods form a circular relationship, the one leading to the other, and the other leading back to the one. Providing that this relationship is maintained—that the internal goods are of a sufficient standard of excellence to attract clients prepared to pay for them, and that the external goods are sufficient to maintain the organization and the architectural practice at its core—then the organization will, at the very least, survive.

But, of course, employees in DesignCo receive some of these external goods in return for their contribution to the realization of the internal goods of the practice. And while they might spend some of this on items directly related to the practice—Elaine maintains her membership of a professional body and a subscription to the *Architectural Review*, for example—most of the external goods they receive will be spent on other practices—maintaining family life and playing cello in a local orchestra in Elaine's case, for example. As a result, we can see the complexity of the relationship, with external goods received from engagement in one practice facilitating participation in potentially a whole range of other practices from which further internal goods are obtained. This also, of course, relates to the idea of life being lived by engaging in a variety of practices, and we can perhaps also begin to see that these may not be entirely unrelated; one practice might facilitate another by providing external goods, and perhaps the internal goods of the other practice might somehow facilitate the first. Elaine's involvement in an orchestra is made possible from the salary she earns by working at DesignCo, but it may be that something about the internal goods of playing in an orchestra might feed her creative side, which then re-emerges in the harmony and resonance of her architectural designs.

Back to the characteristics of a virtuous organization, and the fifth characteristic is to do with an organization's 'mode of institutionalization'. We have already discussed this in some depth in Chapter 6 where we saw that it was one of the characteristics of the virtuous manager to seek a mode of institutionalization which would be most conducive to organizational virtue. However, while we recognized there that it was unlikely that more junior managers would be able to influence this, at senior management and the organizational level this is clearly of concern. Obviously there are still constraints on action here, so that, for example, DesignCo's decision to move to a shareholder-owned model, together with the capital it received as a result, means that it is unlikely to be in a position to buy itself back out of these arrangements to become, for example, a limited liability partnership again. If it felt that the pressures from shareholders were such as to 'crowd out' virtue, then it might have to make do as well as it can, at least for the time being. Nonetheless, endeavouring to ensure that the legal form of institutionalization, or that the practical implications of the particular mode of institutionalization which the organization is 'under', are as conducive as possible to organizational virtue will clearly be a concern for a virtuous organization.

In relation to the capitalist forms of business organization which have emerged, MacIntyre was particularly concerned about this. His argument was that, in effect, the institution and its pursuit of external goods had 'won' over the practice and its pursuit of internal goods, such that 'much modern industrial productive and service work is organized so as to exclude the features distinctive of a practice', and in such a way that this type of activity is 'at once alien and antagonistic to practices'.[4] Indeed, MacIntyre makes a more general point, in relation to practices of all kinds, when he warns that, 'practices are often distorted by their modes of institutionalisation, when irrelevant considerations relating to money, power and status are allowed to invade the practice'.[5] This goes back to MacIntyre's more general concern about the state of the modern world, and we will explore some examples of this issue, and of how organizations have grappled with it, particularly in Chapter 8.

This particular concern, for what we might call the 'internal' environment, links to the sixth characteristic of a virtuous organization which is to do with the external environment. Again, we explored this in some depth when looking at the characteristics of the virtuous manager in Chapter 6. So we can be relatively brief in saying that this is also an organizational-level concern and, assuming that the environment is to some degree hostile to organizational virtue, we would expect the organization to attempt both to resist the environment and to position itself perhaps within 'interstitial spaces'[6] where virtue might flourish. And, like virtuous managers, a virtuous organization would also attempt to create a more conducive environment, not just take it as a given. Again, we will explore some examples of how organizations have attempted to tackle this issue in Chapters 8 and 9.

The seventh and last characteristic of a virtuous organization is that it will seek to develop an appropriate organizational character which will support the organization in achieving all the other characteristics of a virtuous organization which we have identified. We noted in Chapter 3 that it is possible to speak sensibly, albeit in metaphorical terms, about virtues, vices, and character at the organizational level. And we have also noted previously that character is how we describe the way in which various virtues and vices have been combined in an individual or organization—character is, we might say, a way of summarizing this combination.

So, a virtuous organization is one which will possess and exercise appropriate virtues, and avoid particular vices, in such a way that it pursues a good purpose, focuses on the core practice and its internal goods, seeks to provide meaningful work and so 'perfect' its members, pursues external goods but only

---

[4] MacIntyre (1994: 286).　　[5] Ibid.: 289.

[6] Interstices are intervening spaces, chinks, or crevices, for example between the molecules forming an atom.

to the extent necessary for the maintenance and development of the core practice, seeks an appropriate mode of institutionalization which is supportive of virtue, and seeks an environment which is conducive of virtue. But so far, we have said relatively little about the specific virtues which are required of a virtuous organization, and so it is to that which we turn next. And this will, in turn, allow us to define and discuss the concept of organizational character more fully.


## A TAXONOMY OF ORGANIZATIONAL VIRTUES AND ORGANIZATIONAL CHARACTER

Referring back to Figure 7.1, we might begin to consider which organizational virtues are needed by asking a number of questions: 'Which virtues enable the pursuit of both excellence and success, but also their correct ordering and balance?'; 'Which virtues enable the pursuit of a good purpose?'; and 'Which virtues enable the pursuit of a good purpose across all activities and over time?'

The four cardinal virtues which we have considered provide a good initial set. In order to pursue excellence in the core practice, it is fairly clear that courage, temperance (self-control), justice, and practical wisdom will be required. But equally, these may each also be required in order to pursue success. DesignCo, for example, may need to invest in some new software and associated training which will enhance its design capability. In this sense, it is pursuing excellence in its core practice. But this may not have a suitable payback, or even pay back at all, in which case to go ahead with the investment requires temperance (a willingness to temper the pursuit of profit), and potentially some courage in withstanding pressure from senior management or shareholders who might see this as an expensive and unnecessary luxury. But *vice-versa*, courage might be needed in the pursuit of success, for example in DesignCo continuing with a marketing plan, despite initial set-backs, to reach a new set of clients which are not yet aware of DesignCo. This marketing plan may not 'come off', but DesignCo needs the courage of its own conviction that this is an appropriate set of clients to approach. Justice is, using stakeholder terminology, about balancing the interests of different stakeholders, making sure that the benefits arising from the organization's activities are fairly distributed. Excellence for DesignCo might best be achieved by prioritizing the interests of its employees and clients, but justice demands that shareholder interests, normally found on the success side of the equation, are also properly taken into account, for example.

It will be apparent, even from this brief discussion, that there might be judgements to be made between the virtues—that the organization might both use them in combination (temperance with courage, for example), and that there might occasionally be some degree of conflict between them (something we saw in relation to the Good Samaritan experiment discussed in Chapter 3). And what this suggests is that there will be a need for a 'higher' virtue which enables such a judgement to be made. This is typically the role that practical wisdom is understood to play. Practical wisdom was a central virtue for Aristotle[7] and, as we saw in Chapter 6, has also been called 'the nurse of all the virtues'[8] in the sense that it 'may be said to regulate the other virtues by directing them towards their true end'.[9] Practical wisdom is therefore understood to be the key *intellectual* virtue, which provides the ability to think through which virtues should take precedence in a particular situation.

But, again as we saw in Chapter 6, practical wisdom also plays another role in that it is the key virtue which directs the organization towards the achievement of a good purpose. At the individual level, as we saw, the exercise of practical wisdom enables the individual to direct her activities towards the common good. If we transfer that understanding to the organizational level, it is practical wisdom which enables the virtuous pursuit of the organization's good purpose, enabling the organization to think through how it is that the products or services it provides, and the way in which it develops organizational members, make a contribution to the common good, and what more and what else it might do in this regard.

The four cardinal virtues, therefore, provide a good basis for organizational virtues, but we have perhaps not yet found a virtue which enables the organization to pursue external goods and achieve success to a sufficient degree. In some discussions of lists of virtues there are proposals for virtues which seem to be rather instrumental such as ambition, being achievement-oriented, having determination, being competitive or entrepreneurial, and being tough. But these don't seem to be genuinely moral virtues at all. The virtue which does seem to fill this gap, however, is a virtue called zeal. Zeal has been characterized as making the most of any challenge and getting the job done,[10] and having 'a passionate, intentional, rational, diligent pursuit of what is good'.[11] While being zealous or, worse still, a zealot (with its association to religious fundamentalism) are not particularly helpful derivations, perhaps it is possible to rehabilitate the genuine virtue of zeal, and to speak of zeal as an important organizational virtue. As we noted with the other virtues, zeal will be relevant in the pursuit of both excellence and success, but perhaps with zeal the emphasis will be appropriately directed more towards success, while requiring practical wisdom to help retain the proper balance between excellence and success.

---

[7] Beabout (2012: 419).    [8] Dewey, cited in Westbrook (1991: 161).
[9] Porter (1994: 155), see also Beabout (2012: 420).    [10] Solomon (1999: 114).
[11] Horner and Turner (2012: 81).

We have answered two of the three questions set out at the beginning of this section and have so far identified five organizational virtues which will enable the balanced pursuit of success and excellence and the pursuit of a good purpose. So we turn now to consider the last question which was to do with which virtues will enable the pursuit of a good purpose across all activities and over time. For an organization of any size or complexity, ensuring consistency across its various activities is clearly not straightforward, and it will be one of the roles of the institution, and therefore of the managers whose role it is to keep the institution in good order, to try to ensure that the organization is virtuous in all its parts. And we have already met the virtue which is required in this respect in Chapter 5 where we came across integrity at an individual level which, to repeat, MacIntyre describes as follows:

> To have integrity is to refuse to be, to have educated oneself so that one is no longer able to be, one kind of person in one social context, while quite another in other contexts. It is to have set inflexible limits to one's adaptability to the roles that one may be called upon to play.[12]

In the organizational context, we can think of this virtue as being related to the different activities, perhaps even the different practices, which an organization may be engaged in, such that it displays the same virtuous characteristics across all of these activities. This places a requirement for consistency on organizations that is not easy even for small organizations, let alone across geographically and culturally dispersed organizations, and so integrity is a particularly challenging organizational virtue.

If integrity is the virtue for consistency across all activities at any particular point in time, then constancy is the virtue which enables consistency over time. We met this virtue at an individual level in Chapter 5 where, again to repeat, it was described by MacIntyre as follows:

> Constancy, like integrity, sets limits to flexibility of character. Where integrity requires of those who possess it, that they exhibit the same moral character in different social contexts, constancy requires that those who possess it pursue the same goods through extended periods of time, not allowing the requirements of changing social contexts to distract them from their commitments or to redirect them.[13]

In the organizational context, possessing and exercising constancy should enable the organization to pursue its contribution to the common good over time. In particular, as the environment and significant individuals within the organization change, constancy should help to ensure that the virtuous organization is not deflected from its commitment to the common good. And as with integrity, this may be particularly challenging for organizations given the kinds of pressures which can be exerted both internally and externally.

[12] MacIntyre (1999b: 317).     [13] Ibid.: 318.

DesignCo may be an example, where the new managing director and the particularly pushy shareholder we met in Chapter 6, may be exerting pressure in a direction which Elaine, for one, is uncomfortable with.

Of course, it is also worth saying that constancy is not an appropriate virtue if the organization is not pursuing a good purpose in relation to its contribution to the common good. In such a case the organization needs to review what it is all about and seek to pursue a better purpose—and then seek to develop the virtue of constancy to maintain that direction.

We have answered all three questions and derived a taxonomy[14] of seven organizational virtues as a result—courage, temperance (self-control), justice, zeal, integrity, and constancy, with practical wisdom as the key intellectual virtue 'sitting over' each of these, helping to judge both which virtues should take precedence in any particular situation, and directing the organization to make its contribution to the common good. But there is one additional organizational virtue which, in a sense, plays a role alongside constancy that we need to consider. And to do this will require something by way of a digression to appreciate what it is and why it is necessary.

We have, up to this point, considered MacIntyre's goods-virtues-practices-institutions framework at length, but without adding one final component of his framework. And this final component sets a historical context which has been lacking so far, except in making the point in Chapter 4 that practices have histories. MacIntyre refers to this historical component of his framework as a 'tradition', and his point is that our own narrative quests, which are set, as we have seen, in the context of our own narrative histories, are themselves set within a broader tradition, or set of traditions. We have had occasion in earlier parts of this book to critique the modern liberal individualism within which our society operates, and this represents one of the traditions which MacIntyre refers to, as would a religious tradition to which we might be committed.

MacIntyre defines a tradition, in a characteristically complex way, as:

> an historically extended, socially embodied argument, and an argument precisely in part about the goods which constitute that tradition. Within a tradition the pursuit of goods extends through generations, sometimes through many generations. Hence the individual's search for his or her good is generally and characteristically conducted within a context defined by those traditions of which the individual's life is a part, and this is true both of those goods which are internal to practices and of the goods of a single life.[15]

Another way of putting this is to say that traditions never stand still—they are always being redefined by arguments from within them as well as by

---

[14] The term 'taxonomy' is used deliberately, since it carries a sense of being based on a theory, rather than just being a list. See Moore (2015) for this point and for a broader discussion of corporate virtues and character.
[15] MacIntyre (2007: 222).

challenges from outside of them (often other, competing traditions). But, allowing for this level of argumentation and change, a tradition must have achieved a relative degree of stability to be accorded the status of a tradition. So these traditions are influential in our lives, and it is within these traditions that we live and pursue our own narrative quests.

We saw in Chapters 3 and 4 that MacIntyre offered us four definitions of virtues. Now, adding the tradition component to his framework, he offers a fifth definition, though one which links easily enough with the others:

> The virtues find their point and purpose not only in sustaining those relationships necessary if the variety of goods internal to practices are to be achieved and not only in sustaining the form of an individual life in which that individual may seek out his or her good as the good of his or her whole life, but also in sustaining those traditions which provide both practices and individual lives with their necessary historical context.[16]

In other words, virtues also sustain traditions and, if this is so, we might expect to find a particular virtue which is associated with this. MacIntyre makes this point explicitly:

> What then sustains and strengthens traditions? What weakens and destroys them? The answer in key part is: the exercise or the lack of exercise of the relevant virtues...Lack of justice, lack of truthfulness, lack of courage, lack of the relevant intellectual virtues—these corrupt traditions, just as they do those institutions and practices which derive their life from the traditions of which they are the contemporary embodiments. To recognize this is of course also to recognize the existence of an additional virtue, one whose importance is perhaps most obvious when it is least present, the virtue of having an adequate sense of the traditions to which one belongs or which confront one.[17]

Unfortunately, MacIntyre does not then name the particular virtue which does this job, so we will simply give it the name of being appropriately 'tradition-aware'.[18]

Now why does all this matter in an organizational context? The point is that there are also traditions associated with the way business is done, and there is wisdom within these traditions which the virtuous organization would do well to appreciate and to draw on. To illustrate this, let us take one example, an example which MacIntyre himself has commented on—the US-based Long-Term Capital Management (LTCM). The business of LTCM derived from a highly complex mathematical and economic model which operated through derivative contracts based on arbitrage opportunities.[19] The business,

---

[16] Ibid.: 223.      [17] Ibid.: 223.      [18] Moore (2015: 108).

[19] Arbitrage involves benefiting from differences in prices or yields in different markets, for example short-term differences in interest rates which are expected to be corrected. Arbitrageurs purchase a commodity, currency, security, or any other financial instrument in one place and sell it immediately in another at a higher price to a ready buyer, completing both ends of the

however, fell apart when, in August 1998, Russia defaulted on its debt. The Russian government 'simply decided it would rather use its rubles to pay Russian workers than Western bondholders'.[20] The Federal Bank had to bail out the company, and it survived just long enough to meets its debts prior to being liquidated in early 2000. MacIntyre comments:

> What [LTCM] lacked was historical knowledge of two different kinds of contingency: knowledge in depth of the histories of risk-taking firms and of the vicissitudes encountered in those histories and knowledge of the politics of the different cultures within which markets operate, so that, most notably, they misinterpreted events in Russia.[21]

In other words, having the virtue of being appropriately tradition-aware might have saved LTCM, or it might even have persuaded its originators that the risks were so great as to not be worth launching it in the first place. Thus, this virtue in an organizational context would involve being aware of what history teaches as to how to 'do' business at its best, and of the distortions which might be present in the tradition, some of which might arise when the relevant virtues have been suppressed. We will see a particular example of this in Chapter 8.

Figure 7.2 summarizes the above discussion, showing the organizational virtue mapping together with the virtues which we have identified. And it is worth repeating a point we saw in Chapter 3 in relation to individuals, which is that there should be a sense of unity about the virtues so that, even allowing for occasional conflicts between them, the virtuous organization needs to possess and exercise all of them in harmony.

It is also worth noting that Figure 7.2 refers to vices, and the need for the virtuous organization to avoid these. We have generally not talked about vices, but the simplest way to think of them is as being in opposition to the respective virtue. So, instead of courage, the organization which did not possess the virtues might display either cowardice or recklessness. Instead of justice, the organization might display injustice, and in the place of temperance it might display *pleonexia*, the desire to have more and more.[22] The virtuous organization, quite clearly, would not possess or exercise such vices.

Drawing on all that has been covered, we are now in a position to return to the notion of organizational character, and to offer a definition. Organizational character is:

---

transaction usually within a few seconds. Hence the claim that LTCM would function like a giant vacuum cleaner sucking up nickels which everyone else had overlooked.

[20] Loewenstein (2000: 144).     [21] MacIntyre (2009).

[22] A good deal of the business ethics literature is taken up with a consideration of moral vices, even if it does not express it directly in these terms. See, for example, Hine (2007), and Hine & Preuss (2009).

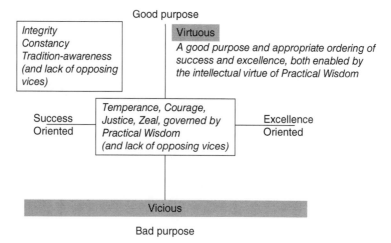

**Figure 7.2.** The organizational virtue mapping with indicative virtues

Source: This diagram first appeared in Moore (2015). This is copyright John Wiley and Sons and is reproduced here with permission, although with one small amendment to 'tradition-awareness' rather than 'tradition-aware'. © 2015 John Wiley & Sons Ltd, 9600 Garsington Road, Oxford OX4 2DQ, UK and 350 Main St, Malden, MA 02148, USA

the summary of characteristics that develop over time in response to an organization's challenges, opportunities and its own pursuit of virtue. An organization can be characterized by the extent to which it possesses and exercises moral virtues (and lacks the associated vices) and by the extent to which it draws on the intellectual virtue of practical wisdom in its pursuit of a good purpose and to enable the correct ordering and balance in its pursuit of excellence and success.[23]

As we saw above, the seventh characteristic of a virtuous organization is that it possesses a virtuous character. And the definition above alerts us to the fact that this is not necessarily something which an organization simply 'has', but is something which has to be worked at over time. But this also implies that organizational character can go either way; as the organization responds to its own challenges and opportunities, and as it pursues virtue or otherwise, any organization can find itself moving in a more virtuous direction, or the opposite. Organizational character may, in that sense, be more malleable than individual character since, for a person, we usually understand that character becomes reasonably 'set' over time.

But what, then, is the difference between organizational character and organizational culture? We explored this briefly in Chapter 3 where we saw that culture is the much more common metaphor for thinking about the way

---

[23] Moore (2015: 109–10). In the original this referred to 'corporations', but this has been changed here to the more generic 'organizations', and another minor change, to reinforce the notion of balance between the pursuit of excellence and success, has also been made.

that organizations do things. An example we used there was of saying that organizational culture might be to blame for some malfeasance, and that restoring a good culture might be important by way of resolution. Culture is also often linked to organizational values, so that we might say that an organization's values are embedded in its culture. But we also said in Chapter 3 that we needed both organizational culture and character, in effect implying that they somehow do different jobs. So what are these?

A way of thinking about this is to refer back to Figure 7.2. Organizational culture has been analysed using this framework,[24] from which the conclusion was that culture tends to be success-oriented. In other words, culture is understood in a somewhat utilitarian sense—get the culture 'right' and the organization will be successful. There is a parallel here with values which we might think of as external standards to which we might aspire. So an organization might aspire to the standard of justice and seek to embed it in its culture, but with the objective in mind of thereby becoming more successful.

From all that we have said about virtues and character, it is probably apparent that these operate somewhat differently from values and culture. There is something deeper here, to do with what an organization really aspires to be at its very core. Recall that virtues are 'dispositions not only to act in particular ways but also to feel in particular ways',[25] so that virtues differ substantially from values which have an external, rather than internal, focus. So a virtuous organization would seek to be just to the very core of its being, and irrespective of whether this led to success. On this understanding, as the definition of organizational character states, organizational virtues and character tend to be excellence-oriented, guiding the organization towards achieving its good purpose, while also recognizing the role which external goods (success) play in achieving this.

On balance, then, while we are likely to continue to use organizational culture since it has become such a common way of speaking about organizations, organizational character offers something more profound by way of a metaphor for thinking about, and seeking to develop, organizations. Get the organizational character 'right', and most other things should fall into place.

## CROWDING IN VIRTUE

But how do we get the organizational character 'right'? While we have defined the seven characteristics of a virtuous organization and explored which

---

[24] See Moore (2005a), particularly 665–9.    [25] MacIntyre (2007: 149).

organizational virtues are required for it to have a virtuous character, there is more to say about how this approach might be operationalized in practice.

The generic term for how to ensure that an organization does what it is meant to do is 'governance'. Governance has thereby become a largely organizationally focused concept, and one which is really all about control. Corporate governance mechanisms, for example, are traditionally about how to ensure that the senior managers of an organization do what the shareholders want of them, and do not pursue their own interests instead—in other words engage in what is technically known as rent-seeking behaviour. Control is exercised by means such as having non-executive directors on the board, share options, and so forth, as ways of aligning incentives.

Interestingly, however, seeking control of this kind by aligning incentives is often thought to 'crowd out' virtue. For example, paying donors to give blood reduced the amount donated; paying children a proportion of the money collected for charitable purposes reduced the amount collected; paying people compensation for locating a nuclear waste repository in their community reduced acceptance levels.[26] It seems that in each case people were offended by the effort to convert their intrinsic motivation to cooperate into extrinsic motivation—being paid to do good. The question which this finding raises, therefore, is whether we can design governance systems which 'crowd in' rather than 'crowd out' virtue.

Some interesting results from what are known as 'social dilemma' games help here. These are games, a little like prisoner's dilemma games but with multiple participants, which offer players the opportunity to cooperate, such cooperation generally maximizing collective returns, or to follow self-seeking behaviour, which free-rides on others. These games typically demonstrate that there are three types of player. 'Strong reciprocators' play for the common good, and typically represent about 15 percent of players; free-riders play for themselves, and make up about one third of players; and in-between are 'conditional cooperators' who may choose either to play for the common good or to free-ride, depending upon which 'side' seems to be winning. These make up the other half of the players. The key to the common good being chosen as the strategy is, therefore, to get the conditional cooperators to side with the strong reciprocators—and this can then even have the effect of changing the behaviour of free-riders.[27] As with the examples of crowding out in the previous paragraph, the question of people's intrinsic versus extrinsic motivation is obviously a factor here, with strong reciprocators displaying very significant intrinsic motivation.

One other feature of these social dilemma games which is worth commenting on is when the games are set up so that players have some other players

---

[26] These examples, with their original references, are given in Moore (2012b: 306).
[27] This is summarized in Moore (2012b: 307–8) where the original references are given.

with whom they are partners, while the remainder are strangers. Not surprisingly, cooperation with those who are designated partners is stronger than with strangers, and the implication of this finding is that generating 'in-groups', where organizational members feel connected to others and to the organization in general, is likely to lead to greater levels of cooperation.

Drawing on these findings in relation to organizational governance systems which crowd in virtue, a first parameter[28] is the recruitment of a sufficient proportion of strong reciprocators, those with a pro-social intrinsic motivation who naturally pursue the common good. This, then, focuses on the recruitment strategy of the organization, and encourages it to find mechanisms for assessing the character of potential members. And, given the distinction we have drawn between the core practice and the institution which houses it, this would need to apply at both the practice and institution levels; virtuous agents are required both in the core practice and in managerial roles. And this is not only about recruitment, but also about the continued development of members of the organization. We noted in Chapter 5 that organizations are, in their very nature, institutions for the formation of character, and so this is to take this point seriously, and build into the structure of the organization mechanisms for character assessment and development.

Of course, it is easier to recruit members with strong pro-social intrinsic motivations to an organization whose internal goods make an obvious contribution to the common good, in other words whose purpose is seen to be a good one. We have already discussed this at length, but the point which needs to be made here is that a parameter for crowding in virtue is to develop inclusive mechanisms for enabling the debate about what the internal goods of the organization are (both the excellence of the products or services and the 'perfection' of individual members), and how they contribute to the common good. An obvious place to start is with the board or governing body since here one might expect the most influence to lie. A regular (perhaps annual) discussion about the organization's purpose, its internal goods, and whether and how they are changing, being added to, or developing, and how the organization perceives this as contributing to the common good, would be a good start. But beyond this there is the need for mechanisms both within the organization to enable organizational members to contribute to this discussion, and outside of the organization to enable members of the community or communities of which the organization is a part to discuss, debate, and challenge the organization in this regard.

These two parameters for crowding in virtue link directly to two others. The third is to do with providing meaningful work for members of the organization. As we saw in Chapter 5, meaningful work has both objective and

---

[28] This section is taken largely from Moore (2012b: 309–11).

subjective dimensions. The objective dimension is covered by the previous discussion; so long as the organization has a good purpose and contributes to the common good, organizational members, at both the core practice and institutional levels, should experience their work as objectively meaningful. Ensuring that work is experienced as subjectively meaningful will require the features of job design which we also explored in Chapter 5. For those strong reciprocators who already possess pro-social intrinsic motivation, both dimensions being in good order should reinforce this motivation. And this should, in turn, encourage the conditional cooperators also to side with the strong reciprocators, and with the organization in general, enabling them to pursue meaningful work rather than to treat work as merely a career or a job.

The fourth parameter for crowding in virtue relates to internal governance systems more generally. As well as involvement in the debate about organizational purpose, organizational members, at both practice and institution levels, need to be involved in the decision-making processes of the organization. One helpful description of this is that organizations need to put in place 'deliberative structures of participatory governance'.[29] This will involve ensuring that the views of particular constituencies, and in particular those of the institution, are not privileged over those of others, and in particular those who participate in the core practice, and this will therefore require that 'power-balanced structures'[30] are put in place. Indeed, we already noted (in relation to the second characteristic of a virtuous organization), that practices are in their nature relatively self-contained, so that as much self-governance as possible should be afforded to the core practice.

The fifth parameter for crowding in virtue again follows logically from this. If self-governance is to be put into effect as far as is possible, then this will involve a measure of trust. In other words, trusting organizational members by limiting the extent of performance monitoring will be important, and the virtuous organization can expect its members to respond appropriately. As some commentators have put it, 'low levels of legal contract enforcement crowd in trustworthiness'.[31] But what this also points to is that trust is never only on one side. To expect this level of trust from organizational members requires that managers at all levels, and particularly senior managers, are themselves trustworthy. And they can demonstrate this particularly by seeking to engender long-term relationships with organizational members, and standing by them when serious circumstances—illness for the individual, redundancies for a group, for example—threaten. For the organization to be seen to be trustworthy in these kinds of situations is likely to generate reciprocal trust in organizational members, even if there will always remain a few free-riders.

---

[29] Bernacchio & Couch (2015: 137).     [30] Moore (2012b: 310).
[31] Osterloh & Frey (2004: 203).

This discussion also points to a broader point about the self-reinforcing nature of these parameters for crowding in virtue. An organization which has a good purpose, employs those with a pro-social intrinsic motivation, gives them meaningful practice-based work, and engages them in the governance of the organization, is unlikely to have too much difficulty with performance-related issues.

The sixth parameter for crowding in virtue then follows. We noted, in relation to the social dilemma games, that identifying as part of an 'in-group' led to more cooperative behaviour. The key to this, therefore, is encouraging group identity so that organizational members feel they are genuinely part of the organization, and can see how the role which they play connects to, and is valued by, others. Engagement in the governance systems of the organization is, of course, one way of helping to achieve this, and again points to the interrelated nature of these parameters.

This then leads to a seventh, and rather cautionary, parameter which is to do with pay and, in particular, executive pay particularly at board level or equivalent. First, it is worth noting that the emphasis on intrinsic motivation above does not mean that extrinsic motivation can be ignored. As we have seen in Chapter 5, pay for organizational members is the principal external good they receive by way of recognition of their contribution towards the internal goods of the core practice, and/or of the secondary practice of making and sustaining the institution. And these external goods enable them to participate in other practices, thereby gaining other internal goods. So the extrinsic motivation of pay should not be underestimated, and in practice most organizational members will be motivated by a combination of both intrinsic and extrinsic motivations—although we might hope that it is the contribution of the organization to the common good, and the meaningfulness of the work itself, which are the primary determinants of the desire to undertake a particular role within a particular organization, rather than the pay itself.

But what, then, about executive pay? It goes without saying that this has been a highly contentious issue over a number of years, with levels of executive pay rising apparently with little restraint. Figures for chief executive officers of large corporations are typically several hundred times greater than remuneration for the average worker.[32] MacIntyre, in characteristic fashion, makes reference to the absurdity of this: 'for you have to be a fool to believe that you should be paid that amount of money'.[33] And he goes on to say that these are 'absurdities that are treated with great solemnity. We are not supposed to laugh at the foolishness of the rich'.[34]

But the effect of high levels of pay may well be that senior executives are not seen to be part of the 'in-group', but are regarded as operating to different standards (on pay, but sometimes also on behaviour) to regular organizational

---

[32] Some relevant figures are cited in Moore (2012b: 298).
[33] MacIntyre (2015: 14).     [34] Ibid.: 14.

members. One effect of this is that these organizational members may well be less willing to cooperate if 'they observe that their superiors feather their own nests'.[35] But another problem with executive pay, and the performance-based share options which often go with it, is the short-term nature of directors' behaviour (typically within a three-year time horizon), and the consequent lack of attention to organizational purpose over the long term.[36]

A possible solution to this is to pay largely fixed and fair salaries with both lower absolute levels of remuneration and smaller incentive components, these based largely on purpose-based performance metrics.[37] Clearly, such a move is in opposition to the trend in executive pay, but if the problems with pay, particularly in relation to the loss of legitimacy which senior managers can experience, and the consequent effects on the organization, are as serious as this suggests, then a radical solution may be required.

The eighth and final parameter for crowding in virtue is transparency. As with some of the other parameters, this follows from much of what has been said already. Internal transparency will be needed on matters such as those related to pay, the ways in which 'in-group' behaviour is encouraged, and governance and decision-making structures, including the outcomes of the internal and external debate on the extent to which the internal goods of the core practice contribute to the common good of the community. External transparency will also be required in relation to this specific debate, as well as in matters such as the financial position of the organization, including disclosure of all of its liabilities, and in the provision of honest information about the range of the organizations' activities and its social and environmental impacts—through the provision of an independently audited set of social accounts, for example.

These eight parameters set a demanding agenda for an organization which wishes to pursue virtue. And, while we have provided an outline of each of these, there is, of course, much more detail to be worked out in relation to the particulars for any specific organization. But then, as will have become clear by now, pursuing virtue at work was never going to be easy.

## SUMMARY

In this chapter we have built on the understanding of organizations as practice-institution combinations to consider what the characteristics of a virtuous organization might be. Having established these, we explored a taxonomy of organizational-level virtues which might be required for an

---

[35] Frey & Osterloh (2005: 104).        [36] Big Innovation Centre (2016: 82).
[37] The idea of purpose-based performance metrics is taken from Big Innovation Centre (2016: 88). For a wider discussion of executive pay see pp. 81–8 and pp. 123–4.

organization to be considered virtuous, and concluded that section by exploring the idea of organizational character and contrasting it with organizational culture. In order to ground this discussion, we then considered eight parameters which would enable the crowding-in of virtue.

Even though these might be regarded as design parameters, enabling the practical application of these ideas, we have still said relatively little about how all of this understanding of 'virtue at work' might work out in practice. This chapter concludes Part II, which has established the implications of MacIntyre's goods-virtues-practices-institutions framework for individuals in their lives in general but particularly when at work, for managers operating within organizations, and now for organizations. Part III develops from this point by giving examples of many different occupations, organizations, and organizational types to show how these ideas have been, and could be, put into practice.

# Part III

# Organizational Virtue Ethics in Practice

# 8

## Virtue Ethics in Business Organizations

### INTRODUCTION

Up to this point we have established the organizational framework for virtue ethics which MacIntyre's approach offers (Part I), and seen how this can be applied to individuals, managers, and organizations (Part II). In doing so, however, we have not drawn on many examples from 'real' organizations. So it is now time, in Part III, to explore how this approach has been applied to occupations and organizations of many different types, and to see what we may be able to learn from this (Chapters 8 and 9), before drawing conclusions (Chapter 10).

As MacIntyre's work, and its individual, managerial, and organizational implications, have become better known, quite a number of studies have been carried out seeking to apply the framework he offers to different types of organizations and practices. Many of these are empirical studies in that they explore whether and how this approach applies in practice. Others are more reflective, seeking, for instance, to apply MacIntyre's concepts to particular occupations—investment advising, accounting, and nursing being just three examples—without conducting empirical work within these.

Given the large number of studies which have now been undertaken, we will need two chapters to consider them. So we will explore business organizations and practices in this chapter and non-business organizations and practices in Chapter 9. Having said that, this division is somewhat arbitrary for two reasons. First, some organizations are hard to categorize along these lines—is a Fair Trade organization, as a form of social enterprise, a business or a non-business organization? Is a circus a non-business or a business organization? (In practice, we will consider Fair Trade organizations in this chapter and circuses in the next.) Second, the way we will approach this is partly thematic, in other words we will, particularly in this chapter, explore themes which have emerged from these studies rather than consider each organization or occupation in turn. (In Chapter 9, by contrast, we will tend to focus on occupations or types of organization, and explore the issues which arise from these.) But what we will find is that the themes or issues, whether they arise from the studies of business or non-business organizations, seem mostly to apply across this somewhat artificial divide—in other words, they generally apply to organizations and practices of all types. The first theme which we consider below is a good example of this; although it arises principally in the context of business organizations and occupations associated with them (which is why it is considered here), it also has general application.

## IS ANYTHING AND EVERYTHING A PRACTICE?

One of the issues which we have come across in previous chapters is whether anything and everything can be considered a practice under MacIntyre's definition. It is probably apparent from the many examples which we have already come across (chess, medicine, architecture, physics, family life, for example) that the concept is a broad one and, indeed, as we have already seen, MacIntyre himself argues that, 'the range of practices is wide: arts, sciences, games, politics in the Aristotelian sense, the making and sustaining of family life, all fall under the concept'.[1] These examples even extend the types of activity which are practices beyond just the organizational applications which are the focus of this book. But MacIntyre has also set lower limits to practices in that particular activities, requiring particular skills, are not in themselves practices—recall that bricklaying, for example, is not a practice while architecture is.[2]

One of the interesting aspects of the studies mentioned above is that they *all* seek to make the case for the particular organizational activity they focus on as being a practice within MacIntyre's definition. While, of course, it is unlikely that anyone would wish to make a public case for an activity *not* being a practice, the fact that activities as disparate as investment advising, banking, open source software, accounting, human resource management, pharmaceutical research and manufacturing, and car manufacturing are argued to be practices suggests a deep-seated desire for the activities to be accorded the status of a practice. Why so? Perhaps what this indicates is a genuine moral concern for meaningful work. In other words, if the activities one undertakes at work are not accorded the status of a practice, it implies that they are, at best, amoral activities, and it seems that no one wants to believe that the activities which typically take up so much of a person's time and effort are not, to some extent at least, morally praiseworthy.

But are all of these organizational activities indeed practices? How would we decide? Consider, for example, the case of investment advising, and of

---

[1] MacIntyre (2007: 188).     [2] Ibid.: 187.

financial services including banking more generally. The reason for beginning here is that there has been what almost amounts to a dialogue between MacIntyre on the one hand and a protagonist for investment advising on the other, resulting in two publications both in 2015.[3] MacIntyre's focus was on financial 'traders' although he extended his argument to the financial sector in general. As will be familiar to readers by now, he was rather forthright in his views: 'the making of money, whether for oneself or for others, can . . . never be a practice.'[4]

MacIntyre's view probably stems from a mediaeval understanding of the sterility of money in which money, as a concrete substance in the form, for example, of coins, was for use merely in exchange; it was understood that it was not in the nature of money to breed money.[5] If this is the case, this would then leave investment advising as merely a set of technical skills falling short of a practice.[6]

The counter-argument in favour of investment advising being a practice drew on Isaiah Berlin's notion of positive liberty as the freedom to fully realize oneself,[7] and made a case for the role of an investment adviser as being *'to enable the positive liberty of his or her clients'*.[8] And, so it was argued, 'only one resource genuinely enables positive liberty in the fullest sense: *money'*.[9] But, this did not quite answer MacIntyre's critique that there is a more fundamental problem which he described as a 'vice that informs the financial sector of the globalizing economy: growth both for the sake of growth and at the service of and as an expression of acquisitiveness'.[10] The point which MacIntyre was making is a familiar one if we rewrite it in the language of internal and external goods. He had argued elsewhere that it is 'always possible for a particular individual or social group systematically to subordinate goods of the one kind to goods of the other',[11] from which we can infer that it is usually internal goods which are subordinated to external goods. And, in the case of the financial sector, that is precisely what MacIntyre was saying; it is always about the external good of money. Recall that for an organization to have a good purpose its internal goods (the excellence of its products or services and the 'perfection' of its practitioners) needs to contribute to the common good. MacIntyre was arguing that the financial sector's concerns are not about internal goods, but only about external goods and private gain.

---

[3] MacIntyre (2015) and Wyma (2015). MacIntyre was writing a chapter entitled 'The irrelevance of ethics' and gave Wyma a draft copy. They then engaged in personal correspondence, some of which is recorded in Wyma's paper.

[4] Personal correspondence cited in Wyma (2015: 233).

[5] See, for example, Langholm (1984).    [6] Wyma (2015: 233).

[7] As opposed to negative liberty as freedom from the interference or intervention of others. See Wyma (2015: 237).

[8] Ibid.: 237, emphasis in original.    [9] Ibid.: 237, emphasis in original.

[10] MacIntyre (2015: 17).    [11] MacIntyre (1988: 35).

But is it quite as black and white as all that? Two other studies have considered retail banking which, although different from investment advising, is still in the financial-services sector. In one study it was argued specifically that there *are* internal goods which arise from the practice of banking. These are 'the provision of an efficient payment mechanism (in which the bank facilitates transactions, transferring its depositors' money to those from whom they buy goods and services), and [more particularly] the assessment and management of risk and giving loans'.[12] We might want to add that the safe 'storage' of depositors' money is also an internal good of banking. And, assuming that we can identify genuine internal goods such as these, the argument in favour of banking being a practice, particularly in relation to its investment and risk-management aspects, would then run along the following lines. Wisely investing financial resources benefits those who have capital, providing them with opportunities not only to protect but also potentially to increase these external goods, not for their own sake but so that the investors, or possibly those who might inherit from them in the future, can engage in various practices leading to the achievement of a variety of internal goods, and hence contribute to the achievement of these individuals' *telos*.

But not only this. There will then be those who are able to access the investments of others, by borrowing from the bank (whose expertise lies in assessing and making loans so that all three parties benefit), and these people will have the opportunity to use these external goods to engage in other practices potentially gaining the internal goods from these. In addition, the banking system should provide for the stability of the financial system in general, and this is its more general responsibility in relation to the common good of society[13]—something which it patently failed to do during the global financial crisis of 2007–8. All in all, banking done in the right way could well be for the common good.

The other banking study is interesting in this regard. This involved interviews with ten leaders in Scottish banking, most of whom had careers which had spanned several decades.[14] These interviewees distinguished between 'old' or traditional banking, as it had been when they started their careers, and 'new' banking as it had become. The differences were stark:

> a culture of customer service was replaced by a sales culture; a strong aversion to risk was replaced by entrepreneurial programmes of merger and acquisition; new technologies and management styles were introduced; professional apprenticeships and qualifications were eroded; and professional skills and knowledge became less important than skills in selling and in generic corporate management.[15]

[12] van de Ven (2011: 555).　　[13] Ibid.: 558; 564.
[14] Robson (2015).　　[15] Ibid.: 120.

The implication of this, using MacIntyre's categories, is that traditional banking was, at the very least, practice-like, whereas new banking is not. And it is worth noting that the very terminology of traditional banking reminds us of MacIntyre's point about practices having histories, and of traditions, which we saw in Chapter 7, and of the need for virtues to sustain and strengthen traditions.

Perhaps, however, the corruption of traditional banking should not surprise us. The 1946 American film *It's a wonderful life*[16] made the same point. (Interestingly, the film is one of the most acclaimed ever made and was nominated for five Academy Awards including Best Picture, but it was a box-office disappointment. This might be taken as evidence that excellence in the pursuit of internal goods does not always lead to success in obtaining external goods.) But this is not to say that all financial institutions have necessarily lost all practice-like features. An organization which provides loans to Fair Trade organizations across the world, Shared Interest Society,[17] is an example of a financial services provider set up specifically with the common good of 'fighting poverty through trade'[18] in mind and, in pursuit of its social objectives, it imposes limits on the returns which investors might make.

But this leaves us with a question: is there a point at which we could say that an organization has stopped being a practice, or that it was set up in such a way that it could never have been considered to be a practice in the first place? Certainly, there are examples of the latter, a concentration camp being an obvious one, and MacIntyre specifically acknowledges that there may be practices which *are* evil, although he then doubts that these are, in fact, practices.[19] So it seems that we can quite legitimately dismiss some activities as non-practices.

But is new banking no longer a practice? It may be possible to argue, using the criteria of the extent to which the internal goods of the practice contribute to the common good, that traditional banking was a practice, and that new banking may still contain the vestiges of a practice. In other words, if a bank

---

[16] See https://en.wikipedia.org/wiki/It%27s_a_Wonderful_Life, accessed 20 September 2016.

[17] See http://www.shared-interest.com/, accessed 20 September 2016. I had the privilege of being involved in the start-up of this organization in 1990, and served as a non-executive director on its board 1996–2004.

[18] This is the mission of the UK's leading Fair Trade organization Traidcraft, about which there is more below. Shared Interest grew out of Traidcraft, so it is appropriate to use the strapline in this context. Shared Interest's own mission is not so succinct but makes the same point: 'Our mission is to provide financial services and business support to make livelihoods and living standards better for people as they trade their way out of poverty. We work collaboratively and innovatively with those who share our commitment to fair and just trade. With a community of investors and the support of donors and volunteers, we seek to contribute to a world where justice is at the heart of trade finance'.

[19] MacIntyre (2007: 200), emphasis in original.

failed to sustain the practice on which it is founded, and made absolutely no contribution to the common good, then it would have failed or, more dramatically, would have, in effect, 'killed' itself from inside.[20] The fact that banks, with certain notable exceptions such as Lehman Brothers and Northern Rock, have generally survived, suggests that there may yet be elements of the original practice of traditional banking. And this might seem to hold out the possibility that organizations which have largely lost their practice-like features, focusing almost exclusively on external goods and losing any sense of serving the common good, still have within themselves the possibility that they might be redeemable.

This certainly fits with MacIntyre's own view that some practices as actually carried out at particular times and places do stand in need of moral criticism,[21] with the implication that this moral criticism might then help them to become more genuinely practice-like once again, even if this contradicts his rather pessimistic conclusion, which we already met in Chapter 7, that, 'much modern industrial productive and service work is organised so as to exclude the features distinctive of a practice'.[22]

The conclusion we have reached, therefore, is a rather nuanced one. Not everything is a practice; some activities are excluded because they do not have internal goods which serve the common good (concentration camps, for example). Some activities clearly are practices even if, sometimes, they stand in need of moral criticism (chess, medicine, architecture, for example). And some activities may have been practices in the past, or could have the potential to be practices in the future, but institutional corruption and acquisitiveness is such that there is barely any evidence of practice-like features (banking, for example). But in the latter case, it may yet be possible to redeem these activities so that they, at least, begin to exhibit practice-like features.

## TWO SPECIFIC PRACTICES

Let us reinforce this point about what are and are not practices by considering two specific activities, both of which, it has been argued, are practices in the sense which MacIntyre uses the term. The first, which follows from the discussion above about financial services, is accounting.[23] The second, taking us into interesting and rather broader territory, is open source software.[24]

[20] See Moore (2005a: 679).   [21] See MacIntyre (2007: 200).
[22] MacIntyre (1994: 286).   [23] West (2016).
[24] von Krogh, Haefliger, Spaeth, & Wallin (2012).

The first question when considering whether an activity is a practice is, as we began to see above, to consider whether it has internal goods and whether these might contribute to the common good. In the case of accounting:

> the most obvious candidate for such an internal good would be high-quality financial statements (i.e. financial statements that fairly present an organisation's financial affairs as far as is possible). Acknowledging that the product of accounting goes beyond traditional financial statements, this would also include high-quality management accounts, budgets, forecasts, performance measures and other accounting information used within organisations, as well as non-financial information that responds to the interests of non-shareholder stakeholders (including corporate social responsibility reporting, and measures related to employee diversity and well-being).[25]

This seems to be both a reasonable description of what accounting (including social accounting) is all about, and makes a reasonable case for the excellence of the products and services which accounting provides. However, it is also worth making the point that accounting is always the accounting *of something*. In other words, just as we saw in Chapter 6 in relation to management—that management is never an isolated activity but is always the management of something—so too accounting fits this description. This means that we should refer, strictly speaking, to accounting as a domain-relative practice, and we should always ask what other domain, and therefore what other practice(s), the domain-relative practice of accounting is being applied to. And this would apply as much to auditing as to organizationally based accounting. Auditors and accountants, in other words, would need to gain, at the very least, an appreciation of those other practices, and indeed organizationally based accountants could, in addition, be considered to be practitioners in that other practice. So, for example, a management accountant in a paint manufacturing company would need to come to an understanding of the practice of paint making, and of its internal goods and standards of excellence, in order to be able to do his job as an accountant well.

What then of the other aspect of internal goods, the 'perfection' of the practitioner—the accountant in this case? Recalling that we met MacIntyre's discussion of the seven-year-old child learning to play chess in Chapter 4, the study of accounting as a practice describes this as follows:

> Drawing on MacIntyre's example of the chess player we can suggest that the internal goods of accounting also include the concomitant intellectual skills, imagination and judgement that accompany the pursuit of quality reporting and better accounting. Beyond the identification of relevant internal goods, however, the example of the chess player has greater applicability to accounting. Replacing the chess player with an accounting graduate, the desire for candy with

---

[25] West (2016: 8).

a desire for wealth, we can paraphrase MacIntyre, stating that... so long as it is the money alone which provides the graduate with a good reason for practicing accounting, the graduate has no reason not to cheat and every reason to cheat, provided he or she can do so successfully.[26]

This, then, points both to the internal goods which contribute to the 'perfection' of the accountant, and to the potential for their corruption if external goods come to dominate. We will return to this latter point shortly, but what is worth noting is that, *when the practice of accounting is in good order*, these internal goods (both the excellence of the products or services and the 'perfection' of the practitioners in the process) do contribute to the common good. Given, as we noted in Chapter 2, the ubiquity of organizations in modern society, it really is important that these organizations are run well (and management accounting has an important role to play here), and that we know accurately and with confidence what their financial position is (the role of financial accounting). And it is not surprising, therefore, that an accounting organization which fails to maintain the practice at its core, but instead allows it to be corrupted, might fail—Arthur Andersen in relation to Enron being the obvious case in point.

Of course, to realize the potential for accounting to be a practice will require that particular virtues are possessed and exercised by its practitioners, and this particular study identified courage, justice, and honesty as the three key virtues for accountants.[27] Courage would be required to write a report which reflects badly on a particular project's viability or to qualify an audit report. Justice is required in reflecting the interests of different parties (shareholders, creditors, suppliers, management, for example, in a set of financial statements). And honesty is required both in presenting a true and fair view, and in being open to validly different interpretations of particular 'facts' (whether a pension scheme is adequately funded, for example).

We have also seen how, to be described as a practice, the activity would need to be institutionalized, and in the case of accounting this is fairly easy to observe; the accounting standards and the professional bodies which make up the institutional framework within which accountants operate are the most obvious of these.[28] This, however, points to another consideration in relation to the practice-institution combination which we have been using as the key metaphor to describe organizations. As we noted in relation to physics in

---

[26] Ibid.: 8. The chess analogy is taken from MacIntyre (2007: 188).

[27] West (2016: 9).

[28] For example, the International Financial Reporting Standards published by the International Accounting Standards Board http://www.ifrs.org/About-us/IASB/Pages/Home.aspx, and professional bodies such as the Institute of Chartered Accountants in England and Wales https://www.icaew.com/, the Association of Chartered Certified Accountants http://www.accaglobal.com/uk/en.html, and the International Accounting Education Standards Board http://www.iaesb.org/, all accessed 20 September 2016.

Chapter 4, practices span more than any single organization. And now we can add, so too do institutions. In other words, all organizations of the kinds we are considering here (specifically business organizations in this chapter, and non-business organizations in the next) are engaged in practices which are 'bigger' than they are, and the institutionalization of those practices, while most noticeable in relation to an institution such as a particular bank or accounting firm, for example, is also 'bigger' than any one institution. And, of course, this also reinforces the point that to be a practitioner is to have commitments to the practice and to the institutions which house it, which extend beyond the particular organization one may be employed by. And these other commitments might occasionally come into conflict with organization-ally based ones. In the case of an accountant working for a particular firm, the commitment to the professional body of which she is a member, and to the practice and institutions of accounting in general, might lead to the need to exercise the virtue of courage if the organization wished her to engage in some creative accounting which was at odds with professional standards.

But this also takes us back to a point about institutions which is, of course, fundamental to the practice-institution framework—that institutions are necessarily concerned with external goods and so have the potential to corrupt practices. In relation to accounting, as we have seen in the example above, this might arise for an accountant working in a particular organization. But it might also be the case that the broader institutions within which the practice is set also have a tendency to corrupt the practice. There is a concern, for example, about the commercialization of accounting,[29] and whether account-ing is in servitude to capital, and so may be 'complicit in the oppression and exploitation of various groups and individuals . . . with the consequence that those without access to capital are, at best, ignored and excluded, but at worst, are harmed in the pursuit of financial gain facilitated by accounting'.[30] This is a severe criticism but it points to another issue which we have come across in earlier chapters—the need for a continuing debate about the internal goods of the practice and how they contribute to the common good. As the study of accounting as a practice that we have been drawing on here put it:

> it is noticeable that outside the realm of academia, there is, in fact, little debate on
> the goods and purpose of accounting . . . [and this is] to point out that without
> such debate within the actual practices and institutions of accounting, the trad-
> ition of accounting is, according to MacIntyre's scheme, in a state of decay.[31]

Let us leave the domain-relative practice of accounting there, in effect with a warning which applies to all practices—to do with sustaining the tradition in a virtuous form—and consider the very different practice of open source soft-ware (OSS). OSS is software which allows users to access and modify source

---

[29] West (2016: 10).    [30] Ibid.: 11.    [31] Ibid.: 12.

code and then redistribute it; OSS products are available in relation to operating systems and desktop environments, graphics and multimedia, office software, internet-related software, and content-management systems.[32] Many of these products are linked to familiar proprietary software provided by for-profit organizations such as Google and Microsoft. And perhaps even more obviously than with accounting, OSS contributes to the common good since these products are valuable in themselves for the help they provide in running all kinds of computer systems, and because they are free. In that sense, they are what economists would call a public good.[33]

But why would software practitioners choose to make these goods freely available, when they could clearly be used for private gain? The answer seems to be, in MacIntyre's terms, that software practitioners regard themselves as involved in a social practice in which the internal goods—both the products themselves and the 'perfection' of the practitioners, together with the contribution these then make to the common good—are more important than the external goods which might be derived from them. The social practice is, in the words of a study which has been undertaken on OSS using MacIntyre's work as a framework, 'saturated with ethical aspects',[34] and we will observe a number of these in what follows.

Perhaps at the core of OSS is what has been referred to as 'beautiful code'.[35] In other words, practitioners strive to produce technically beautiful solutions to software problems, and there is clearly something both highly stimulating in the task, and enormously satisfying about the product, when this is achieved. Of course, this can lead to practitioners becoming known for their expertise and receiving recognition as a result. Reputation is an external good, and it is always the case that the giants of any practice are afforded due reverence. But this is clearly not the driving motivation for OSS practitioners. Instead, we can understand this as a search for new standards of excellence (recall MacIntyre's definition of a practice). This also reinforces the point that if external goods are to be obtained, there is no short cut involved; one needs to engage with the practice and strive to achieve the standards of excellence associated with its internal goods before external goods can be obtained. It is also the case here, as we have discussed previously, that it is particularly other practitioners who are able to appreciate those standards of excellence—the beautiful code in this case. Users of the code may appreciate the functionality of the program that results, but it is unlikely that they will be able to appreciate the way in which this is achieved.

It is in the nature of OSS, as with all practices, that one needs to be apprenticed into it; that only through practice and over time will practitioners

[32] See, for example, http://www.adciv.org/Examples_of_free_and_open-source_software, accessed 20 September 2016.
[33] von Krogh et al. (2012: 666).     [34] Ibid.: 651.     [35] Ibid.: 667.

learn about, internalize, and eventually improve upon the standards of excellence.[36] In this, there is the sense of the narrative quest and the logic of the unity of a life which we came across in Chapter 5—in other words, how this practice fits within a particular practitioner's sense of who she is, and how this practice should be ordered with other practices to realize her overall *telos*. In addition, OSS practitioners seem to acquire an identity associated with the practice and this instils a sense of moral obligation to both support and further develop it.[37] Associated with this, we would expect the virtue of constancy to be particularly important in relation to OSS, and in general OSS might be considered as a 'school of virtue'; it has even been suggested that, in addition to justice, courage, and truthfulness, love for the social practice is a key virtue.[38]

But how, then, is OSS institutionalized, and what are the potentially corrupting effects of this? In practice, OSS has established licences, organizations, and foundations—for example, the Free Software Foundation[39]—as institutional frameworks which sustain the practice. The creation of the Free Software Foundation is an interesting case in point, arising as it did out of Massachusetts Institute of Technology (MIT) deciding to licence some of the code produced in its Artificial Intelligence Laboratory in the 1980s. As a result, MIT restricted access to the source code, even excluding those who originally developed it. The pursuit, in MacIntyre's terms, of external goods by MIT provoked a reaction, one result of which was the creation of the Free Software Foundation.[40]

This is an excellent example of practices and practitioners standing against the acquisitiveness of, and potential corruption by, the institution (MIT in this case) in order to protect themselves and so allow the continued development of the practice and attainment of internal goods—and setting up alternative institutional arrangements in order to do so. As the study into OSS concluded: 'Thus, the "good and right thing to do", according to the social practice's standards of excellence, may be to change the institution and risk losing external goods in favor of internal goods if standards of excellence are threatened'.[41]

One final point which is worth making in relation to the practice of OSS is the lack of hierarchy, administrative structures, and even formal project-management techniques which it employs.[42] This links back to a point in Chapter 7 where we noted that practices are relatively self-contained and self-organizing and should, to a large extent, be trusted to get on with producing

---

[36] Ibid.: 666.    [37] Ibid.: 664.
[38] Ibid.: 660. Love is a key virtue in theological understandings of the virtues, where faith, hope, and love are usually added to the four cardinal virtues we have come across previously—temperance, courage, justice, and practical wisdom.
[39] See https://fsf.org/, accessed 20 September 2016.
[40] This story is told in von Krogh et al. (2012: 665).
[41] Ibid.: 668.    [42] Ibid.: 659.

the internal goods of the practice themselves. While OSS is clearly exceptional in this regard, it perhaps helps in seeing the reason behind this; that practitioners generally know best how to organize themselves and need no externally imposed incentives or controls to do so.


## ORGANIZATIONAL PURPOSE AND MAPPING THE VIRTUOUS ORGANIZATION

We saw back in Chapter 4 how we might think about the extent to which an organization's internal goods contribute to the common good by making some kind of judgement on the good purpose (or otherwise) of an organization. In other words, we might make some kind of judgement as to the 'goodness of purpose' of any particular organization in terms of the extent to which the internal goods of the practice at the core of the organization contribute to the overriding good of the community. We also saw how, along a second dimension, we could then judge the extent to which the organization pursued these internal goods, and most generically excellence, versus the extent to which it pursued external goods, and most generically success; in other words, the extent to which it prioritized internal over external goods, the practice over the institution, or *vice-versa*. And this led to the virtuous organization mapping with purpose on one dimension and success-excellence on the other.

Figure 8.1 shows this mapping again but this time populated with some data from two empirical studies.[43] In the diagram, AB represents Alliance Boots, an organization which had emerged from the merger of Alliance Unichem, a leading European pharmaceutical wholesaler, with Boots, a largely UK-based manufacturer and retailer of health and beauty products. The second study was essentially the same but carried out in Sri Lanka and involving two companies. In this study, anonymity was required, but it is possible to say that Company A was the local subsidiary of a global pharmaceutical company while Company B was a locally owned garment manufacturer. The positioning of these companies on Figure 8.1 has some quantitative basis arising from the data collected during the empirical study, but the points which arise do not require precise numerical values so the axes are drawn without scales. The arrows emerging from AB and B show the anticipated direction of travel from the (then) current position. (In Company A's case there were forces pulling in both the excellence and success directions and these were judged to be in balance.)

---

[43] Moore (2012a) and Fernando & Moore (2015).

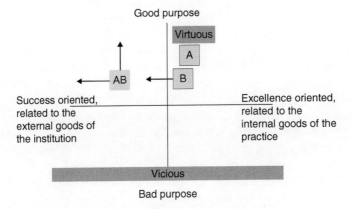

**Figure 8.1.** Organizational virtue mapping with examples

*Source*: This diagram first appeared in Fernando & Moore (2015). This is Copyright Springer and is reproduced with permission of Springer. © Springer Science+Business Media Dordrecht 2014

The interviews with managers which formed the basis of the data for these studies asked them about the purpose of the organizations for which they worked. Perhaps not surprisingly, some answers, particularly from managers in Alliance Boots, mentioned financial success as the purpose of the organization. Given the framework we have developed in this book, this should *never* be the purpose of an organization—financial success is, quite literally, on another dimension. But it is common for people (both employees and others outside the organization) to assume that the purpose for business organizations is to make money, often expressed as the maximization of profits.

Nonetheless, managers in these studies did recognize a 'higher' purpose for their organizations, a kind of *raison d'être* which extended beyond just making money. For Alliance Boots this centred around the provision of healthcare, and this was the same for Sri Lankan Company A, while for Company B this was around the provision of branded clothing. And these managers could also relate this purpose to the good of the community— directly in the case of Alliance Boots and Company A since their products and services help people to live more fulfilled lives by feeling better, and feeling better about themselves; and less directly in relation to Company B which focused on the benefits of the company's activities to its end customers and its own employees.

When asked about success and excellence, and which was prioritized, the Alliance Boots managers acknowledged that it was success-oriented, and this was partly due to the fact that, shortly after the merger, the company had been taken out of public ownership by the US private equity firm Kohlberg, Kravis, and Roberts. Private equity is well known for its financial orientation, partly because it tends to 'load' the organization with debt which then needs to be serviced.[44] The two Sri Lankan companies, however, judged themselves to be close to the virtuous position with excellence being prioritized over success. Interestingly, the managers of all three companies reckoned the ideal position to be just on the excellence side, in line with where we argued it should be back in Chapter 4. So it was even more remarkable that the Alliance Boots managers acknowledged that they were not where they should be.

And indeed, in terms of future direction, Alliance Boots seemed to be heading even more towards success although the expected increased focus on healthcare suggested a better purpose. But the combined direction of the two arrows seemed to suggest the organization was moving at 90°, as it were, from the direction it needed to take if it wished to become virtuous. And this points to another use of this organizational mapping which was mentioned in Chapter 4. Asking managers to locate their organization as it is currently onto this framework, and then to project forward to where it might be heading, encourages some organizational analysis which might then lead to a consideration of whether it wishes to be where it is and where it is going, and potentially to put in place some of the design parameters which were introduced in Chapter 7 in such a way as to crowd in virtue.

An organization which might well have benefited from just this kind of analysis was Lloyds Banking Group. It was one of a number of UK financial services organizations which was found guilty of mis-selling payment protection insurance (PPI).[45] Between January 2010 and March 2012 the bank sold over 1,094,000 products to over 692,000 customers, many of which its customers did not need or want. The bank had clearly lost sight of its purpose which, as we saw above in relation to banking as a practice, was to do with the provision of financial services and assessing and making loans. Not only that, it was clearly prioritizing external over internal goods—as the incentive schemes imposed on financial advisers (the frontline sales people) demonstrated. Locate Lloyds on the organizational virtue mapping and it would be some way towards the bottom left. And, as we have mentioned already in relation to other examples, get this wrong and the organization is in danger of 'killing' itself from inside. The £28 million fine from the Financial Services Authority was nothing compared with the £6.325 billion which the bank had set aside as at the third quarter of 2013 as a provision for compensating customers. The bank had already got itself into trouble during the financial crisis in 2008, when the UK government had to step in and take a sizeable stake to keep it afloat. By 2010, at the beginning of the PPI mis-selling, it did not seem to have begun to learn the lessons from that episode in its history. All

---

[44] The Kohlberg, Kravis, and Roberts' (http://www.kkr.com/) takeover was the largest ever private equity buy-out when it occurred in June 2007. Alliance Boots' total borrowings increased from £1.33 billion prior to the takeover to £9.32 billion afterwards—see Moore (2012a: 368).
[45] This case is analysed in more detail in Moore, Beadle, & Rowlands (2014).

in all, this is a sorry tale in which even the most basic of organizational analysis based on the virtue approach we have explored here would have shown the organization to be heading in a dangerous direction.

But even this conclusion does not mean that we have to give up on organizations such as Lloyds and simply bemoan, along with MacIntyre, the fact that all practice-like features have been extinguished. As we have seen, it is not as simple as that, and the fact that organizations keep going at all suggests there may be something redeemable there. But that leads to a question: what is required to sustain practices and even to enable organizations to begin to (re)prioritize the practice over the institution, internal over external goods? Drawing on other studies which reinforce points we have already covered in previous chapters, we can explore three issues here: the need for virtuous agents; the importance of the mode of institutionalization of the organization; and the requirement for, but also possibility of, a virtuous environment.

## THE ROLE OF ORGANIZATIONAL MEMBERS IN PROMOTING VIRTUOUS ORGANIZATIONS

We have already noted that the virtuous organization will require virtuous organizational members in both the core practice and the secondary practice of making and sustaining the institution. But we also noted that managers in particular, and by implication other organizational members, may suffer from restricted agency. In other words, within the confines of an organization, they may not be able to act in the way they would prefer. And while this is, to some extent, both understandable and realistic (we wouldn't want a nurse who, in a cavalier fashion, didn't follow well-established hospital procedures because he thought he knew better, for example), it can become problematic when the integrity of the core practice, or the legitimacy of the organization as a whole, is under threat. But for individuals inside bureaucratic organizations this is not easy—though not impossible.

One study which researched this issue ended on a pessimistic note.[46] Interviews with managers working in the financial services and alcoholic beverages industries revealed severe constraints on personal agency. In relation to the effect of shareholder pressure mediated through the financial markets, which led to a significant programme of strategic change in a particular organization, one manager said this: 'Blood on the walls... You could say it was motivated, all of it, by one overwhelming consideration. The share price had been going nowhere, and the boys in the City didn't like it!'[47]

[46] Hine (2007).     [47] Ibid.: 363.

And the effect of that kind of pressure was felt intensely by managers who also, in many cases, had typical responsibilities outside of work: 'Children, school fees, mortgages, grocery bills, keeping up appearances, multiple job applications, meeting head hunters, lying awake at night worrying. What doesn't kill you makes you strong? Oh yeah, right! Umm, more like, once bitten, twice shy!'[48]

Several of these managers had experienced 'career breaks'—a euphemism for having to resign or being made redundant. And the experience was such that they didn't feel able to challenge corporate practices in future—'You compromise or you go'; 'You can't become a serial awkward squadder, you become unemployable'[49]—implying that compromise was always the more likely option.

We need to feel the harsh realities of organizational life, and not just in shareholder-owned and listed companies with all the pressures created by the financial markets as was the case here, but in organizations of all types. But are there more positive examples and what might we learn from these?

One study, as we saw above in relation to the question of banking as a practice, interviewed ten leaders in Scottish banking. As we noted there, they distinguished between old or traditional banking and new banking as it had become during their careers. But how had they responded to this as individuals? They certainly experienced the same kind of conflict as the managers in the previous study, but responded differently—not only with what might be called 'moral discomfort' but also with resistance.[50] Several suffered dislocation to their careers and loss of income as a result, but did so by choosing to seek alternative employment in other financial services organizations. In this they exercised what we called in Chapter 6 'exit' rather than 'voice', but in doing so they were promoting the practice of traditional banking as they saw it, and prioritizing internal over external goods in their own lives. But there was also some evidence of resistance—of remaining and exercising voice—and indeed for four of these managers, having once discovered that they could successfully resist organizational pressures, it became something of a habit.[51] Perhaps it is possible not to compromise, and to argue one's point, without getting a reputation for being an 'awkward squaddie'.

These managers also reflected on what it was in the development of their characters which enabled them to resist these quite powerful organizational pressures. There was consensus that this began with families, schools, and communities, in other words that character was developed particularly in one's early years. But character development also came from their apprenticeship into

---

[48] Ibid.: 366.
[49] Ibid.: 367; 363. 'Squadder' was probably intended to be 'squaddie' referring to a private soldier and the notion of an 'awkward squad' of soldiers.
[50] Robson (2015: 120).      [51] Ibid.: 123.

the standards of the banking profession, at least as it was when they began their careers. The particular virtues which were identified were constancy (pursuing the same goods over time), and integrity (pursuing the same goods across different practices), which were then linked with the virtues of courage (involving struggle and resistance), justice (being clear what was owed to customers), self-control (not being 'too attached to the external goods of pay, status or comfortable working conditions') and practical wisdom (knowing 'when and how to resist particular pressures').[52]

This reaffirms in practice what we have seen not only about individual virtues, but also what this particular study referred to as the 'architecture of virtue'—that virtue aims for some good, that there is a unity to the virtues which means they need to be possessed and exercised together, and that this all relates to the unity of a life and to its *telos*.[53] Virtue is about living, breathing people, where they have come from and who they are, and the commitments they have both to other individuals and to particular practices and institutions, and how to work from there to maintain the good of one's own life.

One final study which is worth looking at in this section reinforces many of these points. This was an ethnographic study carried out over fourteen months in an Australian airline company, the focus of the study being on three human resource (HR) managers and a new CEO.[54] In theory at least, HR managers might be described as 'thick' moral agents in the sense that their broad professional responsibilities for the well-being of employees, coupled with a duty of care and responsibility for encouraging the 'just treatment of employees through training, performance management practices or reward systems',[55] all leads to particular moral responsibilities which, one might argue, should be exercised irrespective of organizational priorities. But this is, of course, not always straightforward.

In this particular case, the new CEO initiated a major restructuring of the organization involving a ten per cent reduction in the workforce, laying off around 2,000 employees. This was predicated on 'a rhetoric of financial dire straits and over-expensive labour', despite the fact that the organization was actually 'performing extremely well both financially and operationally, showing record profits during the year and ongoing improvements in productivity'.[56]

The three HR managers were, not surprisingly, shocked by this and, together, began to offer some resistance. Their first action was to produce a report showing the hidden costs of downsizing, something they did by using the language of strategic HRM—people being the key resource and the need for trust if people were to work together effectively—which they presented to the CEO and the senior management team. But more significantly, they

---

[52] Ibid.: 124–5.    [53] Ibid.: 126.    [54] Wilcox (2012).
[55] Ibid.: 88.    [56] Ibid.: 90.

fiddled the books so that the actual numbers who were laid off were around 20 per cent less than the numbers presented to the CEO. In addition, they sought redeployment of those affected where possible, and worked closely with managers in the business units to ensure staff who were being laid off were informed honestly about the situation, ensuring that their redundancy and pay entitlements were maximized, and offering them support in finding a new job.[57]

Beyond this, following the first round of layoffs, the CEO and senior executive team awarded themselves a 35 percent pay rise, bypassing normal corporate governance processes for approval of such an action along the way. Unsurprisingly, one of the HR managers in particular reacted strongly: 'It makes me sick...I went and told [a senior executive] that this was just wrong. How could they do this? I think I overdid it, I'm sure I've just ruined my career and reputation. But somebody had to say it.'[58]

This is a remarkable story. But what was it that led these HR managers to offer such resistance to the organization's and the new CEO's actions, taking risks which could quite possibly have led to their own dismissal and even, as the last quote recognizes, to the end of their careers? As with the Scottish banking executives, part of this stemmed from their own backgrounds. One had worked in the public sector, and members of his family had also been senior civil servants; another had recently converted to Catholicism; the third had also worked in the public sector as well as for a trade union. These backgrounds helped them to keep the impacts of corporate policies on the individuals affected at the forefront of their minds; we might say that they retained their humanity while the organization lost its. In addition, they drew from their background as HR professionals to employ the norms of valuing employees as people; another example (like accounting above) of how professions may act as mediating institutions supporting their members to withstand organizational pressures when these compete with professional values.

As well as these, however, and at a practical level, the three HR managers managed to create what were referred to as 'relational spaces', such as informal afternoon meetings between the three of them, as well as meetings with other HR managers in the organization.[59] These provided opportunities to develop a collective sense of identity focused on their opposition to the organizational changes. These also helped to develop a collective understanding of what being an HR professional as a manager in the organization implied for them at this particular juncture.[60]

All of this indicates that, while constrained, moral agency is possible. But it also indicates that this might well require collaborative action—it is difficult to stand as an individual in these kinds of circumstances—as well as other

---

[57] Ibid.: 91.     [58] Ibid.: 92.     [59] Ibid.: 94.     [60] Ibid.: 94.

supporting mechanisms such as those which professional bodies might be able to provide.

There is, however, another point which neither the banking nor HR managers' studies makes explicitly, but is at least implicit in the stories they tell. This is that each of the individuals involved was attempting to ensure that the work they were engaged in was meaningful work. We explored this in detail in Chapter 5, of course, so there is no need to rehearse this here. But it is clear that both objectively in the purpose of the activities in which they were engaged and, perhaps even more obviously, in relation to the subjective dimension of their work, these practitioners were striving to find meaning in their lives through their work. And finding genuinely meaningful work, or holding onto it when it is under threat, is clearly a task which requires the virtues.

And all of this reinforces the key point of this section which is that, if practices are to withstand the potentially corrupting power of the institutions which house them, this will require the exercise of the virtues by at least some of the practitioners, both those within the core practice and those within the secondary practice of the making and sustaining of the institution.

But are virtuous agents enough?

## A CONDUCIVE MODE OF INSTITUTIONALIZATION

We came across the notion of the mode of institutionalization in Chapter 6, where we saw that it should be a concern particularly of senior management, and in Chapter 7, where we saw that a good mode of institutionalization was one characteristic of a virtuous organization. We noted that this is partly about the legal structure of the organization, but that it extends to other considerations besides.

Picking up the legal point, it is interesting to note how this relates, in the UK and USA at least, to whether companies are incorporated and listed on a stock exchange, thereby allowing them the benefits of access to capital, while also making them susceptible to the constraints which the financial markets impose. The Body Shop, for example, was floated on London's Unlisted Securities Market[61] in April 1984. Anita Roddick, the founder, described the decision to become a public company as 'a pact with the devil', which meant that an emphasis would now be placed on the bottom line when it would previously have been one factor in competition with other criteria.[62] It also, of course, opened up Body Shop to being taken over, and when L'Oréal did so in

---

[61] As it was then; it subsequently became the Alternative Investment Market.
[62] Bakan (2004: 51–3).

2006 this attracted criticism over L'Oréal's testing of cosmetics on animals and its environmental performance more generally.[63] Would the Body Shop's leadership on social and environmental issues suffer as a result?[64] On the reverse side, Levi Strauss took itself back into private ownership via a leveraged buy-out in the mid-1980s in order to avoid the restraints imposed by the financial markets,[65] and remains a privately held company owned by descendants of the family of Levi Strauss to this day.[66] The mode in which an organization is institutionalized is clearly important, and it would not be surprising if some modes (mutualization rather than being shareholder-owned, in the case of UK building societies, for example) are more conducive to organizational virtue than others.

The concern with the pressures imposed by financial markets is obviously, in MacIntyre's terminology, that it forces an overemphasis on external goods to the detriment of the internal goods of the practice, such that corporations in that position may tend to get the balance wrong. An organization which has perhaps got the best of both worlds in this respect is the UK's leading Fair Trade organization Traidcraft.[67] Its corporate structure is that of a public limited company with the benefit of limited liability which that entails. It also has the benefit of having shareholders and the capital which they have provided, but the shares are not expected to offer a significant financial return, and are not publicly traded—instead shares can be bought and sold on a matched-bargain basis via an intermediary.[68] The company has also put in place a golden share mechanism which prevents a hostile takeover, thus allowing it to focus on its mission of 'fighting poverty through trade' without concerns that its brand, which might well be attractive to other organizations, will be under threat.

This mode of institutionalization allows it to pursue its good purpose, making an obvious contribution to the common good through the sourcing and sale of products from the developing world, and in such a way that it offers a good example of a virtuous organization. It is focused on internal rather than external goods; making a profit remains an objective, but only in order to enable the core practice of sourcing and wholesaling Fair Trade goods to

---

[63] See, for example, http://www.cosmeticsdesign-europe.com/Business-Financial/L-Oreal-s-Body-Shop-acquisition-meets-with-mixed-reaction, accessed 20 September 2016.

[64] See http://www.loreal.com/brand/the-body-shop/the-body-shop, accessed 20 September 2016, where it is claimed that its commitment to a policy of 'enrich not exploit' is stronger than ever.

[65] Waterman (1994: 143).

[66] http://www.levistrauss.com/investors/#corporate-governance, accessed 20 September 2016.

[67] This was originally written up as a case study in Moore & Beadle (2006: 381–4), but has been updated from published material, and also on the basis of internal knowledge and observation; I was a non-executive director from 2004 until 2013 and from 2014 a trustee of the Traidcraft closed pension scheme.

[68] http://www.traidcraft.co.uk/become-a-shareholder, accessed 20 September 2016.

thrive. In that sense a limit on external goods has been, quite deliberately, institutionalized. Offering work which is objectively and, so far as is possible, subjectively meaningful, with a strong emphasis on employee well-being is a further characteristic, and overall it has a good organizational character, with appropriately developed organizational virtues, which supports all the other characteristics of a virtuous organization.

Traidcraft also demonstrates those parameters by which an organization can crowd in virtue: the recruitment and development of people with a pro-social intrinsic motivation, attracted by the mission and Christian basis of the organization; a continuing debate, often evidenced in its impact and performance report,[69] about the organization's contribution to the common good; more generally, a participatory governance system which encourages employee and stakeholder engagement, including a staff director on the board, for example; a restriction on executive pay which, as a guideline, does not expect the best paid member of staff to be paid more than six times the full-time equivalent salary of the lowest paid member of UK staff; and transparency not only internally, but also externally in the publication of its impact and performance report.[70]

But while Traidcraft may well offer a good example of a virtuous organization, and of the way in which this can be reinforced by its mode of institutionalization and other characteristics, it may be objected that, as a social enterprise not subject to the constraints of the financial markets, it is atypical of most business organizations. Let us, then, turn to one more example to illustrate that, while the mode of institutionalization is important, it need not necessarily impose impossible constraints.

Volvo was a conventional shareholder-owned and stock market-listed company and, when it was still an independent company, it developed an alternative to the assembly-line production processes that were and are common in the automobile industry.[71] This was at the Uddevalla plant in Sweden where groups of between seven and ten workers assembled entire cars, as opposed to the typically 700 workers involved on an assembly line. This obviously required significant levels of training—up to sixteen months—so that workers could perform multiple tasks. These groups were then given considerable autonomy to decide how best to organize themselves, involving planning the whole process and sequencing of assembly, and including the instruction of new workers, quality control, and personnel issues such as recruitment and holidays. This all sounds much more like car making as a practice than a

[69] http://www.traidcraft.co.uk/media/59fa746f-ab32-4e8a-a7bc-72339670bb26, accessed 20 September 2016.
[70] Ibid.
[71] The story is told in numerous documents, but for this purpose see Breen (2012) from which most of this sub-section is drawn.

conventional assembly line, and indeed one of the other effects of this self-organization of the practice was that the role of management changed. Instead of controlling the performance of workers, management was involved in 'coordinating and supporting a work process that was now the responsibility of "autonomous" assembly teams.'[72] As a result, the distinction between blue- and white-collar workers tended to dissolve.

Not surprisingly, worker satisfaction was high—they were, after all, engaging in work which met many of the criteria for meaningful work which we explored in Chapter 5. And associated with this, staff turnover, absenteeism, and repetitive strain injuries showed significant reductions, while productivity, product quality, and flexibility were at least equal to, and in some respects better than, conventional assembly-line plants.

Despite all this, the plant was closed down after only four years for reasons which had much to do with macro-economic policies in Sweden, Volvo's increasing number of plants outside of Sweden, coupled with the temporary alliance with Renault, and the replacement of senior managers committed to the ideal of meaningful work with others who had grown up with assembly-line production techniques.

We will come back to these points shortly, but the point of relating the story of what turned out to be really only an experiment in the 'practice-like conduct of production'[73] was that, despite the conventional mode of institutionaliza- tion and for-profit motivation of the organization, ways could be found to organize work in such a way that provided evidence of what a practice might look like in an industrial setting, proving along the way that it was not only possible but actually efficient to organize production in this manner, and in such a way as to provide genuine opportunities for meaningful work. It demonstrates that, while it might take quite a bit of imagination, and a certain amount of courage, crowding in virtue is not impossible.


## A CONDUCIVE ENVIRONMENT

The Volvo story also demonstrates the need for a conducive environment if virtuous organizations are to flourish. Those conditions existed when the Uddevalla plant was established, but they had disappeared when it was shut down. And without these conditions, virtuous organizations are always likely to struggle.

As with the concept of the mode of institutionalization, we have already come across the need for a conducive environment in Chapter 6, where we saw

---

[72] Ibid.: 625.       [73] Keat (2008: 83).

that managers are both part of that environment and hence help to create or re-create it. And we saw there a need, potentially, for managers to resist the environment and inappropriate constraints on their agency which it may impose. Similarly, in Chapter 7, we explored briefly the need for a virtuous organization on occasions to resist the environment, but also to attempt to create a more conducive environment—in other words, not to take it as a given. We also noted the possibility of an organization occupying an 'interstitial space' where virtue might flourish.

Returning to the example of Traidcraft, it is possible to argue that this is precisely what it achieved. By positioning itself in such a way that its suppliers (the producer groups in developing countries which were actually the key stakeholders), employees, customers, and shareholders (and not being subject to the pressures of the financial markets), it developed an environment in which all were supportive of its mission. In this sense, it had created what might be termed a 'micro-climate'[74] within which it could flourish. Potentially, other organizations could do the same.

Another way of understanding this is to say that Traidcraft stood in 'reciprocal opposition' to prevailing globalizing tendencies.[75] In other words, it quite deliberately set itself up in order to challenge the conventional way of doing business, and has remained resistant to the general business environment in this respect, as well as, in its own way, attempting to influence that environment for the common good. In other words, it is not just selling products from developing countries, but also selling ethics.[76]

A similar finding in relation to challenging the conventional way of doing business emerged from the Sri Lankan study which we explored above. One of the interesting aspects of that study was that the two Sri Lankan companies were remarkably similar in the way in which they did business, and quite different from the way Alliance Boots did it. In brief, Alliance Boots was very focused on financial performance, whereas the Sri Lankan companies were very focused on their people.[77] This was perhaps not too surprising in the case of Company B which was locally owned, and where the strong Buddhist influence in Sri Lankan society clearly influenced its culture. It was more surprising in the case of Company A which was the subsidiary of a global pharmaceutical company, where the influence of a Western business culture, similar to Alliance Boots, might have been expected to have an impact on its culture. That it did not is encouraging, suggesting that organizations may be able to draw on conducive elements in their environment while resisting others.

---

[74] Moore & Beadle (2006: 384).
[75] Ibid.: 380; 384. The phrase originates in Nelson & Gopalan (2003).
[76] This point was made by the British Ambassador to Bangladesh on the occasion of the launch of the Traidcraft office there in 2005; I was part of the Traidcraft delegation.
[77] Fernando & Moore (2015: 194–5).

More generally, there is gathering evidence that some political economies are more conducive to virtuous organizations than are those of the UK and USA; Anglo-American capitalism does not necessarily get a good write-up in this respect. In the study of Alliance Boots it was found that the managers who were from continental Europe placed a greater emphasis on excellence (and hence on internal goods and the practice) compared with their UK counterparts who emphasized success (and hence external goods and the institution).[78] And more generally, the German version of capitalism provides an example of what is sometimes referred to as a coordinated market economy in which a number of features are more supportive of practice-based business organizations than liberal market economies such as the UK and USA.[79] These include its patterns of share ownership, access to finance, the form of corporate governance with its two-tier board structure, and the consensual form of management which flows from this, together with approaches to apprenticeship and training.[80]

Even within less conducive environments, however, there may still be features of those environments which encourage organizational virtue. In the Lloyds case which we considered earlier, part of its environment was the Financial Conduct Authority. And this regulatory body had 'for many years been warning firms of the need to manage and control risks to customers arising from financial incentives given to sales staff',[81] in particular over payment protection insurance. Had Lloyds listened to this voice in its environment, it might have acted more virtuously, and not suffered the severe consequences which we saw above.

Overall, then, we have examples of environments which may, in whole or in part, be reasonably conducive to organizational virtue. But we have other examples which are less conducive and here the need for business organizations to resist these environments if they are to remain virtuous becomes apparent.

## SUMMARY

In this chapter we have explored various studies of business organizations and practices which have helped to illustrate many of the features of the virtues-based approach to organizations. We have seen that not all activities can be counted as practices, but also that the net may be cast rather wider than MacIntyre himself would allow, even if in some cases there is considerable

[78] Moore (2012a: 381).     [79] Keat (2008: 80–2).     [80] See Moore (2012a: 382).
[81] Financial Conduct Authority 'Final Notice 2013', cited in Moore, Beadle, & Rowlands (2014: 799).

need for improvement. We looked at two particular examples—accounting and open source software—and explored, amongst other things, which virtues might be required by practitioners engaged in these practices. We then explored three other features which arose out of other studies: the need for virtuous agents; the importance of the mode of institutionalization of the organization; and the requirement for, but also possibility of, a virtuous environment.

All of these studies were in the context of business organizations. What, then, of the application of this approach to other types of organization, and what may we learn from these? It is to this that we turn next.

# 9

## Virtue Ethics in Non-Business Organizations

### INTRODUCTION

In this chapter we will extend the exploration of virtue ethics in 'real' organizations by looking at non-business organizations. As we noted at the beginning of Chapter 8, the divide between business and non-business organizations is somewhat arbitrary, so while we will tend here to explore particular occupations and organizational types, grouping these together where possible, the issues which arise from them are mostly transferable across all organizational types and so can be applied to business organizations just as well. We start by considering a number of organizational types which fall within the general category of the performing arts, before considering organizations and occupations within the health sector. We will end by looking at two other examples: churches and journalism.

### EXAMPLES FROM THE PERFORMING ARTS

We have already seen that MacIntyre has given the arts in general as an example of practices,[1] and he has used portrait painting (albeit not itself a performing art) as a specific example.[2] It is probably not surprising, therefore, that the performing arts have been the subject of exploration employing the MacIntyrean framework we have been using. MacIntyre's concept of a practice seems to have immediate and attractive application in these activities, and the ideas of possessing and exercising the virtues in the pursuit of excellence, and in order to achieve the internal goods of the practice, seem intuitively to 'work'.

---

[1] MacIntyre (2007: 188).     [2] Ibid.: 189.

The first example we will look at is symphony orchestras. The study we will draw on here[3] is somewhat unusual in that it did not employ a specifically MacIntyrean framework for its own analysis. But this, in itself, is instructive because we can discern MacIntyrean themes within the study very clearly; a MacIntyrean analysis clearly 'works' with these organizations. And this ought not to surprise us if MacIntyre's framework is genuinely generic, that is, is applicable to many organization types, subject to the limitations which were discussed in Chapter 8.

The study was based on seventy-eight symphony orchestras from the USA, the UK, the former West Germany, and the former East Germany, and treated each of these as organizations in their own right. Unsurprisingly, there was evidence that the members of the orchestra experienced the work in which they were engaged as meaningful and intrinsically motivating; indeed they scored higher on this dimension than any of twelve other occupations.[4] It is straightforward to characterize the work of symphony orchestras as practice-based, fundamentally associated with the pursuit of excellence in musical performance, and with a strong social element—cooperation among members of the orchestra is obviously key to good performance, and indeed the study found that members were generally well satisfied with the quality of their relationships with their colleagues.[5]

But the most interesting findings from the study related to the interaction between the members of the orchestra and those who were in managerial positions—in other words, between the practice and the institution which housed it. One of the first points the study made was that authority for managing the work of an orchestra is typically spread across three roles: the music director, the managing director, and the chair of the governing board.[6] There is obviously a need for close coordination between these roles, and we can easily see, in MacIntyrean terms, that while each of them needs to be concerned for both the internal goods of the core practice and the external goods of the institution, the primary concern for internal goods lies with the music director, while for external goods it lies with the managing director and the chair of the board—although we will consider the role of the managing director in more detail below. But returning to the discussions in Chapters 4, 7, and 8 about the relative priority and ordering in the pursuit of success and excellence, one of the interesting findings was that financial strength was seen

[3] Allmendinger, Hackman, & Lehman (1996).
[4] Ibid.: 201. The other occupations comprised professional string quartets, airline cockpit crews, economic analysts in federal government, mental health treatment teams, airline flight attendants, federal prison guards, industrial production teams, beer sales and delivery teams, an amateur theatre company, operating room nurses, semiconductor fabrication teams, and a professional hockey team.
[5] Ibid.: 204.     [6] Ibid.: 194.

as the pre-requisite for excellence. In answer to the question, 'What factors predict an orchestra's overall standing?', the study concluded:

> The answer is straightforward: its financial strength. Well-off orchestras are able to attract and retain the finest players, conductors, and guest performers. They have adequate facilities, music libraries, and staff support. And, according to our experts' ratings, it shows in their playing. This finding holds both within and between nations, with few exceptions. It is the tangibles, the money and the resources, the things that provide stability, that make the most difference in an orchestra's overall excellence.[7]

A factor here may be that many orchestras 'are constantly on the brink of financial disaster, with orchestra resources and player remuneration ever subject to shifting philanthropic and political priorities'.[8] But what this points to is the essential role of external goods in enabling practices to flourish. While we might want to criticize some organizations, particularly some business organizations, for prioritizing external over internal goods, the opposite position—inadequate external goods—simply means that the practice is starved of resources, and its practitioners will therefore find the pursuit of excellence difficult if not impossible.

But how did those orchestras which were both successful and excellent generate sufficient external goods? The answer lay in the division of responsibilities: a strong board which was focused on the financial position, and did not extend its influence into musical and operational areas; and a strong music director whose role was in setting the orchestra's 'artistic direction and in its development as a musical ensemble'.[9] Indeed, the study found that, 'orchestras that are *dominated* by their music directors tend to get into trouble financially'.[10]

This provides an interesting commentary on how an organization, as a practice-institution combination, needs to operate. Of course, the orchestra is, to the external world, judged by the standards of its performances, but to achieve that excellence it also needs to have the institutional side of the organization in good order. The two, as MacIntyre maintained, form a 'single causal order'[11] and ought therefore to work together in harmony. But while, in a virtuous organization, it ought to be difficult to see the join between the two, recognizing, and even concentrating on, the distinction between the practice and the institution, ensuring that there are particular individuals who are focused on the achievement of internal goods, and others who are focused on the achievement of external goods, may actually be the best way of achieving such harmony. Interestingly, the role of the managing director was then picked out as being crucial to 'balance these sometimes competing sources of influence',[12] ensuring

---

[7] Ibid.: 213.      [8] Ibid.: 194.      [9] Ibid.: 214.
[10] Ibid.: 214, emphasis in original.      [11] MacIntyre (2007: 194).
[12] Allmendinger, Hackman, & Lehman (1996: 214).

that each kept to their own domain of expertise. This may seem somewhat unusual because, in business organizations at least, the role of the managing director would more normally be considered to be focused on the institution, and on securing external goods. But the point about the role of the managing director as being, as it were, at the intersection of the practice and institution, leads neatly into another organizational type where the same role is required.

The organization concerned is the circus and the role is the ringmaster.[13] In traditional circuses ownership of the circus is by a director, in fact, often the director's family, who hire other families (seldom individuals) to provide particular acts during the (summer) season. While the director might act as the ringmaster, in richer circuses this role is separate, though clearly the two must work closely together, and will sometimes put the show (which, with its various acts, will last for the whole season) together from the outset.

As with symphony orchestras, it is easy to conceive of the circus as a practice-based organization. But one point to which a consideration of circuses draws attention is that there are actually multiple practices housed within the one institution. Clowns, trapeze artists, equestrian performers, animal tamers, wire walkers, and so on, some individual acts and the whole performance itself often accompanied by music all go into making up a show, and each of these can be characterized as a practice in its own right. That is to say, each has its own standards of excellence, particular exemplars (famous artistes), and hence historical traditions into which new members of circus families will need to be apprenticed.[14] These practices involve particular technical skills but also require virtues for these skills to be used to perform excellently as individual acts, and for the whole show to be excellent:

> Good acts and good shows are defined by their exhibition of the virtues of circus life—they involve complicated artistic displays, physical prowess in versatility, balance, dexterity, strength, grace and dispositions of character involving pride in performance, determination, courage and tacit knowledge of matters such as audience reaction, timing, and the mood of animals.[15]

Circuses, like all other organizations, also need to secure sufficient external goods to survive, and this can, of course, be a point of tension between the director, the ringmaster, and the circus artists. A particular issue can arise over the length of the interval since this provides an opportunity for additional income generation.[16] Getting the balance right is clearly difficult, not just for the financial performance of the circus, but also for the circus artists who need to go through their warm-up routines at the appropriate time, and so need to know when the interval will end. For the ringmaster, the responsibility is to ensure that the overall 'feel' of the event is 'right'—too long an interval and

---

[13] This section is based on Beadle & Könyöt (2006) and Beadle (2013).
[14] Beadle (2013: 684).     [15] Beadle & Könyöt (2006: 129).     [16] Ibid.: 134.

customers might feel they are being exploited, and this could detract from their sense of enjoyment of the show as a whole. In that sense, as with the managing director of a symphony orchestra, the ringmaster occupies 'a boundary position between directors, artists, other workers and consumers of the circus'.[17]

Perhaps not surprisingly, therefore, the key virtue which the study identified as being required of the ringmaster was practical wisdom. To exercise this virtue requires detailed knowledge of the individual acts, flexibility of response to account for particular circumstances which might come up (for example, a 'pull-down' night when the circus is due to move on will put extra pressure on the timing of the show), the ability to judge the characters of others, as well as ethical considerations relating to protecting the internal goods of the practice (the 'perfection' of the artists and the performance of a 'good show') over the external goods of the institution.[18] In such matters, in a reversal of the normal ordering of hierarchies in organizations, the ringmaster's authority must extend to the director as well as to other artists; it is the ringmaster's role to ensure that the show as a whole is as good as it can be, and if this means overriding the director in certain matters, then so be it.[19] Good directors, of course, also realize and accept this point.

The idea of someone occupying a boundary position between the practice and the institution, which we have seen applying in both symphony orchestras and circuses, might well have more general application. The way in which we described the role of the manager in Chapter 6, as being involved in both the core practice and the secondary practice of making and sustaining the institution, might be reformulated to argue that all managers occupy boundary positions, although for some (perhaps 'middle' managers), this will be more acute than for others who are closer to one or the other practice. But the idea of managers as occupying a boundary position might well be a helpful way of thinking about the managerial role.

One further issue which circuses illustrate is to do with the idea of work orientation, and an associated virtue of constancy. Circuses have experienced declining popularity, in the UK at least, and have also suffered from increased bureaucratic demands, for example in relation to health and safety checks. Given that circus directors acknowledged that they were not in it for the money, in other words that it was not particularly financially rewarding as a career,[20] why would they continue? The answer lay around the idea of a calling. Directors understood and appreciated the practices, and all that went into them, which formed their circuses, and felt called to see these continue. But in addition this was because of the effect a good show could have. One director related a story of a parent writing a letter saying:

[17] Ibid.: 132.     [18] Ibid.: 134.     [19] Ibid.: 133.     [20] Beadle (2013: 686).

that's the first time little Jonny has smiled in three years and he's dying of leukaemia and you've made him smile...[and] the fact of our efforts have really made that boy's day...to think you can bring such pleasure into people's lives...it gives me a lot of pleasure to think that I can do something good for people.[21]

In addition to this, the sense of calling was extended partly because directors felt that they received the recognition of the community including other circus directors, artists, and fans, for the quality of the shows they performed, and partly because of their desire to see the circus continue as a way of life.

But to hold to this sense of calling, the key virtue which circus directors needed to possess was that of constancy, in other words a commitment over the long term to the goods of the practice. As MacIntyre has commented, 'without constancy all the other virtues to some degree lose their point'.[22] And again, this might be taken as a general point about practices, which is that they require a commitment to participate in them over the long term if the internal goods of the practice are to be realized, and the standards of excellence extended. And, besides the other virtues we have considered, this will clearly require the virtue of constancy to maintain that level of commitment.

A third performing art which has several similarities with circuses is jazz. As with circuses, the economic rewards from jazz are limited—few artists can earn a living from it—and yet a sense of calling, and a desire to gain the internal goods which 'are obtainable *only* from playing and performing within the jazz community', meant that, in the particular empirical study we are drawing on here, it was common 'to find musicians choosing to endure economic hardship',[23] in defiance of what might usually be taken as rational economic principles.[24] Indeed for many practitioners, the only way in which they could continue to engage in the practice of jazz was by drawing on resources from other activities and reinvesting these. We have seen this before, with external goods deriving from one practice being used to engage in, and obtain the internal goods from, another practice, and jazz provides a particular example of this.

The description of jazz which this study offered, and its analysis using the MacIntyrean concepts we are familiar with, is such that it is worth quoting at length. Jazz is:

a *coherent, rule-bound social activity* (standards and repertoires played by trios, quartets, big bands) through which by application of the *virtues* (in this case, for example, application, perseverance, courage, honesty, diligence) certain specific *internal goods* can be obtained (typically creative, technical and aesthetic (co)accomplishments in the form of embodied skills, idioms, styles, techniques and grooves), which rely upon *education* (jazz training) and some historically

---

[21] Ibid.: 686–7.      [22] MacIntyre (2007: 242).
[23] Banks (2012: 74), emphasis in original.      [24] Ibid.: 75.

developed and proscribed *standards of excellence* (e.g. the jazz tradition or 'canon'; improvisational aptitudes), and further depend upon *institutions* (record companies, labels, broadcasters, magazines, societies and clubs) in order to flourish. *External goods*, largely in the form of money, power, esteem and status, are also present and available, and are pursued by practitioners and institutions to varying extents and ends.[25]

The study gave an even more precise analysis of the internal goods of jazz, which include:

attaining a sense of creative or emotional fulfilment, emulating or surpassing the established standards, the achievement of improvement in skill or technique, the feeling of community or collective unity in the group, recognition and appreciation of technical or aesthetic achievements of others, or simply experiencing the transcendental, 'in-the-zone' power of improvisation and groove.[26]

The point of including these extended quotations is that they offer an excellent example of what the MacIntyrean concepts mean in practice, and so help to fill them out. As is probably obvious from these descriptions, it is a love of jazz and a concern for it *for its own sake*, which dominates—in other words, the practice takes priority over its institutionalization. But, as the first quote above indicates, jazz, like any other practice, cannot survive without being institutionalized, and perhaps unsurprisingly the tension between practice and institution was felt quite acutely:

what most distinguishes contemporary jazz (at least in a UK context) as a particularly acute example of a flourishing modern practice is the sharply delineated contrast and tension between the durable pull of the internal goods of the practice (the virtues of community participation and engagement and the 'good of a certain kind of life' that jazz provides), *against* the contingent external goods that musicians and institutions might seek to accumulate in jazz or by other means.[27]

Having said that, some aspects of the institutional landscape within which the practice of jazz operates were seen positively. In particular, the educational institutions which support the practice of jazz—academies, colleges, and conservatories—were viewed as advancing the skills of younger players, and ensuring a growing number of 'trained and technically adept players'.[28] However, there was also criticism of the same institutions when they led to 'rather clinical professionalization', and where 'graduates with a more commercially oriented attitude were colonizing the practice', such that 'the essentially free, creative and improvisational practice of jazz can only suffer when contained within a formal, academised syllabus'.[29]

---

[25] Ibid.: 73, emphases in original.
[26] Ibid.: 73, original emphasis (the whole quotation) removed.
[27] Ibid.: 73, emphasis in original.     [28] Ibid.: 78.     [29] Ibid.: 78.

This illustrates how hard it can be for institutions to get the balance right—promoting and prioritizing the practice, while ensuring an adequate supply of external goods for their own survival and development and, in this case, also for their students so as to be able to both attract them in the first place with the promise of rewarding (in both senses) careers, and then in delivering on that promise. Perhaps unsurprisingly, the more commercial organizations in the institutional landscape—record labels, for example—were viewed both as supportive and as potentially corrupting of the practice: 'as soon as he started trying to do something a bit different, he suddenly found himself off the label'.[30]

In these studies of various performing arts, we have seen a number of exemplifications of MacIntyre's concepts, providing further evidence that the MacIntyrean organizational framework 'works', as well as being able to draw out a number of additional points which have more general application. We turn now from these to a number of studies which all relate in one way or another to the health sector, to see what more we may learn from these.

## EXAMPLES FROM THE HEALTH SECTOR

The first study we will look at was based on a rather infamous episode in the UK's National Health Service (NHS) which became known as the 'Bristol Babies' case. It concerned a mortality rate among children undergoing cardiac surgery at the Bristol Royal Infirmary (BRI) in the period 1981–95 which was significantly higher than the national average; potentially up to 150 children suffered death or serious injury during this period.

The MacIntyrean analysis of the case which the study conducted[31] began with the question of the purpose of the practice of medicine, in which the priority of the health and well-being of the patients, if necessary over against the practitioners (surgeons in particular), was clearly established. It is worth pausing at this point and exploring this a little further because so far we have described the purpose of an organization as being about the extent to which the internal goods, the excellence of the products or services, *and* the 'perfection' of the practitioners contribute to the common good. This implies that these two go together and should, perhaps, receive equal priority. Indeed, it might be argued that the excellence of the products and services can be achieved only through the 'perfection' of the practitioners: only good surgeons will perform good operations, for example. But in saying so, it should be clear that while the 'perfection' of practitioners is an end in itself, it is also a means

---

[30] Ibid.: 78.     [31] Beadle & Moore (2011).

to what we might consider to be the greater end of the health and well-being of patients. And what was clear from the Bristol Babies case was that this greater end had been compromised, and mainly so because the surgeons were not up to the task.

But several other features of the analysis demonstrated that it was not just the inadequacy of the surgeons which was to blame; the institutional framework was also seriously deficient such that, even when concerns were raised, they were initially 'met with denial and a refusal to investigate by senior managers'.[32] Indeed, it took the action of the principal internal whistleblower, an anaesthetist who in the end could not face 'putting those children to sleep, with their parents present in the anaesthetic room, knowing that it was almost certain to be the last time they would see their sons or daughters alive',[33] to bring the case to a head, leading eventually to significant changes. For this, as with many whistleblowers, he received not commendation but significant damage to his career.[34] As we saw in the case of the HR managers working for the Australian airline in Chapter 8, resistance to institutional pressures requires individual agency and a willingness to act upon it. And this is not easy, thereby requiring the virtues, not least of which in this instance would be courage.

Institutional pressure in this case stemmed partly from an unwillingness on behalf of senior management to take the concerns seriously. The CEO, for example, had a 'hands-off' attitude to clinical issues, regarding them as being in a separate technical domain.[35] A similar unchallenging attitude was evident in a Department of Health official who was sent a dossier of evidence, but simply telephoned the hospital's chief executive, received verbal reassurances that all was well, and took no further action.[36] But as we have seen, a MacIntyrean analysis, while acknowledging the distinction between the practice and the institution, and therefore of the different roles played by clinicians and managers, would not allow this kind of abdication from the core practice of medicine. The core practice, and the expected standards of excellence, *should* have been of direct concern to those who represented the institution, and if that was not the case then it should have sent warning signals, potentially in advance of the catastrophe. In other words, as we saw with the organizational virtue mapping, and the Alliance Boots and Sri Lankan cases in Chapter 8, the framework MacIntyre provides can be used for organizational analysis, potentially thereby heading off problems ahead of time.

The further MacIntyrean analysis which was carried out identified a number of other potential problems. Practices, as we have seen, are social and

---

[32] Ibid.: 106.     [33] Ibid.: 107.

[34] See, for example, http://www.hospitaldr.co.uk/blogs/london-med-student/time-to-honour-the-bristol-whistleblower, accessed 21 September 2016.

[35] Beadle & Moore (2011: 107).     [36] Ibid.: 107.

thereby require the cooperation of practitioners. But these elements were 'missing from the way the two key surgeons behaved in relation to their teams'.[37] In addition, whatever the particular characteristics of significant organizational members such as the CEO, we have noted in Chapter 7 the need for adequate structures of participatory governance in which the views of all constituencies, and particularly those involved with the core practice, are given appropriate consideration. This requires systems and processes which would, amongst other things, identify and protect against poor performance. Again, the BRI case failed to put these in place, forcing the anaesthetist to turn whistleblower.

Finally, we have seen the need for a conducive environment if virtuous organizations are to flourish, and in this case the designation of BRI as one of nine supra-regional services with particular clinical expertise in this area, despite this being somewhat dubious in the BRI's case, and the failure then to put in place adequate systems to monitor and support its development, coupled with the inadequate scrutiny from higher up in the organization which we saw above,[38] all suggests an unconducive environment. Again, a MacIntyrean analysis would have highlighted these issues and might have led to changes which may have prevented some of the deaths and serious injuries to the children involved. MacIntyrean organizational analysis might therefore, on this account, be rather more than just a nice idea, but could have very direct and practical impacts.

We have criticized the two surgeons involved in the BRI case effectively for lacking both the technical skills demanded of the role, and the virtues required to practice it with excellence. But, of course, this is not to dismiss surgeons in general or to dismiss surgery as a practice. Indeed, as with all the examples in this chapter, it is not difficult to conceive of surgery as a particular practice in its own right. The study of surgery which we will draw on here spoke of this in general terms as involving 'particular communities engaged in particular practices ordered toward particular notions of human flourishing', and argued that what it termed 'the fellowship of surgeons' constituted just such a community.[39]

In stressing the community aspect of a practice, the study provided a case study in which a recently qualified American surgeon, called up for military service in Afghanistan, needed advice on a specific surgical decision. He contacted the twelve trauma surgeons who had trained him and received several extensive responses within a matter of hours. This demonstrated a commitment not only to surgery in general but also, of course, to the particular surgeon in question, who was almost like a son to them.[40] Indeed, so

---

[37] Ibid.: 110.     [38] Ibid.: 111.     [39] Hall (2011: 115).     [40] Ibid.: 118.

important is this communal aspect of the practice that it is institutionalized in the Fellowship Pledge for the American College of Surgeons:

> Upon my honor, I declare that I will advance my knowledge and skills, will respect my colleagues, and will seek their counsel when in doubt about my own abilities. In turn, I will willingly help my colleagues when requested.[41]

Had the surgeons in the BRI case operated to the same pledge, things might have been very different. But the general point here is about the level of commitment to one another which is required of practitioners engaged in a social practice. Although surgery may be a somewhat extreme example, the same principle applies to all practices, and we have seen this before in the idea of being apprenticed into a practice (see Chapter 4, for example), and the commitments this begins to entail in relation to other practitioners.

Surgery, of course, requires a great deal of technical skill but, as this study stressed, technical skill is not in itself sufficient:

> Even the most detailed description of the technical steps of an operation will not prepare the surgeon for the hundreds of small decisions that must be made: Where should I cut? How should I dissect this tissue plane? What instrument should I use? How hard can I push, pull or tear this particular piece of tissue?...What can I get away with for the sake of expedience and what limits must I not cross?[42]

While the answers to such questions come, to some extent, with experience, the point is again one we have come across before; that in addition to technical skills, practitioners require the virtues, and they do so partly because there are always choices to be made. And this also reinforces the point that there is an inescapable moral dimension to practices. The study of surgery put it like this:

> Consciously or subconsciously, each little decision made by surgeons regarding the care of patients is a moral decision. That is to say that surgeons choose among the options available to them because they have particular opinions regarding what would be good (or bad) for their patients. Such choice requires practical wisdom, and the formation of that wisdom involves many years of training alongside surgeons who embody proven practical wisdom.[43]

While this picks out one specific virtue—practical wisdom—which, as we saw previously, has been called the 'nurse' of all the virtues,[44] the study identified several other virtues also required of surgeons: courage, humility, assertiveness, gentleness, compassion, tact, industriousness, and honesty.[45] It also commented on the impossibility of developing these within the period of medical and surgical training, and recognized that such moral development

---

[41] See https://www.facs.org/about-acs/statements/stonprin#fp, accessed 21 September 2016.
[42] Hall (2011: 119).      [43] Ibid.: 123.      [44] Dewey, cited in Westbrook (1991: 161).
[45] Hall (2011: 131).

is the work of a lifetime which 'starts well before medical school and lasts beyond the years of active surgical practice'.[46] In particular, however, it felt that there were

> solid grounds for optimism because character formation happens minute by minute in the apprenticeship of residency and subsequent practice among the fellowship of other surgeons. By disciplining ourselves to the practices of surgeons who have proven trustworthy and good, our character is formed to become similarly trustworthy and good.[47]

This reinforces, within the confines of a particular practice, the point we have come across before about the way in which character formation is a crucial aspect of the good life, and of our ability to achieve the internal goods of practices leading to the realization of our own *telos*. It also reinforces the point that we can develop the virtues within practices at work. And, of course, the development of virtues in one practice is transferable to other practices—we might expect surgeons to display the virtues they have developed in the course of their medical careers, and so to be courageous, humble, wise, and so on in all the other aspects of their lives.

But this also links to another of the fundamental components of virtue ethics which we explored in Chapter 3; the search for the ends of and the good in our lives. In the context of the study of surgery, and linked to the key virtue of practical wisdom, this was put so well that it is worth quoting at length:

> Note that practical wisdom does not exist in a vacuum, but in relationship to the specific goal of achieving something truly worthwhile and important: namely, something good. As such practical wisdom is not 'objective', but explicitly value-laden because it functions only in relation to thick notions of what human beings are meant to be and become. In short, the goal of practical wisdom is human flourishing in all the richness that word implies. More than the comparatively thin or limited notions of utilitarian happiness or the socially contracted justice of reciprocal tolerance, Aristotle and MacIntyre develop the concept of human flourishing (*eudaimonia*) as a thick or full notion of genuine happiness, health, integration, and harmony...For Aristotle and MacIntyre, it is impossible to choose wisely without a clear sense of what it means for human beings to flourish, and all moral action is directed toward this goal. Consciously or not, the best surgeons have clear notions of what it means for their patients to flourish.[48]

This is obviously a very demanding, but also potentially inspiring description of what surgery is actually all about, but again it ought to be clear that it has much wider application than just surgery.[49] Substitute for 'surgeons' and

---

[46] Ibid.: 130.     [47] Ibid.: 131.     [48] Ibid.: 124, emphasis in original.

[49] It is worth noting that, in relation to medical practice in general, MacIntyre has argued that the simultaneous pursuit of its three ends ('to stave off the patient's death for as long as possible;...to prevent the patient's suffering pain or physical disability as far as possible; and...to promote the patient's general health and physical well-being', MacIntyre (1978: 38))

'patients' in the last sentence the equivalent from any other practice-based activity and it ought to read, and challenge and inspire, just as well.

Nursing is, of course, another important part of healthcare and, as with surgery, it has been argued that nursing can be considered to be a MacIntyrean practice[50]—although we will come back to explore and extend this below. Many nurses, it was claimed in the particular study we will consider here, enter the profession for what we have previously referred to as pro-social reasons to do with the care of patients; they are motivated more by the internal goods of the practice than the external goods they might thereby obtain.[51] And, as we have seen in relation to several of the practices we have already covered in this chapter, entering the practice entails a particular range of commitments, some of which may be realized by practitioners only over time as nurses immerse themselves in their practice. This was described in the study of nursing as follows:

> To engage with nursing as a practice requires…a commitment to the rules and traditions of nursing, but in the case of nursing this represents a minimum requirement. The additional commitment is explained in part by the promise implicit in the expectations held both by patients/clients and by healthcare professionals that the best interests of any given individual in receipt of care are paramount; and in part by the fact that nursing as a practice requires a physical, emotional and intellectual presence. A presence that encompasses a commitment to the traditions of nursing, a commitment to the well-being of the individual or group of individuals in receipt of care, and a commitment to the development of the practice of nursing. It is within these different commitments that the virtues[52] can be identified as having specific purposes in helping to maintain the practice.[53]

Again, we see the breadth of commitments which engaging in a practice is likely to involve. But one particular point which this study made that is worth dwelling on is its description of nursing as a 'professional practice'.[54] We came across professions and professional bodies in relation to accounting and HR in Chapter 8 and, of course, surgery and medical practice in general, which we considered above, have professional bodies which define part of their institutional environment. We have seen how professional bodies might act as mediating institutions, supporting their members to withstand organizational pressures if and when these compete with professional values. But the study of nursing offers another insight into the role of professions.

---

is such that the choices involved have become 'sufficiently frequent in occurrence and sufficiently harsh in character for moral choice to have become a central medical task' (39). As such, he argues that moral philosophy has more to learn from medical ethics than *vice-versa*.

[50] Sellman (2000).      [51] Ibid.: 28, 30.

[52] Another study of nursing identified compassion, courage to be an advocate for a patient, and respectfulness to empower patients, as the key virtues. See Armstrong (2006: 120).

[53] Sellman (2000: 29).      [54] Ibid.: 29.

As with all genuine professions, nurses in the UK are subject to a code of professional standards laid down by their professional body, the Nursing and Midwifery Council.[55] An interesting feature of this particular code is its insistence that nurses should act in a manner consistent with the values of their profession *at all times*. For example: 'Act in the best interests of people at all times... You uphold the reputation of your profession at all times... Act with honesty and integrity at all times... Be aware at all times of how your behaviour can affect and influence the behaviour of other people'.[56]

Most of the expectations laid down here are clearly intended for the workplace. But it is also clear that they extend beyond it and, at the very least, suggest that nurses should live their lives in a manner which remains consistent with the code. And this links to a point we made particularly in Chapter 5 about the unity of one's life and the key virtue of integrity; that we should endeavour to be the same kind of person in all social contexts. While we tend to think of the virtues as being developed outside of organizations and transferred in, as it were, this is suggesting, as with surgeons, that the opposite move is also possible; that we can come to possess and exercise virtues in and through organizations, and then transfer them to other parts of our lives. And this may be the case particularly where professions are involved, as we saw with traditional banking in Chapter 8.

So far in this section, we have focused almost entirely on the professionals involved in healthcare—surgeons, anaesthetists, nurses—but of course the health sector operates by means of many different types of organizations, and also employs many managers. And while it is often easy to criticize institutional arrangements and the actions of managers, we should also remember the sympathy which MacIntyre showed for managers 'locked up', as it were, inside such bureaucratic organizations. Someone has to carry out these roles. How might MacIntyre's framework help them?

An interesting study with NHS managers who were mostly working in mental health adopted an action-research approach,[57] and used the MacIntyrean framework we have developed here.[58] Twenty-six participants[59] engaged in six sessions over a six-month period. These managers were involved in leading changes to their services and were experiencing this as a frustrating process, finding themselves inundated with change imperatives, many of which were presented as having equal priority and yet which seemed to

---

[55] https://www.nmc.org.uk/globalassets/sitedocuments/nmc-publications/nmc-code.pdf, accessed 21 September 2016.

[56] Ibid.

[57] Action research involves designing and engaging in various interventions in an organization and then reviewing their outcomes.

[58] See Conroy (2009) and Kempster, Jackson, & Conroy (2011).

[59] Conroy (2009) reports 26, Kempster, Jackson, & Conroy (2011), based on the same study, report 24.

conflict with each other, and many of which seemed to increase bureaucracy rather than reduce it.[60]

One of the key issues which the programme the managers were on sought to raise was the question of the purpose of the organizational activities in which they were engaged. This led to what was described as 'the emergence of a communal narrative of what would serve the *telos* of well-being for all in society', but particularly for those 'suffering mental health problems and who live in our community'.[61] As a result of this, the managers 'began to realize that many of the activities they were engaged in were aligned with purposes and values that were in pursuit of the external goods of money, status or power', and this realization 'invoked their anger that they had been following policies and guidelines that did not bring internal goods to them, their staff or their patients'.[62] This 'righteous anger'[63] was cathartic in that it led them to overcome feelings of powerlessness, and to become what the study described as 'leaders with a purpose and a rekindled passion for ensuring that internal goods were not corrupted by the drive for external goods'.[64]

Obviously, for this to take effect, there was a requirement for 'agentic action',[65] in other words for these leaders to claim (or possibly reclaim) and exercise agency in their own right. Again, the programme seemed to give them the courage to do this, and unsurprisingly courage was the key virtue which was identified as being necessary for these leaders. 'Overall, the outcome was that the programme seemed to (re-)construct courage and develop a clearer purpose for them and their organization', as the following quotes from participants demonstrate: 'I am more courageous now in my assertion of doing the right thing in the organization rather than meeting targets', and 'Now I feel it is not about who we commission more about what patients need'.[66]

There are similarities here with the HR managers in the Australian airline case discussed in Chapter 8. And one factor which is the same in both cases, and which should not be underestimated, is that these managers/leaders were doing this together, as well as under the guidance of the programme leaders, and so were presumably encouraged and supported by each other. As we have seen before, being virtuous on one's own is difficult, but given that practices are by definition social in nature, finding support from others ought to be both a priority and a possibility.

One difference between the two studies, however, is that the one reported on here involving NHS managers used a specifically MacIntyrean framework for its action research. This again provides evidence of the possibility and potential benefits of employing this approach for organizational analysis and subsequent intervention.

---

[60]  Conroy (2009: 262–3).
[61]  Kempster, Jackson, & Conroy (2011: 326), emphasis in original.       [62]  Ibid.: 327.
[63]  Ibid.: 327.        [64]  Ibid.: 327.        [65]  Ibid.: 329.        [66]  Ibid.: 328.

## CHURCHES AND JOURNALISM

The final two examples we will look at, both of which have been studied from a specifically MacIntyrean perspective, are churches and journalism. These are, however, grouped together for convenience rather than because they have anything particular in common.

Churches have been studied reasonably extensively as organizations, having many similarities with other types of organization but also some notable differences. For example, small independent churches, particularly in the USA, have been characterized almost as small businesses with organizational objectives (membership numbers and income, for example) which have to be met in competition with other churches and organizations which offer similar 'services' to 'consumers'.[67] At the opposite end of the spectrum, large, international denominations such as the Roman Catholic Church can be thought of as providing an institutional order within which more local forms of organization, 'down' to individual congregations as organizations in their own right, have to operate.

Nonetheless, the claim that individual churches can be considered as organizations, and therefore as practice-institution combinations in their own right, and hence can be subject to the kind of MacIntyrean analysis to which we have put other organizations, has been made in both reflective and empirical studies.[68] One thing which emerged from the empirical study was that, when asked about the main elements of their faith, many respondents (who were a mixture of ordained and lay members of their churches) framed their answers in what we might call a *teleological*/theological framework.[69] In other words, they started by talking about their belief in God, and what they understood God's purposes in the world to be, and then went on to describe what they felt called to do, and hence the practices in which they were engaged.

From all the studies which have been carried out using the framework MacIntyre offers, this is a unique finding, but one which links back to a point which we explored in Chapter 3. There we came across the idea of being able to provide 'reasons for actions' which provided a link from any particular action to be able to explain and justify how it contributed to the overall good which was being aimed at in the person's life. Here we see just that process though in reverse; respondents provided a statement of what they understood the good to be (in terms of God and God's purposes in the world), and hence why they did what they did. While this is, as noted, a unique empirical finding, it does potentially have application in other organizational contexts. If someone in, for example, a business organization, was asked why

---

[67] See White & Simas (2008), for example.
[68] Moore (2011), Moore & Grandy (2016).      [69] Moore & Grandy (2016: 14).

she carried out a particular action, we might reasonably expect her to be able
to speak of the organization's purpose and how its goods or services might
contribute to the common good of the community, and hence how this action
contributed to that good end,[70] in other words to be able to provide reasons for
her action.

Something else which emerged from these studies is that there might well be
more than one practice 'housed' within the institution of the church—
something which we have already come across in relation to circuses. In the
case of the church, these might be referred to generically as the 'practices of
faith', while recognizing that worship, witness (evangelism, for example),
pastoral care, discipleship,[71] and social action are just some of the practices
in which church members engage. We would, however, need to be careful that
each of these genuinely is a practice in its own right, having sufficient
coherency and complexity, and with its own historically established standards
of excellence, to warrant being called a practice.

Although a detailed analysis is not needed for our purposes, the five
practices identified above would each seem to fulfil the requirements for a
practice under MacIntyre's definition. But one interesting thing which has
emerged in addition from these studies is the idea of *sub-practices*. Music,
for example, might be considered to be a sub-practice of the practice of
worship. The singing of hymns, anthems, and other sacred music in churches
and cathedrals obviously has a long and illustrious past, with many famous
composers (Bach, Handel, Mozart, and so on) having contributed to it.
Composing and 'performing', including the musical accompaniment,
clearly have a coherency and complexity worthy of being a practice in its
own right, together with standards of excellence which have been established
over centuries. But sacred music finds its rightful place only in the context of
worship—otherwise it simply becomes a performance much like a symphony
orchestra would provide. And worship involves other things—liturgy,[72] pray-
ing, and preaching being the most obvious—which might also be practices in
their own right. So we have here the idea of a hierarchy of practices, with
an overall practice like worship comprising a number of sub-practices which
need to be ordered and coordinated in order to ensure the integrity of the
'master' practice.

What emerges from this are the general points that there may be sub-
practices to what we have referred to as core practices (to distinguish them
from the secondary practice of making and sustaining the institution); and

[70] Ibid.: 20.
[71] In other words the making of disciples through more or less formal forms of induction and
education including, for example, baptism.
[72] Liturgy refers to the words and actions of the minister and congregation including such
things as confession and absolution.

that, as we saw with circuses, a particular institution may house more than one practice. But this leads to another point which emerged from the study of churches: the possibility that there might be conflict *between* practices. So far, we have commented many times on the fundamental tension inherent in organizations as being between the practice and its focus on internal goods, and the institution and its focus on external goods. But one thing which emerged from the empirical study of churches was conflict between, for example, the practice of music and the practice of discipleship. As one respondent in the study put it:

> Personally my burden is that the institution of the Salvation Army has allowed the traditions of musical performance to highjack the living of faith, whereas they become more important than discipleship, so the institution that kind of nurtures and maintains that set of priorities is counter-productive to growing and moving on in faith, simply because the priority's been the wrong way around.[73]

The question then becomes how such conflict between practices might be resolved, and the suggestion in the study was that this might be a role for those who represent the institution in adjudicating between practices. It might be possible, as we saw in Chapter 7, for those at the institutional level to see 'best practice' for the organization as a whole in a way that individual practitioners, with their concerns for their own particular practices, might be unable to do. So, as with the need for sub-practices to be ordered and coordinated, multiple practices themselves, where they are housed within a single institution, will also need to be properly ordered and coordinated. This would apply, for example, in educational organizations like schools and universities where there are a large number of practices (art, physics, mathematics, and so on).

There are two other aspects of these studies of churches which are worth exploring. The first is an obvious point that those 'professionals' (priests, ministers, and so on), who go 'up' the hierarchy into more 'managerial' positions (as bishops, for example),[74] never lose the requirement to continue to engage fully in the core practices of the church, whatever the nature of their institutional responsibilities may be. While this is particular to churches, it is by no means unique to them. Senior academic managers in universities might well continue to be involved in teaching and research, and the same might well be true of senior managers in other organizations, particularly professional service organizations like accountancy, consulting engineering, and architectural practices. We recognized in Chapter 6 that managers, however senior, should never leave the core practice of the organization behind them, not least

---

[73] Moore & Grandy (2016: 16–17).
[74] It is recognized that the common organizational/managerial terminology does not sit very comfortably in a church context.

because it is the practice which they are managing, and in a sense these examples reinforce and extend this point.

The other aspect of the church studies which is worth looking at develops out of this point. We have stressed the inherent tension between practices and institutions on many occasions, but also made the point that this might be a potentially creative tension and that the two form a 'single causal order',[75] as we saw with symphony orchestras above. An interesting example from the empirical study of churches was of a Roman Catholic Church where, for lack of a male priest, a religious sister had been put in charge of a parish. This meant that masses were restricted to when a priest could attend. This might have represented a source of considerable tension, with the institutional requirement for masses to be presided over only by a man restricting and potentially overriding the practices of faith. But the accommodation which had been worked out clearly prioritized practices and was an excellent example of practices and the institution working harmoniously together.[76] The more general point which emerged from this is that churches might be (or might be expected to be) organizations in which the practices and the institution are so in harmony (or in such creative tension) that the distinction between them is hard to see. And this might be something which churches as organizations have to offer as an example to other organizational types.[77]

The final example we will look at in this chapter is based on a reflective study of journalism which began by making the same claim which we have seen with all the other examples in this chapter; that journalism is a social practice.[78] The key internal good of the practice of journalism which the study identified was the pursuit of truth in the interests of citizens.[79] In its unadulterated form journalism employs techniques such as 'witnessing, verification [and] interviewing' and requires virtues 'such as justice, courage, truthfulness and solidarity'.[80] The study described this as follows:

> [The claim is] that journalism's first obligation is to truth, that its first loyalty is to citizens (especially to provide citizens as members of a public with a forum for criticism), that journalists must be independent of those about whom they write (especially the powerful), that its essence is a discipline of verification and its accessible style of writing, and that its practitioners must be allowed to exercise their personal conscience, [and these] can be read as standards of excellence to which good journalists aspire.[81]

We see here, as we have seen many times before, that it is possible to use MacIntyrean concepts to set down an inspiring vision of what a particular practice entails, what goods it aims for, and to what standards of excellence it

---

[75] MacIntyre (2007: 194).      [76] Moore & Grandy (2016: 15–16).
[77] See Moore (2011: 61).       [78] Salter (2008).      [79] Ibid.: 34–5.
[80] Ibid.: 35.      [81] Ibid.: 36.

aspires. But, as we would then expect, a MacIntyrean analysis cautions about the reality of any practice once it becomes, as it must, institutionalized: 'the bulk of research into journalism argues that the "external goods" pursued by the institutions within which journalists work have come to dominate the practice'.[82] The study argued that the effect of this was that the public goods which might be regarded as the output of a 'pure' form of journalism have come to be replaced by 'managerially ordered customer satisfaction',[83] and this serves the purpose of creating recognizable consumer groups to whom, as well as newspaper copy, advertising may be sold, thereby generating profit for the corporate media groups which control the industry. Journalists and their communities are thereby reduced to one more example of producers and consumers.[84]

But beyond even this, the study also claimed that, 'despite journalistic claims to "objectivity", liberal-democratic understandings of politics pervade the general outlook of corporate news organizations and, all too often, the orientation of individual journalists', and as such:

> news discourses come to presume and protect certain dominant norms and values—the sanctity of property, the basic rights of the state and capital, the benevolence of foreign policy, the idea of the nation state, the legitimacy of standing armies, the 'reasonableness' of political positions, the need for economic efficiency and so on.[85]

This, of course, takes us into much broader political territory than has been the general focus of this book, although we have had occasion to comment on and critique such liberal democratic understandings before. And yet despite these concerns, the study of journalism as a practice argued that 'it is still held by most journalists that they do pursue certain social goods such as the truth, justice, the public interest, checks on the powerful and so on',[86] even if in the end this only amounted to 'critical legitimation ... of the dominant institutional order'.[87]

In the terms in which we have spoken of such things, this points to another example of an environment which is potentially unconducive to virtue and, as we have seen before, this requires the agency of practitioners acting collectively to resist it if practices are to thrive. In particular, the study pointed to alternative modes of institutionalization as enabling just this kind of resistance. Thus the UK newspaper the *Guardian*, owned by the Scott Trust which protects it from commercial or political interference,[88] was given as one mainstream example.

---

[82]  Ibid.: 35.    [83]  Ibid.: 35.    [84]  Ibid.: 35.
[85]  Ibid.: 35–6.    [86]  Ibid.: 36.    [87]  Ibid.: 37.
[88]  See https://en.wikipedia.org/wiki/The_Guardian, accessed 21 September 2016.

But the study focused particularly on Independent Media Centres (IMCs)[89] as an example of alternative institutional arrangements which might enable such resistance to be realized. These operate on the basis of 'public journalism' with an open publishing system which has much in common with open source software that we explored in Chapter 8. While there is an umbrella body which provides the kind of institutional architecture required—including a Mission Statement and Principles of Unity[90]—it operates as a network of local IMCs which are typically city-based.

Of course, even organizational arrangements like these are subject to the kinds of tensions to which MacIntyre's framework draws attention: they suffer from a lack of external goods which can threaten their continued existence; their opposition to the dominant institutional order has led to legal challenges which have caused some IMCs to consider legal incorporation, thus finding themselves drawn into the existing institutional order; there have been occasions of participants putting up disruptive contributions while hiding behind the anonymity considered essential to normal operations, requiring institutional-level intervention; and IMCs find themselves marginalized by internet search engines so that their potential to challenge the existing social order is undermined.[91] Resistance to the mainstream, as we have noted many times before, is not easy, but again this study points to the kind of MacIntyrean analysis and prescription for action which might make such resistance more feasible.

## SUMMARY

In this chapter we have explored various studies of non-business organizations and practices which have extended those of business organizations in Chapter 8. While some points have been reinforced—the need for a conducive environment, for example—a number of new issues have emerged. For example, we saw the benefit of maintaining the distinction between the practice and the institution with sharply defined roles, as became evident with symphony orchestras. We also saw that there may be a requirement for particular individuals to occupy a boundary position between practice and

---

[89] See https://indymedia.org/or/index.shtml, accessed 21 September 2016. It describes itself as follows: 'The Independent Media Center is a network of collectively run media outlets for the creation of radical, accurate, and passionate tellings of the truth. We work out of a love and inspiration for people who continue to work for a better world, despite corporate media's distortions and unwillingness to cover the efforts to free humanity'.
[90] Salter (2008: 41).        [91] Ibid.: 43–4.

institution, as with the circus ringmaster. And we saw the possibility of there being sub-practices, and of conflict between practices, and for the need therefore to keep multiple practices in their proper order, as with churches.

We are now in a position, therefore, to draw all of the themes, issues, and points from Chapter 8 and this chapter together, and to offer some overall conclusions. It is to this that we turn in Chapter 10.

# 10

————

# Conclusions

## INTRODUCTION

We have been on a long journey through some fairly complex territory. We began by thinking about the ubiquity of organizations in our present social order, and hence of the importance of understanding them. We saw that we tend to think about organizations by using metaphors and recognized that the approach in this book represented, in a sense, just one more organizational metaphor. However, the claim was made that it is a particularly important and insightful one, and the remainder of the book has, in effect, been an attempt to substantiate that claim. We also reviewed the CSR and stakeholder approaches to business and organizational ethics, which are the most common way in which such matters tend to be addressed, and recognized some of their inherent weaknesses.

It was at that point that we began to explore what virtue ethics, or at least a MacIntyrean version of virtue ethics, offered and, having considered that in general, we developed the implications of this in terms of a virtues-based metaphor for organizations using the various concepts which MacIntyre provides. We then, in Part II, worked through the implications of this MacIntyrean framework for individuals, managers, and organizations. And in Part III we considered a number of studies which have used that framework in order to analyse various occupations, organizational types, and particular organizations, to see how this approach works out in practice.

The purpose of this concluding chapter is to review and draw some conclusions from all that we have covered. To do so, we will first summarize the MacIntyrean virtue ethics approach. Then we will reconsider the organizational and managerial implications, drawing out some of the themes which have emerged from the various studies we have looked at. In doing so, we will consider a question which has been implicit in the discussions so far, but which now needs to be tackled explicitly: how feasible is this approach in practice, particularly for organizations? In the light of that, we will revisit the earlier critique of current approaches to organizational ethics, before concluding.

# MACINTYREAN VIRTUE ETHICS—A SUMMARY

We have seen that MacIntyre, drawing on but extending Aristotle's ideas, offers a way of thinking about ethics, and of life in general, from a virtues approach. Key to this was the idea of *telos* or purpose; that each of us as individuals can understand our lives as being on some kind of journey—a narrative quest—towards our true end, to become, in that overworked phrase which we use today, what we were 'always meant to be'. This idea of individual journeys towards our own end and good was linked with the understanding that these journeys are always undertaken in a communal setting, and therefore of the need for the realization of the common good as providing the context in which individuals might be able to realize their own *telos*. We extended this approach by considering two different kinds of goods—internal and external. We saw how it was internal goods which we should pursue for their own sake, and which should therefore take priority in our lives if we are to realize our *telos*. But we also recognized that we could not attain internal goods without sufficient external goods, and that therefore obtaining these was also essential to the good life.

But we immediately recognized a danger, in that we might begin to think that the pursuit of external goods was an end in itself, rather than simply a means to the end of obtaining internal goods. And MacIntyre was concerned for societies (and most particularly modern Western societies) in which the pursuit of external goods had become dominant, and the effect which that was having on the virtues, and on our abilities, individually and collectively, to realize our true ends.

In relation to virtue ethics at the individual level, but also linking to the societal level and the idea of the common good, a key concept which MacIntyre introduced was that of practices, defined in a particular way to draw attention to their coherent, complex, and cooperative social form, and their being the locus for the achievement of internal goods. We also came to understand that, in order to achieve these internal goods, there was a requirement to pursue those standards of excellence which were appropriate to, and which partially defined, any particular practice.

We saw that the idea of practices applied to a very wide range of human activities, and that it was possible to conceive of life as lived mainly inside a variety of practices. We also saw that practices have histories, so that being inducted into a practice meant learning about its past, and appreciating that its standards of excellence had been defined by those who had previously excelled at it. Connected with this, we also saw that practices were linked to traditions which changed and developed over time, and the ways in which practices would also therefore change and develop over time, and this gave an historical perspective both to practices themselves and to the lives of those engaged in them.

This historical context linked back to the idea of a narrative quest, in that we could conceive of our lives as being a story, of which we are the subject, but which is set in its own particular historical context, within the traditions which have formed the practices in which we now engage, and which involves a set of interlocking narratives with those with whom we share our lives. These, as we saw, form the 'moral starting point'[1] of our lives, and also indicate the connections and commitments which we have, and which we cannot easily (nor, generally, would want to) escape from.

We then saw how the virtues played an essential part in all of this: virtues enable us to achieve the goods internal to practices; they sustain us in our narrative quest for the good in our lives; and hence they enable us to achieve our purpose in life, summarized as achieving *eudaimonia* or our overall *telos*. Virtues were understood to be deep-seated dispositions to act and feel in particular ways, so that the virtuous person should experience a harmony and unity in their lives, possessing and exercising all of the virtues in concert. We recognized, of course, that this was not at all easy and that the development of the virtues, and the formation of our characters, was a task which, although it began when we were children, would continue throughout our lives.

We also recognized that, among the various practices in which we might engage, those involving work, and often therefore work inside organizations, were likely to be very significant, particularly given the amount of time and effort which this might demand of us. And we noted that, as a result, we should seek, and possibly even demand, meaningful work as a way of ensuring that we were in the best position to gain the internal goods from such practices as we might be involved in at work. Considering the role of virtue at work at this individual level provided the link to consider organizations and indeed management from a virtues perspective, again using concepts which MacIntyre offers us.

Before moving on to the managerial and organizational implications of this approach, however, it is worth pausing and reflecting on what the virtues approach to ethics, and to life in general (since, as will have become evident, the two are essentially intertwined in the virtues approach), implies. And it might be that we could agree that it offers both a realistic and an attractive way of 'coming at' all of this. It is realistic in that it may well reflect quite accurately the way in which we experience life, albeit perhaps now with a set of concepts and terminology which were not previously available to us, and which enable us to articulate this rather better. And it might also be that we could agree that this is attractive in that it perhaps offers an inspiring way of thinking about how we approach life in general, and our working lives in particular, both now and in the future.

---

[1] MacIntyre (2007: 220).

But, if it is both realistic and attractive, we would probably then have to acknowledge that it is also rather challenging. It asks of us which practices we have chosen to engage with, what projects and purposes we have in our lives, how the pursuit of both internal and external goods and the various practices in our lives are ordered, and what part these play within the structure of our lives as a whole. It therefore asks about the unity of our lives and the key virtue of integrity in enabling us not to live compartmentalized lives, but to be the same person in the wide range of practices in which we are engaged and which make up our lives. It also asks of us to be able to give reasons for our actions which we can link to our *telos*, and indeed it asks whether we can give an account of what we think our *telos*, our own particular *raison d'être*, might be. And it asks us occasionally to reflect and to ask questions such as, 'To what conception of my overall good have I so far committed myself? And do I now have reason to put it in question?'[2] And it therefore always asks of us 'what more and what else'[3] the good life for us consists of.

All in all, therefore, this approach to virtue ethics asks hard questions both of us as individuals and of the kind of society we live in, and are partially responsible for building. But maybe that should not surprise us. As Socrates, another great virtue ethicist, is reported to have said, the unexamined life is not worth living. And, as a result of all we have worked through, we do at least have some kind of answer to the question we left hanging in Chapter 1—what does it mean to be a good person?

## MACINTYRE'S FRAMEWORK—ORGANIZATIONAL IMPLICATIONS

The key to developing from the individual and communal virtue ethics approach, to explore what we might call the intermediate level of organizations was, of course, MacIntyre's claim that practices have to be institutionalized if they are to survive for any length of time. And it was this idea of organizations as practice-institution combinations which gave us the particular way of thinking about—this particular metaphor for—organizations which we have explored at length. We saw how practices focus on the achievement of internal goods, and institutions on external goods, and, while they form a 'single causal order', this also exposed a fundamental tension inherent in all organizations—the tension between the pursuit of internal versus external goods, in which 'the ideals and the creativity of the practice are always vulnerable to the acquisitiveness of the institution, in which the cooperative

---

[2] MacIntyre (1992: 8).      [3] MacIntyre (2007: 219).

care for common goods of the practice is always vulnerable to the competitiveness of the institution'.[4]

Nonetheless, we saw in several of the organizational examples which we
looked at, that there were ways of managing this tension: ensuring that
different practitioners were focused on the achievement of the different
goods (as in the best symphony orchestras); and recognizing the 'boundary
position' occupied by some which 'held' that tension (the ringmaster, for
example). It seemed, therefore, that this could become a creative rather than
destructive tension, but only so long as both sets of practitioners were committed to the core practice, and recognized the secondary, though essential,
nature of the institution in housing the practice. Indeed, in the virtuous
organization, we recognized that the 'join' between the practice and the
institution ought to be hard to see (churches, perhaps).

But we also saw examples of this inherent tension erupting on occasion, for
instance in the studies of banking, and the way in which 'traditional' banking
had given way to 'new' banking. We saw this tension also in open source
software and Independent Media Centres, and the alternative institutional
arrangements which had been put in place to try to protect the practice. And
we saw, in the cases of Lloyds Bank and the Australian airline company, the
ways in which, in these situations, the pursuit of external goods seemed to
have become overriding. These examples all reinforced the point that this
tension remains. Organizations, we might say, are 'unresolved dilemmatic
spaces'[5] where the central dilemma between practices and institutions is
never resolved, but has to be continuously worked at.

We also noted several other aspects of this way of thinking about organizations.
We saw that it is not possible to say that anything and everything can be
considered to be a practice, and that the deciding factor is the extent to which
the internal goods of the practice (the excellence of the goods or services and the
'perfection' of practitioners) contribute to the common good. We saw that, while
this might allow the boundary to be drawn reasonably widely (and probably more
widely than MacIntyre would allow), it did challenge activities such as banking
where it seemed that the practice had been corrupted to the extent that 'new'
banking may contain only the vestiges of a practice. But we also saw that this then
opens up banking not only to moral criticism but also to the possibility of reform.

Indeed, one of the things we particularly noted was that MacIntyre's
framework can be used for organizational analysis, and can therefore potentially lead to organizational change. The organizational virtue mapping, and
its use to analyse Alliance Boots and the two Sri Lankan companies, was a
case in point, as was the MacIntyrean analysis of the 'Bristol Babies' case.

---

[4] Ibid.: 194.
[5] This is a phrase which originated in a presentation given by Sarah Banks of Durham
University.

Equally, the use of the MacIntyrean framework to conduct action research in the case of the NHS managers working in mental health reinforced the practical potential of applying the framework to make organizational interventions, and thereby to seek change for good.

We also saw that there were examples of good practice which we could observe, and potentially learn from; Traidcraft provided one such case in point, as did the experiment in working practices at Volvo even if over only a relatively short period of time. We also saw positive examples in healthcare, with surgeons and nurses offering examples of practitioners fully engaged in and committed to their practices, and we saw there how practices entailed wider commitments to other practitioners, and to the practice, and to its standards of excellence, which could be realized only if practitioners remained in these practices for extended periods. The virtue of constancy, pursuing the same goods over such extended periods, was seen to be key to this.

Accounting, banking, human resources, surgery, and nursing also raised another set of issues over the role of the professions. An often unanalysed suspicion, particularly in relation to business organizations, is that virtues have to developed, and our characters formed, outside of organizations, and that it is the other practices in our lives—family and community life, religious practices, and so on—which are needed to 'top up' the virtues, before we plunge back into organizational life, where these virtues are soon depleted. But we have seen that, while of course possible, this is not necessarily the case; practice-based organizations offer us the opportunity to exercise the virtues, and to develop them further.

But, again, the potential for the institutional corruption of practices holds out the possibility that this will not always be the case. And while for some practitioners this may be problematic, those practitioners who are also members of professional bodies have an additional source of influence in this regard. Of course, professions are also organizations, and so are also subject to the same process of corruption as any other organization, as we saw might be the case with accounting. But when in good order, professions can, as we saw, act as mediating institutions, both supporting their members in withstanding pressure from within their employing organization, and encouraging them to maintain the integrity of their professional values (what we might now call virtues) in the whole of their lives, as we saw with nursing.

Having worked through the characteristics of a virtuous organization in Chapter 7, and the eight organizational virtues which, it was argued, are the key to the formation of a virtuous organizational character, and having then explored the various parameters which provided a practical set of guidance for 'crowding in' virtue, we saw from the examples in Chapter 8 that there are three pre-conditions for virtuous organizations. These are the presence, in both the core practice and the secondary practice of making and sustaining the institution, of virtuous agents; a conducive mode of institutionalization; and the presence of a similarly conducive environment. And we saw examples of each of these in considering, for example, the HR managers in the Australian airline case; Traidcraft and Volvo in relation to their modes of institutionalization; and Traidcraft again, and the two Sri Lankan companies, in relation to both creating and drawing on a conducive environment.

As with the implications for individuals, we might agree that this approach to organizational ethics is both realistic and attractive. It is realistic in the way that it provides a means of understanding organizations, and a means of opening them up for critical analysis, which makes intuitive sense. It may be attractive particularly in its ethical implications, offering us the possibility of organizations as being '*essentially* moral spaces',[6] with all the implications which that has. But, if it is realistic and attractive, we would probably also have to agree that it is challenging. Creating a virtuous organization, with all that that implies, may well be a rewarding task, but it is clearly by no means an easy one. As a result of all we have worked through, however, we do at least have some kind of answer to the question we left hanging in Chapter 1—what does it mean to be a good organization?

## MACINTYRE'S FRAMEWORK—MANAGERIAL IMPLICATIONS

We have seen that, as well as enabling us to give some kind of answer to what it means to be a good organization, MacIntyre's framework also gives us a particular way of locating and understanding the role of management. By drawing the distinction between practices and institutions, and by following MacIntyre's contention that the making and sustaining of institutions had all the characteristics of a practice, we saw that this was indeed the practice in which managers are engaged. And the most important point to note from this is that, if the making and sustaining of institutions is a practice, it must have its own internal goods, and its own historically determined standards of excellence. Hence, being a manager holds out the possibility of exercising the virtues in pursuit of those standards of excellence, and of those internal goods, of these being some of the constitutive goods of the individual manager's overall good, his or her 'perfection', and therefore of the role of manager as contributing to the realization of an individual's own *telos*. This therefore offered, in a sense, a 'high' view of management, apparently far removed from MacIntyre's criticism of managers as, at best, morally neutral efficient achievers of pre-determined ends.

---

[6] Beadle & Moore (2011: 103).

We also saw that management is always domain-relative, that it is never 'management in general' but always 'management in the particular'. And this implied that managers always have another practice, the core practice at the heart of the organization, with which they have to engage and, indeed, from which they may also be able to gain internal goods.

This positive potential role for management was, however, tempered somewhat by appreciating that part of the role of managers, as with the institutions they serve, is the pursuit of external goods. And this, therefore, takes us back to the same discussion as above about the priority of external goods, of managers finding that their agency is restricted in being able to pursue internal goods, and of the requirement but also the difficulty of influencing the purpose of the organization and how it contributes to the common good. And hence we saw the danger that managers might end up living conflicted lives, compartmentalized into at least two different social spheres, with being a manager inside a bureaucratic organization forcing one set of virtues and vices (and perhaps mainly vices) to the fore, while other parts of their lives perhaps enabled them to exercise the virtues more fully.

Two possible answers to this emerged. One was to work for a virtuous organization where these kinds of tension were limited by design. The other was to resist or, to put it another way, to accept the boundary position which managers occupy between the core practice and the institution. And we saw in the cases of the Scottish bankers, the Australian HR managers, the whistleblower in the Bristol Babies case, and the NHS managers working in mental health, the possibility of doing so. But we also saw the potential damage to careers which this involved. And hence we recognized the need for two virtues in particular: practical wisdom to know when an issue could not be ignored, and courage to do something about it.

As we might expect, therefore, the role of manager within MacIntyre's framework has similar characteristics to those which we saw for individuals and organizations. It is, we might agree, realistic in its portrayal of what it is actually like to be a manager. It may also be attractive, particularly in the idea of management being a domain-relative practice through which internal goods may be obtained which form part of an individual's narrative quest towards their true *telos*.

But we would then also need to acknowledge that the role of manager is rather challenging. Attempting to be a good manager, seeking to influence the purpose of the organization, prioritizing the core practice over the institution, and hence internal over external goods, while ensuring an adequate supply of the latter, seeking to provide meaningful work for others, while resisting those inside the organization and outside of it who might have other priorities, is a challenging position to be in. But, as a result of all we have worked through, we do at least have some kind of answer to the question we left hanging in Chapter 1—what does it mean to be a good manager?

## IS MACINTYREAN VIRTUE ETHICS UTOPIAN?

This summary of all that we have covered leads to one other question which we have so far not addressed directly. We cannot dismiss lightly the charge that this whole approach to ethics and life, to organizations and managers within them, which we have advanced here, is utopian. Indeed, MacIntyre himself acknowledges just such a charge: 'What you will be told by those who represent established power is that the kind of institutions that you are trying to create and sustain are simply not possible, that you are unrealistic, a Utopian'. But, he continued, in characteristic fashion, 'And it is important to respond by saying "Yes, that it exactly what we are"'.[7]

MacIntyre went on to justify this statement by making a distinction between a utopianism of the future and a utopianism of the present. Future utopianisms 'are always apt to and almost invariably do result in a sacrifice of the present to some imaginary glorious future, one to be brought about by the sacrifice of the present'.[8] But this is not the only possibility and, MacIntyre argued, that a refusal to sacrifice the present to the future needs to be accompanied by 'an insistence that the range of present possibilities is always far greater than the established order is able to allow for'.[9]

In other words, MacIntyre holds out the possibility of reform, or perhaps even of revolution, along the lines he suggests, if only the established order could be encouraged to open its eyes to such alternative ways of seeing and doing things. Another way of putting this is to say that we need an alternative metaphor for organizations and organizational ethics, one which can capture the imagination and lead to positive change. And that is, of course, precisely what we have sought to advance here.

But this still leaves a question which, put in its most basic form, is whether organizations which sought to adopt the approach we have explored in this book, and perhaps particularly business organizations in the highly competitive world which they inhabit, would simply vanish, crowded out by other more aggressive and seemingly efficient organizations.

In an attempt to answer this, some have gone down the route of claiming, in effect, that virtue leads to success.[10] In other words, just as we saw in the discussion of strategic CSR in Chapter 2, the claim is that, in becoming virtuous, an organization will automatically become more successful in conventional terms. But this seems to miss entirely the point and nature of the virtues. As MacIntyre has put it:

> It is of the character of a virtue that in order to be effective in producing the
> internal goods which are the rewards of the virtues it should be exercised without

---

[7] MacIntyre (2008: 5).     [8] Ibid.: 5.     [9] Ibid.: 5.
[10] Examples include Arjoon (2000), Chun (2005), and Solomon (1999).

regard to consequences...cultivation of the virtues always may and often does hinder the achievement of those external goods which are the mark of worldly success.[11]

But does this then mean that virtuous organizations will not survive? Part of the answer to this is that, as we saw in the ability to attract organizational members with pro-social interests and therefore lower control costs in Chapter 7; in some of the benefits of meaningful work in Chapters 5, 6, and 7; and in the possibility of creating a 'micro-climate' within which the organization might flourish (Traidcraft in Chapter 8), there are benefits to this approach. This does not guarantee success, of course, but it does suggest that it may not be impossible.

In addition, as we have seen, it is in the nature of the virtuous organization to pursue sufficient external goods to enable its own survival, and the survival and flourishing of the practice(s) at its core. Virtuous organizations should not be naive in this respect and, as we saw with symphony orchestras, the best organized themselves to ensure they procured sufficient external goods to flourish. Furthermore, we have seen a number of examples of existing practices and organizations in Chapters 8 and 9 where the pursuit of organizational virtue seemed to lead to more than just survival.

Beyond this, however, it is clear that an unconducive environment, a society in which the pursuit of external goods had become dominant, for example, would be problematic for organizational virtue. It has been suggested that part of the answer to this is government regulation to level the playing field.[12] This already occurs, of course, in areas such as environmental regulation and health and safety legislation, for example. We also noted in Chapter 5 that the state should take some measure of responsibility for the provision of meaningful work. So there ought to be other mechanisms, besides action at the organizational level, which could help to ensure the survival and flourishing of virtuous organizations.

All of this does not mean, however, that virtuous organizations would necessarily be particularly successful when measured in conventional terms such as financial performance. The preclusion from seeking to maximize external goods, ensuring only that there are sufficient for the institution to survive and the core practice to flourish, would mean that such organizations might well be 'satisficers' rather than 'maximizers' in this regard. But on the other hand, the claim is that virtuous organizations would be better in many respects than conventional organizations. Their focus on the excellence of their products and services, the 'perfection' of organizational members via the

---

[11] MacIntyre (2007: 198).
[12] See O'Toole & Vogel (2011: 72), for example, although the argument there is made from the perspective of Conscious Capitalism (see Chapter 2, footnote 61) rather than from a virtue perspective *per se*.

provision of meaningful work, the concern for the extent to which they make a contribution to the common good, are the parameters by which they would wish to be measured. And against these, they would be likely to be shown to measure up rather well.

## MACINTYREAN VIRTUE ETHICS VERSUS CSR AND THE STAKEHOLDER APPROACH

We spent some time in Chapter 2 looking at the most common current approach to organizational (although more directly business) ethics—CSR and the stakeholder approach. It was suggested there that this approach suffers from a number of problems. First, by concentrating on the 'business case' for CSR, organizations will only 'do' ethics if, and in so far as, it pays. Second, by focusing on the organizational implications and benefits of doing CSR, there is an assumption that what is good for the organization is also good for society. Third, this conceived of ethics-as-strategy rather than ethics-as-ethics leading to the conclusion that ethics had been 'captured' by (particularly business) organizations. Fourth, there was no explicit consideration in the CSR and stakeholder approaches of the purpose of the organization, and therefore how it generated the value which it created. Any activity would do, apparently, so long as it led to the creation of (economic) value, and provided that that value was shared out among the stakeholders involved in a way that could be regarded as fair.

It is probably already clear that the approach which we have worked through in this book is both very different from CSR and the stakeholder approach and answers each of these objections. It does not offer a utilitarian, calculating approach to ethics, although it would not eschew entirely calculations of some kind as one possible contributory factor in making decisions. The concern for the contribution which the organization makes to the common good takes us back much more closely to the macro-social concerns which were a feature of early CSR than the organizationally focused concerns of strategic CSR. The approach argued for here does not conceive of ethics-as-strategy, indeed quite the reverse, even though working through the implications of this way of approaching organizational ethics might very well have strategic implications. And finally, the purpose of the organization could well be argued to be the starting point of this approach, in contrast to the CSR and stakeholder approaches.

In addition to these points, it is also possible to argue that MacIntyrean virtue ethics offers an *integrated* framework which CSR and the stakeholder approach do not really attempt. As we have seen, there are implications here for individuals as individuals, and how one might approach life as a whole, including one's working life in organizations. There are also implications for individuals as managers, but these are integrated with the implications for the individual as individual. And in addition there are implications for organizations, and indeed for society as a whole. The claim is that MacIntyrean virtue ethics offers not only a better approach than CSR and the stakeholder approach, but that it offers an integrated and coherent approach which works across all of these different 'levels'.

## A CONCLUDING STORY

We began this book by considering Elaine's story, and we have learned more of Elaine and her family during its course. So, in the nature of the narrative-based character of virtue ethics, it seems appropriate to end with an update.

First, Elaine's father, who was seriously ill, passed away. Obviously, this was a traumatic time for Elaine and her mother, and meant that Elaine had to take time off work to support her, and to help with all the practicalities including, over the following year or so, helping her mother to move to a smaller house closer to where Elaine and Fred live. In addition, of course, Elaine needed time for her own grieving process; she had been particularly close to her father. Her husband Fred was wonderfully supportive of Elaine, and took on prime responsibility for running the house and looking after their three children during the immediate period following her father's death.

As she emerged from this initial period, Elaine realized that her weekend visits to provide her mother with time off from caring for her father would no longer be necessary, and gradually, as the demands on her time from that direction became less, she was able to put more time back into family life. And, as she did so, she found again the delight she took in this, and the pleasure from seeing and helping her children to grow up. She even started playing the cello again—something she had not been able to do for a while.

But at work the storm clouds were gathering. The managing director of DesignCo was putting more pressure on the architectural practice to achieve higher financial returns, to the point where minimizing internal costs seemed to become the only criterion during a building's design. Creativity in design seemed no longer to be valued at DesignCo at all. At one point, Elaine was so concerned about the quality of the designs, and the impact this might have on the firm's reputation in the medium term, that she tackled her immediate boss over this. And this led to a 'conversation' with the managing director, in which Elaine stuck to her point but felt that he wasn't really listening—or perhaps worse.

As a result, Elaine began to make contact with other architects she knew from organizations she had worked for previously, going even as far back as college days. But, out of the blue, she was contacted by another architectural practice which had recently started on a commission to extend and refurbish a building which Elaine had worked on when in a previous organization. To her surprise, one of the clients had mentioned a particular feature of the building which had really 'worked'—it was both very aesthetically pleasing and functional. And this client had remembered Elaine as a young, aspiring, but also inspiring architect, and the part she had played in the design, and had mentioned her to one of the senior partners of the new architectural practice. And, needing to recruit, the partner had sought her out.

The new architectural organization was a young and relatively small practice. The role which needed to be filled involved managing a small team of architects, and key to the new practice was establishing a reputation for design excellence; it had already made its mark in the creativity of some of its designs, but wanted to embed this further. And the senior partner in this new architectural practice, in an initial conversation with Elaine, stressed the need not only for creativity, but also the importance of bringing on the younger architects. And she had already done her homework and discovered enough to know that Elaine's managerial style would fit well. It became clear that, if she wanted it, the job was hers. It all sounded almost too good to be true.

But there was a catch. The salary on offer was some way below what she was currently earning. And this led to a long evening with Fred as they discussed whether she should take the new job. Again, Fred was highly supportive, dismissing the impact on the family income, and the possible difficulty of paying the mortgage, as being a minor concern. They could always down-size if need be, he argued. And, in the course of that evening, Elaine was also reminded of all that she and Fred had been through together, and it left her feeling that perhaps they could make their marriage work after all.

The following day, she sat in her office at work thinking through all the implications of this major decision, and its impact on her, Fred, the children, her colleagues at DesignCo, but also the possibility of being a creative architect again, and of managing a new team of more junior architects with all the possibilities which that offered. And, as she did so, she glanced up and noticed for the first time in ages a plaque on the wall which her father had had framed and given her when she had first graduated as an architect. It contained a quote from Jørn Utzon, the Danish architect best known for designing the Sydney Opera House:

> The architect's gift to society is to bring joy to the people from the surroundings they create.

And that was, in the end, just what she needed to make the decision.

# References

Aguinis, H. & Glavas, A. (2012), 'What we know and don't know about Corporate Social Responsibility: A review and research agenda', *Journal of Management*, 38, 4: 932–68.

Allmendinger, J., Hackman, J., & Lehman, E. (1996), 'Life and work in symphony orchestras', *Musical Quarterly*, 80, 2: 194–219.

Alzola, M. (2015), 'Virtuous persons and virtuous actions in business ethics and organizational research', *Business Ethics Quarterly*, 25, 3: 287–318.

Anscombe, E. (1958), 'Modern moral philosophy', *Philosophy*, 33, 1: 1–19.

Aristotle (1955), *The ethics of Aristotle: The Nichomachean ethics*, translated by J. A. K. Thomson, Harmondsworth: Penguin Books.

Arjoon, S. (2000), 'Virtue theory as a dynamic theory of business', *Journal of Business Ethics*, 28, 2: 159–78.

Armstrong, A. (2006), 'Towards a strong virtue ethics for nursing practice', *Nursing Philosophy*, 7, 3: 110–24.

Bakan, J. (2004), *The corporation*, London: Constable.

Banks, M. (2012), 'MacIntyre, Bourdieu and the practice of jazz', *Popular Music*, 31, 1: 69–86.

Beabout, G. (2012), 'Management as a domain-relative practice that requires and develops practical wisdom', *Business Ethics Quarterly*, 22, 2: 405–32.

Beabout, G. (2013), *The character of the manager: From office executive to wise steward*, Basingstoke: Palgrave MacMillan.

Beadle, R. (2002), 'The misappropriation of MacIntyre', *Reason in Practice* 2, 2: 45–54. (The journal has been subsequently renamed *Philosophy of Management*.)

Beadle, R. (2013), 'Managerial work in a practice-embodying institution: The role of calling, the virtue of constancy', *Journal of Business Ethics*, 113, 4: 679–90.

Beadle, R. & Knight, K. (2012), 'Virtue and meaningful work', *Business Ethics Quarterly*, 22, 2: 433–50.

Beadle, R. & Könyöt, D. (2006), 'The man in the red coat—management in the circus', *Culture and Organization*, 12, 2: 127–37.

Beadle, R. & Moore, G. (2011), 'MacIntyre: Neo-Aristotelianism and organization theory', *Research in the Sociology of Organizations*, 32: 85–121.

Beinhocker, E. & Hanauer, N. (2014), 'Redefining capitalism', *McKinsey Quarterly*, 3rd quarter, 3: 160–9.

Bernacchio, C. & Couch, R. (2015), 'The virtue of participatory governance: A MacIntyrean alternative to shareholder maximisation', *Business Ethics: A European Review*, 24, S2: 130–43.

Big Innovation Centre (2016), 'The purposeful company: Interim report', available at http://www.biginnovationcentre.com, accessed 21 September 2016.

Blackburn, S. (Ed.) (1994), *Oxford dictionary of philosophy*, Oxford: Oxford University Press.

Blau P. & Scott, W. R. (1962), *Formal organizations*, San Francisco, CA: Scott, Foreman.

Bosma, H., Marmot, M., Hemingway, H., Nicholson, A., Brunner, E., & Stansfield, S. (1997), 'Low job control and risk of coronary heart disease in Whitehall II (prospective cohort) study', *British Medical Journal*, 314: 558–65.

Bowen, H. (1953), *Social responsibilities of the businessman*, New York: Harper.

Breen, K. (2012), 'Production and productive reason', *New Political Economy*, 17, 5: 611–32.

Brewer, K. (1997), 'Management as a practice: A response to Alasdair MacIntyre', *Journal of Business Ethics*, 16, 8: 825–33.

Bright, D., Winn, B., & Kanov, J. (2014), 'Reconsidering virtue: Differences of perspective in virtue ethics and the positive social sciences', *Journal of Business Ethics*, 119, 4: 44–60.

Cameron, K., Bright, D., & Caza, A. (2004), 'Exploring the relationships between organizational virtuousness and performance', *American Behavioral Scientist*, 47, 6: 766–90.

Carroll, A. & Buchholtz A. (2000), *Business and society: Ethics and stakeholder management*, 4th ed., Cincinnati, OH: Thompson Learning.

Cartwright, S. & Holmes, N. (2006), 'The meaning of work: The challenge of regaining employee engagement and reducing cynicism', *Human Resource Management Review*, 16, 2: 199–208.

Chalofsky, N. (2003), 'An emerging construct for meaningful work', *Human Resource Development International*, 6, 1: 69–83.

Chun, R. (2005), 'Ethical character and virtue of organizations: An empirical assessment and strategic implications', *Journal of Business Ethics*, 57, 3: 269–84.

Clarkson, M. B. E. (1995), 'A stakeholder framework for analysing and evaluating corporate social performance', *Academy of Management Review*, 20, 1: 92–117.

Conroy, M. (2009), 'Narrative-ethics informed approach to health services leadership development', *Leadership in Health Services*, 22, 3: 259–72.

Crane, A., Palazzo, G., Spence, L., & Matten, D. (2014), 'Contesting the value of "creating shared value"', *California Management Review*, 56, 2: 130–53.

Crockett, C. & Anderson, A. (2008), 'A grounded theory of virtue: From purpose to praxis', unpublished working paper.

Darley, J. M. & Batson, C. D. (1973), 'From Jerusalem to Jericho: A study of situational and dispositional variables in helping behaviour', *Journal of Personality and Social Psychology*, 27, 1: 100–8.

Dempsey, J. (2015), 'Moral responsibility, shared values, and corporate culture', *Business Ethics Quarterly*, 25, 3: 310–40.

Department for Business & Skills (2014), 'Corporate responsibility: Good for business and society: Government response to call for views on corporate social responsibility', available from: https://www.gov.uk/government/uploads/system/uploads/attachment_data/file/300265/bis-14-651-good-for-business-and-society-government-response-to-call-for-views-on-corporate-responsibility.pdf, accessed 21 September 2016.

DesJardins, J. (1993), 'Virtues and business ethics', in G. Chryssides and J. Kaler, *An introduction to Business Ethics* (pp. 136–42), London: Chapman and Hall.

Donaldson, T. & Preston, L. (1995), 'The stakeholder theory of the corporation: Concepts, evidence and implications', *Academy of Management Review*, 20, 1: 65–91.

Doris, J. (2002), *Lack of character: Personality and moral behaviour*, Cambridge: Cambridge University Press.

Eliot, T. S. (1969), 'The waste land', in *The complete poems and plays of T. S. Eliot*, London: Faber.

Encyclical Letter (2015), '*Laudato si*' of the Holy Father Francis, on care for our common home', available from http://w2.vatican.va/content/dam/francesco/pdf/encyclicals/documents/papa-francesco_20150524_enciclica-laudato-si_en.pdf, accessed 21 September 2016.

Endrikat, J., Guenther, E., & Hoppe, H. (2014), 'Making sense of conflicting empirical findings: A meta-analytic review of the relationship between corporate environmental and financial performance', *European Management Journal*, 32, 5: 735–51.

European Commission (2011), 'A renewed EU strategy 2011–14 for corporate social responsibility' COM (2011) 681 final, available from: http://eur-lex.europa.eu/LexUriServ/LexUriServ.do?uri=COM:2011:0681:FIN:EN:PDF, accessed 21 September 2016.

Fernando, M. & Moore, G. (2015), 'MacIntyrean virtue ethics in business: A cross-cultural comparison', *Journal of Business Ethics*, 132, 1: 185–202.

Foot, P. (1978), *Virtues and vices and other essays in moral philosophy*, Oxford: Blackwell.

Freeman, R. E. (1984), *Strategic management: A stakeholder approach*, Boston, MA: Pitman.

Frey, B. & Osterloh, M. (2005), 'Yes, managers should be paid like bureaucrats', *Journal of Management Inquiry*, 14, 1: 96–111.

Froud, J., Johal, S., & Williams, K. (2002), 'Financialisation and the coupon pool', *Capital and Class*, 78 (Autumn): 119–51.

Ghoshal, S., Bartlett, C., & Moran, P. (1999), 'A new manifesto for management', *Sloan Management Review*, 40, 3: 9–20.

Grayson, D. & Hodges, A. (2004), *Corporate social opportunity! Seven steps to make corporate social responsibility work for your business*, Sheffield: Greenleaf.

Griffin, R. W. & O'Leary-Kelly, A. M. (2004), *The dark side of organizational behaviour*, San Francisco, CA: Jossey-Bass.

Hackman, J. & Oldham, G. (1975), 'Development of the job diagnostic survey', *Journal of Applied Psychology*, 60, 2: 159–70.

Haldane, A. (2015), 'Who owns a company?', speech given at University of Edinburgh Corporate Finance Conference, available at http://www.bankofengland.co.uk/publications/Pages/speeches/2015/833.aspx, accessed 21 September 2016.

Hall, D. (2011), 'The guild of surgeons as a tradition of moral enquiry', *Journal of Medicine and Philosophy*, 36, 2: 114–32.

Hannan, M. T. & Kranzberg, M. (no date), 'History of the organization of work', available from: http://www.britannica.com/topic/history-of-work-organization-648000, accessed 21 September 2016.

Harman, G. (2003), 'No character or personality', *Business Ethics Quarterly*, 13, 1: 87–94.

Hartman, E. (2013), *Virtue in business: Conversations with Aristotle*, Cambridge: Cambridge University Press.

Hasnas, J. (2012), 'Reflections on corporate moral responsibility and the problem solving technique of Alexander the Great', *Journal of Business Ethics*, 107, 2: 183–95.

Hine, J. (2007), 'The shadow of MacIntyre's manager in the Kingdom of Conscience constrained', *Business Ethics: A European Review*, 16, 4: 358–71.

Hine, J. & Preuss, L. (2009), '"Society is out there, organisation is in here": On the perceptions of corporate social responsibility held by different managerial groups', *Journal of Business Ethics*, 88, 2: 381–93.

Hinings, C. & Mauws, M. (2006), 'Organizational morality', in J. Bartenuk, M. Hinsdale, & J. Keenan (Eds), *Church ethics and its organizational context: Learning from the sex abuse scandal in the Catholic Church* (pp. 115–21), Oxford: Rowman & Littlefield.

Hirschman, A. (1970), *Exit, voice and loyalty: Responses to decline in firms, organizations, and states*, Cambridge, MA: Harvard University Press.

Hirschman, A. (1982), 'Rival interpretations of market society: Civilising, destructive, or feeble?' *Journal of Economic Literature*, 20, 4: 1463–84.

Hoggett, P. (2004), 'A service to the public: The containment of ethical and moral conflicts by public bureaucracies', in P. du Gay (Ed.), *The values of bureaucracy* (pp. 167–90), Oxford: Oxford University Press.

Horner, D. & Turner, D. (2012), 'Zeal', in M. Austin & R. Douglas Geivett (Eds), *Christian virtues for everyday life* (pp. 72–103), Grand Rapids, MI: Wm. B. Eerdmans Publishing.

Horvath, C. (1995), 'Excellence v. effectiveness: MacIntyre's critique of business', *Business Ethics Quarterly*, 5, 3: 499–532.

Hursthouse, R. (2001), *On virtue ethics*, Oxford: Oxford University Press.

Husted, B. & Salazar, J. (2006), 'Taking Friedman seriously: Maximising profits and social performance', *Journal of Management Studies*, 43, 1: 75–91.

Ip, P. K. (2009), 'Is Confucianism good for business ethics in China?', *Journal of Business Ethics*, 88, 3: 463–76.

Ip, P. K. (2011), 'Practical wisdom of Confucian ethical leadership: A critical inquiry', *Journal of Management Development*, 30, 7/8: 685–96.

Ireland, P. (2010), 'Limited liability, shareholder rights and the problem of corporate irresponsibility', *Cambridge Journal of Economics*, 34, 5: 837–56.

Jensen, M. & Meckling, W. (1976), 'The theory of the firm: Managerial behavior, agency costs and ownership structure', *Journal of Financial Economics*, 3, 4: 305–60.

Keat, R. (2000), *Cultural goods and the limits of the market*, London: MacMillan Press.

Keat, R. (2008), 'Practices, firms and varieties of capitalism', *Philosophy of Management*, 7, 1: 77–91.

Kelly, K. (2016), 'Organizations and violence: The child as abject-boundary in Ireland's industrial schools', *Organization Studies*, 37, 7: 939–61.

Kempster, S., Jackson, B., & Conroy, M. (2011), 'Leadership as purpose: Exploring the role of purpose in leadership practice', *Leadership*, 7, 3: 317–34.

Keynes, J. M. (1932), 'Economic possibilities for our grandchildren (1930)', in *Essays in persuasion* (pp. 358–73), New York: Harcourt Brace.

Koehn, D. (1995), 'A role for virtue ethics in the analysis of business practice', *Business Ethics Quarterly* 5, 3: 531–9.

Langholm, O. (1984), *The Aristotelian analysis of usury*, New York: Columbia University Press.

Lawrence, D. H. (1974), *Selected essays*, Harmondsworth: Penguin.

Lee, M.-D. P. (2008), 'A review of the theories of corporate social responsibility: Its evolutionary path and the road ahead', *International Journal of Management Reviews*, 10, 1: 53–73.

Loewenstein, R. (2000), *When genius failed: The rise and fall of long-term capital management*, New York: Random House.

MacIntyre, A. (1977), 'Epistemological crises, dramatic narrative, and the philosophy of science', *Monist*, 60, 4: 453–72.

MacIntyre, A. (1978), 'What has ethics to learn from medical ethics?' *Philosophic Exchange*, 9, 1: 37–47.

MacIntyre, A. (1979), 'Corporate modernity and moral judgement: Are they mutually exclusive?' In K. E. Goodpaster & K. M. Sayer (Eds), *Ethics and problems of the 21st Century* (pp. 122–35), Notre Dame, IN: University of Notre Dame Press.

MacIntyre, A. (1982), 'Why are the problems of business ethics insoluble?' In B. Baumrin & B. Friedman (Eds), *Moral responsibility and the professions* (pp. 350–9), New York: Haven Publishing.

MacIntyre, A. (1984), 'Does applied ethics rest on a mistake?' *Monist*, 67, 4: 498–513.

MacIntyre, A. (1988), *Whose justice? Which rationality?* London: Duckworth.

MacIntyre, A. (1990), *Three rival versions of moral inquiry: Encyclopedia, genealogy, tradition*, Notre Dame, IN: University of Notre Dame Press.

MacIntyre, A. (1992), 'Plain persons and moral philosophy: Rules, virtues and goods', *American Catholic Philosophical Quarterly*, 66, 1: 3–19.

MacIntyre, A. (1994), 'A partial response to my critics', in J. Horton and S. Mendus (Eds), *After MacIntyre* (pp. 283–304), Cambridge: Polity Press.

MacIntyre, A. (1995), *Marxism and Christianity*, London: Duckworth.

MacIntyre, A. (1998), 'The *Theses on Feuerbach*: A road not taken', in K. Knight (Ed.), *The MacIntyre reader* (pp. 223–34), Cambridge: Polity Press.

MacIntyre, A. (1999a), *Dependent rational animals: Why human beings need the virtues*, London: Duckworth.

MacIntyre, A. (1999b), 'Social structures and their threats to moral agency', *Philosophy*, 74, 3: 311–29.

MacIntyre, A. (2006), *The tasks of philosophy: Selected essays*, Volume 1, Cambridge: Cambridge University Press.

MacIntyre, A. (2007), *After virtue: A study in moral theory* (3rd ed.). London: Duckworth.

MacIntyre, A. (2008), 'How Aristotelianism can become revolutionary: Ethics, resistance, and Utopia', *Philosophy of Management*, 7, 1: 1–7.

MacIntyre, A. (2009), 'The very idea of a university: Aristotle, Newman and us', lecture given at Blackfriar's Hall, Oxford, 9 June.

MacIntyre, A. (2010), 'Intolerance, censorship and other requirements of rationality', lecture delivered at London Metropolitan University, 28 October, http://www.londonmet.ac.uk/research-units/hrsj/events/public-events/.

MacIntyre, A. (2015), 'The irrelevance of ethics', in A. Bielskis and K. Knight (Eds), *Virtue and economy: Essays on morality and markets* (pp. 7–22). Farnham: Ashgate.

MacIntyre, A. & Dunne, J. (2002), 'Alasdair MacIntyre on education: In dialogue with Joseph Dunne', *Journal of Philosophy of Education*, 36, 1: 1–19.

Mackey, J. & Sisodia, R. (2013), *Conscious capitalism: Liberating the heroic spirit of business*, Boston, MA: Harvard Business Review Press.

McCann, D. P. & and Brownsberger, M. L. (1990), 'Management as a social practice: Rethinking business ethics after MacIntyre', *Annual of the Society of Christian Ethics*: 223–45. (This journal has been renamed *Journal of the Society of Christian Ethics*.)

McWilliams, A., Siegel, D., & Wright, P. (2006), 'Corporate social responsibility: strategic implications', *Journal of Management Studies*, 43, 1: 1–18.

Michaelson, C., Pratt, M., Grant, A., & Dunn, C. (2014), 'Meaningful work: Connecting business ethics and organization studies', *Journal of Business Ethics*, 121, 1: 77–90.

Moore, G. (1999), 'Tinged shareholder theory, or, what's so special about stakeholders?' *Business Ethics: A European Review*, 8, 2: 117–27.

Moore, G. (2002), 'On the implications of the practice-institution distinction: MacIntyre and the application of modern virtue ethics to business', *Business Ethics Quarterly*, 12, 1: 19–32.

Moore, G. (2005a), 'Corporate character: Modern virtue ethics and the virtuous corporation', *Business Ethics Quarterly*, 15, 4: 659–85.

Moore, G. (2005b), 'Humanizing business: A modern virtue ethics approach', *Business Ethics Quarterly*, 15, 2: 237–55.

Moore, G. (2008), 'Re-imagining the morality of management: A modern virtue ethics approach', *Business Ethics Quarterly*, 18, 4: 483–511.

Moore, G. (2011), 'Churches as organisations: Towards a virtue ecclesiology for today', *International Journal for the Study of the Christian Church*, 11, 1: 45–65.

Moore, G. (2012a), 'Virtue in business: Alliance Boots and an empirical exploration of MacIntyre's conceptual framework', *Organization Studies*, 33, 3: 363–87.

Moore, G. (2012b), 'The virtue of governance: The governance of virtue', *Business Ethics Quarterly*, 22, 2: 293–318.

Moore, G. (2015), 'Corporate character, corporate virtues', *Business Ethics: A European Review*, 24, S2: 99–114.

Moore, G. (2016), 'Corporate agency, character, purpose and the common good', in K. Akrivou & A. Sison (Eds), *The challenges of capitalism for virtue ethics and the common good: Inter-disciplinary perspectives* (pp. 159–65), Cheltenham: Edward Elgar.

Moore, G. & Beadle, R. (2006), 'In search of organizational virtue in business: Agents, goods, practices, institutions and environments', *Organization Studies*, 27, 3: 369–89.

Moore, G. & Grandy, G. (2016), 'Bringing morality back in: Institutional theory and MacIntyre', *Journal of Management Inquiry*, DOI: 10.1177/1056492616670754.

Moore, G., Beadle, R., & Rowlands, A. (2014), 'Catholic social teaching and the firm. Crowding in virtue: A MacIntyrean approach to business ethics', *American Catholic Philosophical Quarterly*, 88, 4: 779–805.

Morgan, G. (2006), *Images of organization*, London: Sage Publications.

Morrell, K. (2012), *Organization, society and politics: An Aristotelian perspective*, Basingstoke: Palgrave Macmillan.

Morrell, K. & Brammer, S. (2016), 'Governance and virtue: The case of public order policing', *Journal of Business Ethics*, 136, 2: 385–98.

Nash, L. (1995), 'Whose character? A response to Mangham's "MacIntyre and the Manager"', *Organization* 2, 2: 226–32.

Nelson, R. & Gopalan, S. (2003), 'Do organizational cultures replicate national cultures? Isomorphism, rejection and reciprocal opposition in the corporate values of three countries', *Organization Studies*, 24, 7: 1115–51.

O'Sullivan, M. (2003), 'The political economy of comparative corporate governance', *Review of International Political Economy*, 10, 1: 23–72.

O'Toole, J. & Vogel, D. (2011), 'Two and a half cheers for conscious capitalism', *California Management Review*, 53, 3: 60–76.

Orlitzky, M. (2011), 'Institutional logics in the study of organizations: The social construction of the relationship between corporate social and financial performance', *Business Ethics Quarterly*, 21, 3: 409–44.

Orlitzky, M., Schmidt, F. L., & Rynes, S. L. (2003), 'Corporate social and financial performance: A meta-analysis', *Organization Studies*, 24, 3: 403–11.

Osterloh, M. & Frey, B. (2004), 'Corporate governance for crooks? The case for corporate virtue', in A. Grandori (Ed.), *Corporate governance and firm organization: Microfoundations and structural forms* (pp. 191–211), Oxford: Oxford University Press.

Ouchi, W. (2007), 'Markets, bureaucracies and clans', in Wharton (2007), pp. 13–22.

Phillips, R., Freeman, R. E. & and Wicks, A. (2003), 'What stakeholder theory is not', *Business Ethics Quarterly*, 13, 4: 479–502.

Pollard, A. (Ed.) (2000), *The representation of business in English literature*, London: Institute of Economic Affairs.

Pontifical Council for Justice and Peace (2004), *Compendium of the social doctrine of the church*, Rome: Libreria Editrice Vaticana, available from http://www.vatican.va/roman_curia/pontifical_councils/justpeace/documents/rc_pc_justpeace_doc_20060526_compendio-dott-soc_en.html, accessed 21 September 2016.

Porter, J. (1994), *The recovery of virtue*, London: SPCK.

Porter, M. & Kramer, M. (2002), 'The competitive advantage of corporate philanthropy', *Harvard Business Review*, December: 56–68.

Porter, M. & Kramer, M. (2006), 'Strategy and society: The link between competitive advantage and corporate social responsibility', *Harvard Business Review*, December: 78–92.

Porter, M. & Kramer, M. (2011), 'Creating shared value', *Harvard Business Review*, January–February: 62–77.

Rhodes, C. (2016), 'Democratic business ethics: Volkswagen's emissions scandal and the disruption of corporate sovereignty', *Organization Studies*, 37, 10: 1501–18.

Robson, A. (2015), 'Constancy and integrity: (Un)measurable virtues?', *Business Ethics: A European Review*, 24, S2: 115–29.

Ryan, S. (2009), Report of the commission to inquire into child abuse (CICA). Dublin: Stationary Office. Available from http://www.childabusecommission.ie, accessed 21 September 2016.

Salter, L. (2008), 'The goods of community? The potential of journalism as a social practice', *Philosophy of Management*, 7, 1: 33–44.

Scott, W. R. (2007), 'Reflections on a half-century of organizational sociology', in Wharton (2007), pp. 2–12.

Sellman, D. (2000), 'Alasdair MacIntyre and the professional practice of nursing', *Nursing Philosophy*, 1, 1: 26–33.

Simmons, J. (Ed.) (1951), *Letters from England*, London: Cresset Press.

Slote, M. (1996), *From morality to virtue*, Oxford: Oxford University Press.

Smith, J. (Ed.) (2009), *Normative theory and business ethics*, Lanham, MD: Rowman and Littlefield.

Solomon, R. (1999), *A better way to think about business: How personal integrity leads to corporate success*, Oxford: Oxford University Press.

Solomon, R. (2003), 'Victims of circumstances? A defense of virtue ethics in business', *Business Ethics Quarterly*, 13, 1: 43–62.

Swanton, C. (2003), *Virtue ethics: A pluralistic view*, Oxford: Oxford University Press.

Terkel, S. (1975), *Working*, London: Wildwood House.

van de Ven, B. (2011), 'Banking after the crisis: Towards an understanding of banking as a professional practice', *Ethical Perspectives*, 18, 4: 541–68.

Velasquez, M. (2003), 'Debunking corporate moral responsibility', *Business Ethics Quarterly*, 13, 4: 531–62.

von Krogh, G., Haefliger, S., Spaeth, S., & Wallin, M. (2012), 'Carrots and rainbows: Motivation and social practice in open source software', *MIS Quarterly*, 36, 2: 649–76.

Waterman, R. (1994), *The frontiers of excellence: Learning from companies that put people first*, London: Nicholas Brearly.

Weaver, G. (2006), 'Virtue in organizations: Moral agencies as a foundation for moral agency', *Organisation Studies*, 27, 3: 341–68.

Webber, J. (2006), 'Virtue, character and situation', *Journal of Moral Philosophy*, 3, 2: 193–213.

West, A. (2016), '*After Virtue* and accounting ethics', *Journal of Business Ethics*, DOI 10.1007/s10551-016-3018-9.

Westbrook, R. (1991), *John Dewey and American democracy*, Ithaca, NY: Cornell University Press.

Wharton, A. (Ed.) (2007), *The sociology of organizations: An anthology of contemporary theory and research*, Los Angeles, CA: Roxbury Publishing.

White, D. & Simas, C. (2008), 'An empirical investigation of the link between market orientation and church performance', *International Journal of Nonprofit and Voluntary Sector Marketing*, 13, 2: 153–65.

Wilcox, T. (2012), 'Human resource management in a compartmentalized world: Whither moral agency?' *Journal of Business Ethics*, 111, 1: 85–96.

Williams, K. (2000), 'From shareholder value to present-day capitalism', *Economy and Society* 29, 1: 1–12.

Wyma, K. (2015), 'The case for investment advising as a virtue-based practice', *Journal of Business Ethics*, 127, 1: 231–49.

Yeoman, R. (2014), 'Conceptualising meaningful work as a fundamental human need', *Journal of Business Ethics*, 125, 2: 235–51.

# Index

academic
  appointments 8
  articles 6
  career 8
  community 9
  context 60
  journals 6
  managers 183
  papers 5
  studies 29
  work 5n.3
academics 6, 26, 109
academies 172
accountancy 183
accountants 109, 147–9
accounting 11, 30n.53, 141–2, 146–50, 158,
    165, 178, 193
accounts 72, 147
acquisitiveness 64–6, 102, 143, 146, 151, 191
action
  -centred 34
  -guiding 46, 48, 53
  -oriented 36
  -research 179–80, 193
actions 2, 9–11, 21, 24, 26–7, 29, 32n.61, 33–4,
    36–7, 44–53, 71, 82, 88, 90, 95n.47, 101, 111,
    122, 157–8, 174, 177, 180–2, 186, 191, 197
activities 4–5, 11, 32, 38–9, 43, 58–62, 79–80,
    86, 90, 93, 98, 102, 108–9, 115–17, 124–6,
    142, 145–6, 153, 159, 164, 166, 171, 180,
    189, 192, *see also* practices
actor
  -centred 46
  -oriented 36, 39, 44
actors 26, 81, 102
aesthetic
  accomplishments 171
  achievements 172
  dimension 37
aesthetically pleasing 37, 57, 72, 200
Afghanistan 175
agency 10, 51–3, 104, 106, 108, 114, 120,
    155, 158, 163, 174, 180, 185, 195
  corporate moral 51–2
aggregation 53
  of individuals 17, 50–1
airline
  company 157, 174, 180, 192, 194
  crews 167n.4

Alliance Boots 152–4, 163–4, 174, 192
Alliance Unichem 152
alliances 16, 162
Alternative Investment Market 159n.61
ambition 1, 4, 115, 125
American Catholic Philosophical
    Association 9n.16
American College of Surgeons 176
American Philosophical Society 9n.16
anaesthetists 174–5, 179
Andersen, Arthur 148
Anglo-American
  capitalism 164
  corporate governance 100
appraisal 3, 104
apprentices/apprenticeship 62–3, 116n.54,
    150, 156, 159, 164, 176–7
arbitrage 128
architects 1, 2n.2, 4, 39–40, 44, 57, 59,
    63–4, 71–2, 101, 103–5, 111,
    114–15, 200
architectural
  degree 105
  designs 93, 104, 122
  firms 63, 66, 68
  organization 200
  practices 1, 2n.1, 3, 18, 106, 113n.44,
    121–2, 183, 199–200
  projects 63
architecture 2–5, 7, 57, 59–61, 63, 66, 68–9,
    72, 80, 83–4, 91, 104–5, 107–9, 142, 146,
    157, 186
*arête* 43, 93
Aristotelian
  approach 5n.4
  philosophy 9
  politics 61, 88, 142
  tradition 38
  virtue ethics 38
  virtues 42n.31
Aristotle 8, 33, 37–8, 40, 47, 49, 56, 78, 125,
    177, 189
arts 57, 61, 142, 166, 173, 183
Association of Chartered Certified
    Accountants 148n.28
attentiveness 39, 64
Australian airline 157, 174, 180, 192, 194
autonomy 90, 92, 161–2
avarice 23

*Index*

Printed and bound by CPI Group (UK) Ltd, Croydon, CR0 4YY